365
Mary

*Happy Birthday to Kit —
with a delightful new look
at Mary. In friendship,
Nancy*

365

Mary

A DAILY GUIDE TO MARY'S WISDOM AND COMFORT

Woodeene Koenig-Bricker

HarperSanFrancisco
A Division of HarperCollins*Publishers*

365 MARY: *A Daily Guide to Mary's Wisdom and Comfort.* Copyright ©
1997 by Woodeene Koenig-Bricker. All rights reserved. Printed in the
United States of America. No part of this book may be used or repro-
duced in any manner whatsoever without written permission except in
the case of brief quotations embodied in critical articles and reviews.
For information address HarperCollins Publishers, 10 East 53rd
Street, New York, NY 10022.

HarperCollins Web Site: http://www.harpercollins.com
HarperCollins®, ♛ ®, and HarperSanFrancisco™ are trademarks of
HarperCollins Publishers Inc.

FIRST EDITION

Library of Congress Cataloging-in-Publication Data
ISBN 0–06–064744–2 (pbk.)
LC: 97–15093

99 00 01 ❖ RRDH 10 9 8 7 6 5 4

ACKNOWLEDGMENTS

To Kris. I owe you BIG time.

To the Round Robins. Thanks for the prayers—and the pitchfork.

To Jii. *Merci beaucoup* for dancing in with chocolate-covered espresso beans when I needed them most.

To my mother. Without all your Rosaries, this book would never have been completed.

When I attended Catholic grade school and Catholic high school in the 1950s and 60s, Mary was an essential part of Church and school life. From the Angelus at noon to May altars to spiritual bouquets filled with rosaries, Mary and Marian devotion pervaded our spiritual focus. The nuns who taught me encouraged all young ladies to become "just like Mary," especially in matters of dress. "Ask yourself if Mary would wear an outfit before you put it on," we were admonished.

I think that's when I first started having a little trouble with Mary. The only pictures I'd ever seen of her showed her wearing a long dress and cloak. No matter how hard I tried, I couldn't picture Mary in the blue and gold plaid skirt and white knee socks that made up our school uniform, and I certainly couldn't imagine her in a bathing suit (no matter how modest) or Levi 501s.

From that point on, Mary began to seem less relevant to my life. Gradually, I stuck her on a mental shelf, to be brushed off at Christmas and on holy days. It wasn't that I actively disliked her. It's just that most of the pictures and prayers and stories the nuns told us made her seem like a cross between a plaster statue, Pollyanna, and Mrs. America. (Not to mention the fact she never wore anything except a long blue dress with stars on it!)

After I became an adult, I gave Mary nodding recognition as the Mother of Jesus, but she never was central to my faith. So, if I wasn't crazy about Mary, why did I want to write a book about her?

One of the main reasons was my own mother. She's always had a profound devotion to Our Lady. From the time I was a little girl, she would tell me about being able to picture herself with Mary and Jesus as she said the Rosary. I wanted to understand Mary a little more so that I could get to know my mother a little better. In addition, I wanted to write a book that would express my gratitude to my mother for having passed on a measure of her own deep and abiding faith, and what better way to do that than to write a book honoring the Mother of God? Finally, I'll admit the journalist/reporter in me wanted to know what it was about Mary that has made her so appealing over the ages. By researching what others had written and said about the Blessed Virgin, I hoped I might be able to figure out what has inspired such overwhelming devotion.

So I started to read what had been written about Mary and investigate the theology behind Marian devotions. Armed with that information, I began to write what I thought a Mary book *should* be. In the first draft, Mary was totally, completely and utterly holy. She was also gorgeous, unflappable, and perfect in every way, shape, and form.

Every stereotype image of Mary Most Holy that I had created in my mind bubbled to the surface and I felt obliged to try to twist those images into something I personally found positive and encouraging. Ironically, the more I wrote about that Mary, the more I disliked her. And the more I disliked her, the guiltier I felt and the harder I tried to like her.

It didn't work. About halfway through the process, I gave up. I had said everything I could about that saccharine Mary and I was no closer to understanding why my mother and so many millions of others were so in love with her than I was when I began. In fact, I liked Mary even less than when I had begun!

So I put aside all the books I'd collected and the theology I had been reading and I began to concentrate on Mary as I found her in the Scriptures. I read and reread the passages in the New Testament that talked about the Annunciation, the Visitation, and the Nativity until I practically had them memorized. I threw out all the pictures of the Virgin as a flaxen-haired waif and looked at photos of Middle Eastern women in *National Geographic*. I set aside the multitude of prayers I'd collected and instead asked Mary to help me discover who she really was, not what I—or anyone else—thought she should be, but who Marim of Nazareth, a woman of first-century Israel, really was.

Then I began to write: not what I thought I *should* write, but what I felt I *had to* write. Gradually, a very different Mary from the pious statue I had first envisioned began to emerge. I realized that I had subtly (and not so subtly) placed Mary into the role of quasi-goddess. I had been trying to make her into someone or something she never was and never could be. As I let the Mary of Scripture emerge, I met a flesh-and-blood woman who laughed and cried and danced and ate and drank and talked and loved. I met a woman who was indeed worthy to become the Mother of God.

I don't claim any special revelations about the Blessed Virgin. She has not appeared to me (and I probably would die of cardiac arrest if she did!). She hasn't spoken directly to me or sent me any celestial messages, so I can't be certain that the Mary I have discovered would pass theological muster in all areas.

What I am certain about, however, is that I've discovered a woman whose life can inspire my own and a mother whose love is so expansive it transcends time and space.

Regardless of whether you've been devoted to Mary your entire life or if, like me, you've come to know and appreciate her somewhat later, I hope these reflections will help you grow in understanding and affection for this incredible, extraordinary, and unique woman who was chosen by God to be a pivotal figure in the salvation history of humanity. I hope that you will discover, as I did, that Mary is not just the *Theotokos*, the Virgin, the Mother of God, but that she is also Mary, our companion, our friend, and our mother.

(And you might even conclude, as I finally did, that if she were living on earth today, she very well might wear Levis once in a while instead of constantly putting on a long blue dress!)

Woodeene Koenig-Bricker
May 1997

The Solemnity of Mary

Mary is honored by many titles and many names, but her place in history is secured by one fact, and one fact only: she agreed to become the mother of the Messiah. In essence, Mary's entire renown rests on her motherhood.

But Mary isn't just the mother of Jesus. She's also the spiritual mother of all who follow the way of her son. Pope John Paul II, who dedicated his priesthood to Mary, asserted in his encyclical Redemptoris Mater that "the Mother of Christ, who stands at the very center of the mystery—a mystery which embraces each individual and all humanity—is given as Mother to every individual and all mankind. . . . [Mary] is clearly the mother of the members of Christ . . . since she cooperated out of love so that there might be born into the Church the faithful."

As we begin a new year, it's fitting that we look to Mary as an example of the importance of motherhood for humanity. All too often, we forget that being a mother, in the fullest and truest sense of the word, is essential to the continuation of the human race.

While not every person is called to be a mother in the biological sense, we're all called to be life-givers and love-bearers. And isn't that really what a mother is—a person who is willing to nurture life and love? Isn't that what the world really *needs?*

In what ways can I emulate Mary as a life-giver and life-nurturer? How can I model my life on that of Mary?

1 CELEBRATE AND REJOICE IN LIFE. 1 USE MY TALENTS TO BUILD UP RATHER THAN TEAR DOWN, TO CREATE RATHER THAN DESTROY, TO LOVE RATHER THAN HATE.

The Abundant Life

Abundance: a quantity that is more than enough; plenty.
OXFORD AMERICAN DICTIONARY

We're quick to say that we live in a land of abundance, but how many of us really believe we have "more than enough"? The advertising industry is predicated on the principle that we don't have all we need, that there's always room for more.

Yet how much do we really need? And more important, *what* do we really need?

No one would say that Mary lived a life of plenty, yet without doubt she lived an abundant life. She embraced both joy and sorrow, concentrating not on what she could obtain but on what she could become. Her entire life was one continual *yes* to the grace and gifts God desired to give her—the same grace and gifts God desires to give each one of us.

But in order to have space in our hearts to accept God's gifts, we must make a conscious decision to let go of the desire to acquire. We must rouse ourselves from the numbing grip of possession-sickness to experience the liberating freedom of love. Once we do so, we'll discover that we no longer feel the need to find validation in a big-screen TV, the latest fashions, or a fancy new car. Instead, we will find the wholeness we were created to experience in deep and authentic relationships with other people.

After all, it's only in creating authentic relationships based on love that we can discover what it truly means to live the abundant life.

Do I seek fulfillment in an abundance of possessions or in an abundance of love? What material goods can I release today in order to create room for spiritual growth?

TODAY I LET GO OF THOSE POSSESSIONS THAT ARE PREVENTING ME FROM LIVING LIFE TO THE FULLEST.

A Change of Plans

Just imagine the scene. Joseph wakes up in the middle of the night, having had a dream in which an angel tells him to head to Egypt immediately. He rolls over, wakes up Mary, and announces, "We've got to go. Pack up the baby, and let's get out of here!"

Mary undoubtedly had a few rather pointed questions at that moment. It seems likely that she would have asked why they were in such a hurry. She might have wondered if his dream had really been a visit from an angel or was merely the result of too much garlic with the previous night's flatbread. And even after she was convinced that Joseph *had* had a vision, she might have asked about the travel arrangements. ("Have you considered where we're going to find a donkey at this time of night?")

If Mary did indeed question Joseph, that doesn't make her any less holy than if she had meekly put Jesus in a sling and headed out to the desert. After all, she did talk frankly with an angel when he told her she was going to have a baby despite being a virgin. It seems unrealistic to think that she wouldn't have asked her husband a few questions about their sudden, urgent need to head into the desert.

But speculation on her reaction notwithstanding, the fact remains that Mary was willing to change her plans—which probably included a visit to her parents to show off the baby—to accommodate the necessity of following the angel's directive. She understood that being able to adapt at the last moment is sometimes the only way to save your life.

How do I react when I'm faced with a sudden, urgent change
of plans? Can I be flexible enough to accept someone
else's directions once in a while?

TODAY I'LL BE FLEXIBLE AND WILLING TO CHANGE MY PLANS.

Laws of Creation

Many of the classical pictures of Mary and the infant Jesus portray gentle moments of tender affection between mother and child. Mary gazes lovingly at her son, who gazes lovingly back at his mother.

One of the reasons that these paintings have such lasting appeal is that they tap into our universal human desire for affection. It's not enough to be cared for physically; we need to be cared for emotionally as well. We need to *feel* that we're loved. Even Jesus and Mary weren't above that fundamental need.

But how do we go about having that need fulfilled?

One of the universal—and seemingly contradictory—laws of creation is that in order to get, we have to give. In fact, the law is directly reciprocal: we receive what we relinquish.

This principle has entered into our collective wisdom as the proverb "You reap what you sow." Thus, if you're looking for love and affection in your life, start loving others. If you want to feel cared for, start caring for others. If you want to feel valued, start valuing others.

A prayer attributed to St. Francis eloquently expresses this truth:

> . . . for it is in giving that we receive,
> it is in pardoning that we are pardoned,
> and it is in dying that we are born to eternal life.

What do I want to get out of life?
How am I currently giving those things to others?

TODAY 1 WILL SOW THOSE THINGS 1 WANT TO REAP TOMORROW.

Amazement

When angels appear in the Scriptures, the first words they say are generally some variation on "Don't be afraid!" The one exception is the greeting Mary receives. When the angel Gabriel appears to her, to ask her to cooperate in the birth of God's son, his first words are "Hail, favored one! The Lord is with you!" In fact, the word *hail* might better be translated as "Rejoice!"

As intriguing as the angel's greeting is, Mary's reaction is even more fascinating. It isn't rejoicing—but it isn't fear either. We're told that she "was greatly troubled . . . and pondered what sort of greeting this might be." Mary appears to be amazed not so much by the messenger as by the message. It's as if she takes the presence of the angel for granted, though she's confused by his words of address.

Gabriel's next words almost sound superfluous, since they are the usual "Don't be afraid." One can imagine Mary frowning a little and saying, "I'm *not* afraid. I'm just wondering what you're doing here."

We often say that we're amazed when we're really just shocked and scared. What separates amazement from mere surprise is the fact that amazement results in action. Mary's reaction to the angel is a perfect example of true amazement. After an initial sensation of surprise, coupled with curiosity and bewilderment, she doesn't stand slack-jawed, staring at Gabriel; she listens to his message, considers his request, and then makes a decision.

The next time you're feeling shocked and scared, don't let it stop there; ask yourself what you're going to do with your reaction, how you can turn it into action-oriented amazement. You may be "amazed" to discover what God has in store for you!

When was the last time you were amazed?
What did you do about it?

WHEN I'M AMAZED, I USE MY WONDER AND CURIOSITY FOR
MY SPIRITUAL DEVELOPMENT BY CONVERTING THEM
INTO PRACTICAL ACTION.

Epiphany

On the Feast of Epiphany, which we celebrate today, the Christian Church traditionally commemorates the visit of the Wise Men to the Holy Family. The Wise Men—or the Magi, as they're sometimes called—came from the East, following a star that signified the birth of a king. They brought three gifts—gold, frankincense, and myrrh— which is why we traditionally believe (although the Gospel accounts don't mention any specific number) that there were three of them, each bearing one gift. Although the gifts they brought were fit for a king, the Wise Men themselves weren't kings.

So why is this feast called *Epiphany?* The word itself, in its religious connotation, means "the appearance of a superhuman being." Given that definition, it seems that Christmas would be a better time to celebrate. But the word *epiphany* can also mean "a revelation, a realization," and that's exactly what we recall on this day. On this feast, the significance of Mary's son was revealed to all people—not just shepherds and angels, but Jews and Gentiles alike. For the Magi, this day was truly an epiphany. They had followed a star, not knowing what to expect, and it had led them to the desires of their heart.

We too are called to experience epiphanies in our lives—those moments when, for the briefest second, everything seems to make sense; when we catch a glimmer of why we're here and sense the reason behind the plans of the universe.

Like the Wise Men, we're called to follow our star, even when we have no idea where it will lead; for it's only in following our star that we open ourselves to God's life-changing power.

Have I ever experienced an epiphany?
Has any event changed my life-view completely?

¶ FOLLOW MY STAR WHEREVER IT LEADS.

Pets

No verifiable record exists of any pets the Holy Family might have had. In the Israel of their day, however, generally only the wealthy could afford the luxury of an animal that didn't earn its keep. Yet it's pleasant to imagine that when the Holy Family lived in Egypt, Mary experienced the comfort and company of a cat.

Domestic cats have been part of Egyptian households almost since the dawn of Egyptian civilization. During the time that Mary, Joseph, and Jesus lived there, cats would have been commonplace, winding their way through unsuspecting legs, meowing for milk at back steps, curling comfortably on freshly folded piles of laundry—in short, doing just what cats do today.

While cats aren't everyone's favorite pet, companion animals have been part of humanity since the first humans stepped onto the savanna. And rightly so. The lessons of unconditional love and mutual dependence that we learn from our pets help give us a glimpse into the workings of the universe.

As Irving Townsend put it in *The Once Again Prince,*

We who choose to surround ourselves with lives more temporary than our own, live within a fragile circle easily and often breached. Unable to accept its awful gaps, we still would live no other way. We cherish memory as the only certain immortality, never fully understanding the necessary plan.

Do animals have any lessons to teach me?
What have I learned from them?

1 REJOICE AND CELEBRATE ALL LIFE—HUMAN AND ANIMAL.

Anger

Can you imagine Mary being really upset—downright angry—with someone or something? Most likely not. We traditionally picture her as being patient, mild, meek, and happy with everything that came her way.

However, we do Mary a disservice if we assume that she never got angry. Anger itself isn't a sin. The Psalms are full of references to God's righteous anger. Jesus himself was filled with anger when he drove the money-changers from the Temple.

So why do we assume that Mary never got angry? Perhaps it's because we make a leap of illogic. Let's take a look at the faulty reasoning:

A. People generally become angry because someone does something that they perceive as wrong.
B. Mary's son Jesus was God.
C. God can't sin.
D. Therefore, Jesus couldn't do anything wrong.
E. Since Jesus couldn't do anything wrong, his mother had nothing to get angry about.

This argument has two major flaws. First, it assumes that the only person Mary had any dealings with was Jesus; and second, it assumes that everything wrong is sinful. Both of those assumptions are false. When one of Jesus' boyhood playmates tracked sheep dung across Mary's clean floor, Mary probably wasn't the cheeriest mom in the village. She might have raised her voice. She might even have—gasp!—felt quite cross. What sets Mary apart, however, is the fact that even when she felt angry, she never allowed her anger to cause her to sin.

The feeling of anger is just that—a *feeling*. It's what we do with our anger that makes it harmful to ourselves or others.

Do I ever lose my temper? Have I ever let my anger cause me to hurt someone either verbally or physically?

WHEN I'M ANGRY, I ACKNOWLEDGE THE FEELING
BUT DON'T LET IT CONTROL ME.

Picturing Reality

It's a good thing cameras hadn't been invented when Mary was living. If we had a photograph of her, we'd be bound to be disappointed. She'd be either too thin or too fat. Her features would be too pretty or not pretty enough. She'd be too tall or too short, too old or too young, too dark or too fair. No matter what she looked like, she could never match our mental images.

Over the centuries, many artists have tried to bring their visions of Mary to life. While she has been portrayed in innumerable ways by innumerable artists, most of the portraits present a delicate, docile maid (often with Nordic features) who looks too fragile to be allowed outside in a brisk wind.

Such a picture is at odds with reality. Since Mary was Semitic, she would have had the features and coloring of a woman from the Middle East. Since she lived a good deal of her life outdoors, she must have been weathered and tanned. And since she was a working-class woman, she was quite likely sturdy and strong—as capable of planting a field as of sewing a fine seam.

Why, then, do our pictures of Mary so often make her look vapid and ephemeral?

Maybe it's because we don't want Mary to look like a real-life woman. Maybe we want her to look like a carved statue, because then we don't have to emulate her. Who, after all, can emulate a statue? But Mary is *not* a statue. She's an intelligent, forthright woman, marked by determination and holiness. Those are qualities that we can and should emulate.

How do I picture Mary? Do I see her as a real person or as a marble statue? What would happen to my concept of Mary if I saw her as she really is?

1 DON'T JUDGE BY OUTSIDE APPEARANCES. 1 STRIVE
TO SEE WHAT'S UNDERNEATH THE SURFACE.

Ark of the Covenant

One of Mary's traditional titles is Ark of the Covenant. Since the Ark of the Covenant was the Hebrew container for the Tablets of the Law that Moses brought down from Mt. Sinai, calling Mary the Ark of the Covenant may strike us as being a little peculiar. The title seems to imply that she's like a gilded box with stone inside. Not a terribly appealing image until you understand what the title really indicates.

The Ark of the Covenant was the sanctuary for the material sign of God's contract with the Hebrews. Because of its close contact with the Tablets of the Law, the Ark itself was transformed into a holy object.

In traditional Christian belief, Mary's womb became the sanctuary for Jesus, who was the material sign of God's new contract with all people. Like the original Ark, Mary was transformed into holiness through her contact with Jesus. We, through our contact with Mary and her son, can also be transformed into holiness.

As Pope John Paul II said in an address on November 30, 1980, "Has man ever been able to attain to anything more exalted? Has he ever been able to experience about himself anything more profound? Has man been able through any achievement of his being man—through his intellect, the greatness of his mind, or through heroic deeds—to be lifted to a higher state than has been given him in this 'fruit of the womb' of Mary . . . ?"

How can I let Mary's example transform me?
In what ways can I become an ark of holiness for
those around me?

I KNOW THAT I'M FILLED WITH THE HOLINESS OF GOD.

Expecting a Miracle

A popular bumper sticker reads, "Expect a miracle!"

When you pray, do you really expect God to answer? Do you really believe that if you ask for a miracle, you'll get one?

If we're honest, most of us would have to admit to harboring a few doubts—and not without good cause. All of us can cite examples of "failed" prayer: people we know who poured out their heart and soul to God and yet their child still died, or their business still collapsed, or their marriage still failed. In those cases, many well-wishers offer sappy platitudes such as "It must have been God's will" or "I'm certain God has something much better in mind for you."

One wonders if people said similar things to Mary when her only son was condemned as a criminal and crucified on a cross. Undoubtedly she prayed that somehow God would spare her child; and yet, on that Friday afternoon, he was nailed to a cross and left to die a traitor's death.

What must Mary have felt at that moment? She had received a promise thirty-three years earlier that her son would be the Messiah, but she hadn't been given detailed plans. Like us, she had to offer her prayers not knowing what the outcome would be, trusting God to hear and answer. In the midst of her suffering at the Crucifixion, it's likely (human nature being what it is) that someone tried to comfort her at the foot of the cross by saying, "It's God's will."

The irony is that it *was* God's will. Moreover, despite appearances, God was preparing a miracle—the greatest miracle of all time: the Resurrection.

Mary expected a miracle. *And she got one!*

> *Do I trust God enough to believe that my prayers will be*
> *answered? Do I allow God room to answer, or do I*
> *demand a response in a specific time and manner?*

1 KNOW THAT GOD WANTS ONLY GOOD FOR MY LIFE.

Feelings

True or false?

> Mary never complained.
> Mary was never cranky.
> Mary was never tired.
> Mary liked everything and everybody.

If you answered *true* to all the above statements, you may be assuming some mistruths about Mary.

Traditional theology teaches that Mary was conceived without the natural tendencies toward sin that the rest of us are born with. In some mysterious fashion, she was the first to have the saving action of Jesus applied to her soul—applied, in fact, at the moment of her own conception. This Immaculate Conception, as it's called, gave Mary certain graces. For instance, she was able to resist the lure of sin in her life, becoming, as Wordsworth put it, "our tainted nature's solitary boast."

But the fact that she was conceived without a trace of sin doesn't mean that Mary was above all the foibles and frustrations of human life. At the end of a long day's walk into the hill country to see her cousin Elizabeth, Mary might well have complained that her feet hurt. When the crops had to be harvested, the laundry done, and the Sabbath meal prepared—all on the same day—Mary might well have sunk into bed totally exhausted.

In looking to Mary as a role model, Christian believers must be wary not to assume that her special graces caused her to abandon her human nature. Instead, Mary stands as an example of the way each of us can rise above our failings, while still remaining fully and joyously human.

Do I assume that holiness is incompatible
with normal human emotions?

I ACCEPT MY FEELINGS, REALIZING THEY ARE NEITHER
RIGHT NOR WRONG; THEY SIMPLY *ARE.*

Mama

The first words that most children say are pet forms of address for their parents—Mama or Dada—and they result in great parental excitement.

That first name for a maternal parent—Mama—carries a very different connotation than the formal address—Mother. The word *Mama* brings with it a sense of comfort, cuddling, and connection, while *Mother* is stiff, stuffy, and stern.

Just for fun, try thinking of Mary as *Mother*. What sort of picture springs to mind? For many, it's a stately woman dressed in flowing blue robes and seated on a throne. She smiles benevolently on her subjects, since she's as much queen as mother. Although she exudes compassion and understanding, she's nonetheless a bit aloof and distant.

Now picture Mary as *Mama*. Does your image change? Perhaps you now see her in a rough-woven tunic, her face smudged with flour from the day's baking. No longer formally seated in a throne room, she stands in her kitchen amid the clutter of normal family life.

Which Mary appeals most to you?

Perhaps it's Mary the Queen Mother, in charge of an army of angels, confident, powerful, and contained. Or maybe it's Mary the Mama, with open arms, a hug, and a smile.

More than likely, both images have their appeal. When we're in need of a mother, we can turn to Mary, the powerful Mother, who not only knows what's best for us but has the resources to help satisfy our needs. When we long for a mama, we can seek solace in Mary, our Mama, who embraces us with loving arms and kisses away our tears.

Do I generally picture Mary as Mother or as Mama?
Which aspect of Mary do I need to embrace today?

1 ACKNOWLEDGE MY NEED FOR A MOTHER'S LOVE. 1F 1 DON'T HAVE A MOTHER ON THIS EARTH, 1 KNOW THAT 1 HAVE A MAMA IN HEAVEN.

Beauty (and the Beast)

One of the most beloved Disney animated classics is *Beauty and the Beast.* Based on the French folk tale *La Belle et le Bête,* it's a timeless story of the transforming power of a young girl's love. In some ways, *La Belle et le Bête* is also the story of salvation.

According to teaching put forth in the Hebrew Scriptures and reiterated in the Christian New Testament, humanity and God became so separated that reconciliation seemed impossible. Yet God, as ever-loving parent, found a way to restore the shattered relationship. The divine plan was stunningly simple: God would become a human being. God would be born of a human mother, be raised in a human family, and ultimately die a human death. In living out that plan, God would reunite humanity and divinity.

The one small hitch was a little thing called "free will." The girl God chose to set this plan in motion had to freely and willingly say *yes.* God couldn't force her to cooperate; God could only invite her to participate. Fortunately for all of us, Mary's reply was affirmative: "May it be done to me according to your word."

So what does this have to do with *La Belle et le Bête?*

In the folk tale, a prince has been changed from a handsome young man into a horrible beast, and he must remain a beast until someone loves him fully, completely, and freely. Then, and only then, will he be able to resume his rightful form and rightful place. Belle is able to see through his flaws and offer the Beast her love. Her *yes* to love transforms the Beast. Mary was able to see through the flaws of this life, and it's her *yes* to love that transformed the world.

Do I give my love freely and without strings?

I USE MY FREE WILL TO SAY YES TO LIFE AND YES TO LOVE.

Marriage

Anyone who has ever been married knows that marriage isn't something to be entered into lightly. Even the best marriages have their difficult moments. Couples have to struggle to find common ground, to share their lives, to grow together.

The marriage of Mary and Joseph was no different. They too had to have had their trials. Remember that although Mary was blessed with certain graces from the time of her own birth, Joseph wasn't. He was a perfectly normal, ordinary man, which means he could have snored, left his sandals on the hearth, forgotten to tie up the goat—all the ordinary things that can drive a spouse up the wall.

The fact that Mary was unique in the history of humanity doesn't mean that she didn't have to adjust to the strains of living with another human being. Joseph wasn't her clone; he had his own little idiosyncrasies, many of which may have been frustrating to her.

In addition, some traditions say that he was a widower when he married Mary, so it's entirely possible that he had children from his first marriage. How Mary got along with those kids—and how those kids got along with Mary—is something Scripture wisely ignores.

The fact that Mary knew what the day-to-day life of a married woman is like doesn't detract from her holiness; instead, it gives everyone who is married an example of true and lasting commitment.

If I'm married, what can I do to help support my spouse today?
If I'm not married, how can I help someone who is married
live out his or her commitment more fully?

1 KNOW THAT IF 1 TRUST GOD, 1'LL DEVELOP THE KIND OF
RELATIONSHIPS 1 NEED TO MATURE SPIRITUALLY.

Behind Closed Doors

A popular country-and-western song talks about what happens behind closed doors when an apparently prim and proper woman lets her hair down. The song celebrates an expression of love, but not all closed doors conceal passion and affection. In all too many cases, closed doors hide heartache and sorrow. Relationships that appear in public to be placid and peaceful may be, in worst-case scenarios, cauldrons of abuse and violence in private.

In Mary's life, for instance, we haven't a clue what her friends and relatives (with the exception of Elizabeth) said about her being pregnant outside of wedlock. Since we know the end of the story, we *assume* that they were supportive and helpful, but they may have been critical and judgmental. They may have made cutting remarks about her condition and her virtue when no one but Mary could hear them. Conversely, they may have been loving and nurturing, despite what the rest of the village was saying.

The fact is that we simply can't know what goes on behind the closed doors in other people's lives. That's one of the main reasons it's so essential that we refrain from judging other people's lives and behavior. When we're tempted to be critical, it's helpful to remember that what goes around, comes around. It's almost a sure bet that the one thing we're the most critical of in someone else's life will be the one thing that someday someone will be critical of in ours.

Do I tend to make critical judgments about other people,
or am I willing to live and let live?

¶ LET GO OF THE TEMPTATION TO CRITICIZE OTHERS.

Change

Change always creates disruption.

That may sound like an overly simplistic statement, but it's true. Although change is always disruptive, change isn't always bad. Indeed, sometimes change is necessary. If, for instance, you've developed patterns of behavior in your relationships that aren't conducive to your spiritual growth and well-being, you need to make changes. If you're leading a life that's self-destructive or self-deprecating, change is vital. Often change is absolutely essential to spiritual and emotional health. Without change, life itself may be compromised in such cases.

One of the messages Mary brings to the world in her appearances at places such as Lourdes and Fatima is the absolute need to change sinful lives into holy ones. Over and over again she says, "Pray; pray so that you will change."

The changes Mary asks for aren't easy. She asks that we change our attitudes, our prejudices, our selfishness, and our sinfulness.

As you begin to change, count on feeling uncomfortable. Life favors the status quo, after all. As you continue to make changes, those around you may begin to feel uncomfortable as well. Often your changes will force them to make changes too, changes that will promote your—and their—spiritual growth, which is exactly what Mary is counting on!

What do I need to change in my life today?
What will I do when I encounter resistance to
my attempts to change?

I HAVE THE STRENGTH TO CARRY OUT THE CHANGES
I NEED TO MAKE IN MY LIFE.

Hope

For a woman who lived in a podunk village in a backwater part of the world, Mary certainly saw more than her share of marvels. An angel in her living room. Wise Men on her porch. Angels in the sky. During those few blessed months surrounding the birth of Jesus, Mary experienced signs and wonders beyond her most vivid dreams.

Then came the next thirty years. No more angels. No more Wise Men. No more marvels. Just ordinary life in a small village. The memory of the signs and wonders must have faded a bit with the passing years. Doubts must have crept in. *Did I really see an angel? Did he really tell me my son would be the Messiah?* Perhaps Mary brought out one of the chests the Magi had given her and fingered its inlaid surface, remembering, pondering. Thirty years is a long time to go without confirmation of the promise made by the angel. *Is it possible I was mistaken?* she may have said to herself. *Maybe I misunderstood. Maybe I was wrong.*

We don't know what Mary thought, but we do know that she continued to hope. In fact, she's sometimes called the Mother of Hope. She deserves that title because she knows what it means to cling to a promise in the face of doubt, to walk by faith, not sight. In short, more than any of us, she knows what it means to hope.

Is there something that I'm hoping will come to pass?
Do I trust God's promises enough to wait
patiently without confirmation?

I BELIEVE EVEN THOUGH I DON'T SEE, AND I HOPE EVEN THOUGH I DON'T KNOW FOR SURE THAT MY DREAMS WILL BE REALIZED.

Best Behavior

We generally figure that Mary and her son Jesus were always on their best behavior. But exactly what does being on one's best behavior mean? Does it mean acting appropriately in a given situation, or does it mean acting the way others expect us to?

If it means acting appropriately—and most of us would accept that definition—then Mary and Jesus certainly were always on their best behavior. But if it means acting the way others expect us to, they almost never were.

Jesus turned his world upside down—not just by working miracles, but by associating with prostitutes and tax collectors, by blessing Gentiles as well as Jews, by defying the conventions of his day in order to create a new order of consciousness.

When we're on our best (most appropriate) behavior, we're conducting ourselves in the way that's best for us and those around us. Depending on the situation, our best behavior may be silly or serious, daring or demure, boisterous or boring. It all depends.

The key to being on your best behavior is figuring out what behavior is called for at the moment. Sometimes it's obvious—reserved decorum would be essential if you were to meet with the president of the United States in the Oval Office, for example. But if you were to play charades with the president at a private party, a different type of behavior would be best.

God wants us to figure out what our best behavior should be, whatever our circumstances, and to be on that best behavior at all times!

*Do I act appropriately, or do I behave the way I think
others expect me to behave?*

I'M ALWAYS ON MY BEST BEHAVIOR.

Wisdom

Religions based on goddesses recognize three distinct stages of holiness for women: the virgin daughter, the mother, and the wise woman. Christianity has traditionally applied the first two aspects of holiness to Mary but has by and large ignored the third. Mary is honored as the innocent virgin and praised as the nurturing mother, but rarely is she seen as the mature, wise woman.

An overemphasis on Mary's virginity and Christ's virgin birth has the potential to prevent us from making a complete identification with Mary. Yet she didn't remain a young virgin her entire life. As she who was "full of grace" grew older, she developed into a woman of mature grace. She grew, just as all of us do, not only in age but also in wisdom.

That's one of the great lessons Mary has to teach us: that we can and must grow in wisdom. She wasn't a fully developed person at the time of the angel Gabriel's appearance to her. Though mature beyond her years, she was still only about fourteen. At that time, hers was a wisdom given by God, not a seasoned wisdom developed through years of living. Thirty-three years later, at the foot of her son's cross, she was no longer the same person. Life, with all its joys and all its pains, had transformed her. The virgin girl who said yes to an angel had become the mature woman who stood by her son during the agony of the Crucifixion. The teenager couldn't have done what the forty-seven-year-old could. To fully appreciate Mary, we must see her in all stages of her life.

As we grow through our own lives, we need to recognize that we aren't the same person we were five, ten, or twenty years ago. Like Mary, we too need to grow in wisdom and maturity, for Mary's path of growth is our path as well.

How have I grown over the last year?
The last five years? The last ten years?

I APPRECIATE THE WISDOM I HAVE GARNERED
OVER THE YEARS OF MY LIFE.

Righteousness

In the sixth month, the angel Gabriel was sent from God to a town of Galilee called Nazareth, to a virgin betrothed to a man named Joseph, of the house of David, and the virgin's name was Mary.

LUKE 1:26–27

In ancient Israel, the betrothal was more than a mere engagement. It was a serious commitment—almost as serious as marriage itself. In fact, marriage came into being in that culture not as a single act of exchanging vows (as it does today) but as part of a process that began with the promise to marry *eventually.* Such a solemn and binding promise—the betrothal—could take place when both parties were very young and the marriage itself years in the future. The betrothal was both a sign of something to come and a commitment to something that already existed. While the girl continued to live at home during the betrothal, it wasn't unheard of for a couple to have sexual relations during that time.

Most of the emphasis on the angel Gabriel's visit rightly belongs to Mary, but consider Joseph for a moment. There he was, honoring the official terms of the betrothal, and Mary turns up pregnant! He knew *he* wasn't responsible—so what was he to think? You can be sure he didn't say to himself, "Lo, she must have been visited by an angel and is now miraculously pregnant."

Since he "was a righteous man, unwilling to expose her to shame, he decided to divorce her quietly." In those few words lie the key to Joseph's character. Even though he thought that Mary had betrayed her betrothal vows, even though he believed that he had been wronged, he didn't want to hurt Mary: he was willing to have the entire village think that he'd abandoned her when she was carrying his child. Obviously he loved her passionately, for he was willing to besmirch his own character in order to salvage hers. Could anyone's love exceed that?

Am I willing to sacrifice myself for those I love? Would I be willing to do so even for someone I thought had wronged me?

I ALWAYS WANT THE BEST FOR THOSE AROUND ME.

Memories

Memories are one of the greatest treasures any of us can possess. Pictures can be destroyed, videotapes can be erased, but (barring a disease such as Alzheimer's) memories last a lifetime.

Tradition says that Mary spent the last years of her life with the disciple John in Ephesus. Far from her family and home, Mary ended her days as a stranger in a strange place. With little or nothing familiar around her, she must have taken comfort in her memories while waiting to join her son in heaven.

What did Mary remember at the end of her life?

Her memories certainly would have included major events such as the Annunciation, the Visitation, and the Resurrection, but they also would have included simple times in Nazareth—watching Jesus help Joseph in the workshop, talking with her friends at the city well, preparing the table for the Sabbath meal.

Quiet times shared with those we love often make the most lasting memories of all. A cup of tea and a cookie over a heartfelt conversation can create a deeper and more lasting memory than an entire grand tour of Europe.

It's never too late to create memories that will be comforting and sustaining at the end of life. But creating such memories entails taking risks—risks of the heart and soul. These risks are sometimes more difficult to undertake than the most arduous physical challenge, but in the eternal scheme of things they're worth it.

Do I bear grudges, or do I store memories?
What kind of memories do I want to create today?

¶ CREATE MEMORIES THAT SUSTAIN AND NOURISH MY SOUL.

Blessedness

For generations Christians have called Mary hundreds of different names, but perhaps none is more appropriate than the simple word *blessed.* That title is the only one Mary applied to herself—not because she considered herself special but because she recognized that God had done great things through her. Mary said exultantly,

> My soul proclaims the greatness of the Lord;
> my spirit rejoices in God my savior.
> For he has looked upon his handmaid's lowliness;
> behold, from now on will all ages call me blessed.
> The Mighty One has done great things for me,
> and holy is his name.
> His mercy is from age to age
> to those who fear him.
> He has shown might with his arm,
> dispersed the arrogant of mind and heart.
> He has thrown down the rulers from their thrones
> but lifted up the lowly.
> The hungry he has filled with good things;
> the rich he has sent away empty.
> He has helped Israel his servant,
> remembering his mercy,
> according to his promise to our fathers,
> to Abraham and to his descendants forever.
> (Luke 1:46–55)

What great things has God, the Mighty One, done for me in my life? Do I believe that God will fill me with good things, according to God's promises?

TODAY I PROCLAIM THE GOODNESS OF THE LORD
WITH ALL MY BEING.

Courage

Mary isn't often thought of as having been courageous, but she was. From the young girl who stood straight and tall before an angel to the mature woman who waited patiently in the Upper Room with her son's followers, Mary is a model of quiet valor.

What does it take to be brave in today's world?

All too often, we think that courage requires physical risk. We think of a firefighter entering a blazing inferno to rescue a trapped victim. A rescue team rappelling down the side of a cliff to reach an injured climber. A team of divers searching for pieces of a wrecked plane in a dismal swamp.

Those who perform such deeds are indeed brave, but bravery can take many forms. What about a young girl willing to face the task of raising her child alone? Or a mother holding her head high despite the ridicule of neighbors who think her son is crazy? Or an elderly woman pushing aside a police officer to stand beside her wrongly accused child? Are not these women (all of whom could be Mary herself) committing acts of courage as well?

The next time you face a situation that demands courage, remember the example of Mary. Her strength can be your strength, if only you ask for her assistance.

What do I think constitutes real courage?
Who is the bravest person I know?

I HAVE WITHIN ME THE POWER TO BE AS BRAVE
AS CIRCUMSTANCES DEMAND.

Mary's Blessing

The writings of the saints are filled with praises and petitions to Mary.

For instance, in the year 373 St. Athanasius begged, "Remember us, most holy Virgin, and bestow on us gifts from the riches of your graces, Virgin, full of grace." And more than fifteen hundred years later, Pope John Paul II prayed, as reported in *Insegnamenti* on May 12, 1982,

> I wish to repeat now, before you all, *totus tuus*—all yours, O Mother! I ask you to offer me and all these brethren up to the "Father of Mercies," in homage and gratitude, hiding and covering our poverty with your merits and those of your Divine Son. And may we be accepted, blessed, and strengthened in our good resolves, which we wish to bind up, like a bunch of flowers, with a ribbon "woven and gilded" for you, O Mother: "Do whatever he tells you." Give us your blessing, Lady, our most beloved Mother!

The one common thread in all the many praises of and petitions to Mary is the request for her blessing. Why has it been so important to holy men and women throughout the centuries that Mary extend her blessing? Why should we care if Mary blesses us?

We need Mary's blessing because she's more than the mother of Jesus; she's *our* mother as well. In receiving her blessing, we gain the backing of a mother's love, which is one of the most powerful forces in the universe.

Have I ever asked Mary for her blessing?
Do I believe that she'd give it to me if I asked?

TODAY I'LL ASK MARY TO BLESS ME AND ALL THOSE IN MY FAMILY.

Inner Beauty

When we picture Mary, we generally envision a stunning young girl about eighteen years old, with flowing hair, flawless skin, and a to-die-for figure. Childbirth, hard outdoor labor, days in the sun without sunscreen—none of these dares leave a mark on her. Indeed, when Mary appears in visions, she's often described as being young and beautiful.

But the Mary who stood at the foot of the cross must have looked quite different. She would have been nearly fifty when Jesus died—an old woman by standards of the time. She would have had laugh lines around her eyes, her hair would have been streaked with gray, and her figure would have already settled into matronly comfort. She was probably still beautiful, but without the untouched, ephemeral beauty we normally associate with her.

Because Catholic tradition teaches that Mary was preserved from sin, we tend to assume that she was preserved from the ravages of ordinary life. We assume that since her soul was flawless, her body must have been as well. Hence, we picture Mary as eternally young and gorgeous. But as Antoine de Saint-Exupéry says in *The Little Prince*, "What is essential is invisible to the eye." Mary appears as a beautiful woman not because she rivaled Miss America in her earthly life (though she may have) but because of her inner goodness. She appears beautiful because she *was* beautiful where it counts—in her soul.

Do I spend more time cultivating my inner beauty
or my outer appearance?

TODAY I'LL SPEND TIME BECOMING BEAUTIFUL ON THE INSIDE.

Well-Wishing

It's hard to imagine Mary doing much besides praying and taking care of Jesus. (And since Jesus was God, we assume that he probably didn't need much taking care of. We don't imagine him as a stubborn two-year-old balking at potty training, or a sullen teen leaving his tunic draped over a stool.) Because we assume that Jesus didn't need much "mothering," all too often our image of Mary is of a hermit nun rather than a real wife and mom.

To get a more realistic picture of Mary, imagine the scene at the communal city well. Mary is chatting with her neighbors, laughing at a story one of the women is telling, listening to rumors that the Romans are planning on building a gladiator arena in a nearby field. She waits her turn to dip her large jug into the fresh, sweet water. Perhaps she pauses to help an elderly relative with her jug. Nothing on the outside indicates that she's playing a pivotal role in the history of the world. She looks just like an ordinary Jewish mother providing water for her household.

And that's the way it should be. The wonder of Mary is not that she's above us but that she's one of us. She knows how hard ordinary life can be, but she also knows that it's precisely in the ordinary that the most extraordinary spiritual events occur.

Do I think that I have to be doing spiritual things all the time to be "holy"? Do I believe that I can achieve wholeness and holiness in my ordinary activities?

I LOOK FOR WAYS TO BECOME A HOLY PERSON NOT IN "SPIRITUAL" ACTIVITIES BUT IN THE ACTIONS OF DAILY LIFE.

Bread

At the Last Supper, Jesus took bread, broke it, and gave it to his disciples, saying, "Take and eat; this is my body." We hear those words over and over, each time we celebrate Mass or attend a Communion service.

Ever wonder who made the bread that was used that Passover night? Of course, we don't know, but it's pleasant to think that perhaps Mary prepared the loaves.

Earlier in the week, she must have known, with the intuition mothers have, that something was afoot. She must have sensed the uneasiness in her son and his disciples. She had to have heard rumors and rumblings among the other women.

Wondering, worrying, watching, she may have found respite in the ritual of grinding the wheat, kneading the dough, shaping the loaves. She may have found peace in knowing that no matter what happened in the next few days, her son, her baby, would enjoy the taste of bread prepared by his mother.

If indeed Mary was the one to make the bread that Jesus broke at the Last Supper, little did she know that she was helping prepare a miracle. In doing what mothers have done for millennia, she transformed grain into bread for life. That night, before he died, her son transformed her bread for life into the Bread of Life.

How can I allow my life to be transformed by service for others?

I ALLOW MYSELF TO BECOME A NEW PERSON THROUGH
THE POWER OF MARY'S SON JESUS.

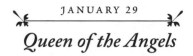

Queen of the Angels

We might think we'd like to be visited by an angel, but it's likely that most of us would prefer to be visited by an angel *in disguise*. Real angels aren't chubby little babies or androgynous creatures in long white dresses who drift to earth on gossamer wings.

Why we've pictured angels as delicate or dainty is a puzzlement, since the angels described in Scripture are a lot more like heavenly Marine commandos—take-charge, no-nonsense beings carrying out divine orders even if that means storming the gates of hell itself.

The angels posted at the gates of Eden, for instance, were armed with flaming swords. The angels described in Ezekiel—with their four faces, four wings, hooves of brass, four hands, and accompanying illuminated spinning wheel—could have come straight from a science-fiction movie. The angel who appeared to Balaam terrified Balaam's donkey into immobility. The angels singing over Bethlehem scared the poor shepherds witless. Not a pudgy-toed baby in the entire angelic lot.

Angel reality gives Mary's traditional title Queen of Angels a fascinating slant. Instead of being queen over a gaggle of fluttering cherubs or fey spirits, Mary is queen of an army of determined, focused, self-assured beings who follow God's will without hesitation.

When we ask Mary to send the angels to help us, we're asking her to dispatch a literal army. Perhaps the reason we don't experience the angels' assistance in our lives is that we fail to see them as the powerful spiritual warriors they really are.

When I ask for angelic assistance, do I believe that I'll be helped?
In what ways have I already been helped by the angels?

1 EXPECT THE ANGELS TO HELP ME WHEN 1 ASK MARY,
QUEEN OF ANGELS, FOR GUIDANCE.

Purchasing Power

If Mary ran out of garlic for the evening meal, she couldn't send Jesus to the corner store to pick up another clove or two. The only time Mary could buy food—or anything else, for that matter—was on market day. The rest of the time she had to either make do with what she had or borrow from one of her neighbors.

With stores open twenty-four hours a day, we Americans no longer have to plan shopping trips in advance. Whenever the mood strikes us, we can dash into a store and buy just about anything our hearts desire (and our pocketbooks can afford). Such spontaneity may appear liberating, but having unlimited access to purchases can actually be confining.

Stop and ask yourself if there's anything you *need* to buy at this very moment. Be honest. Is there anything you absolutely can't live without? Granted, if the cupboard is literally bare, you need to find something to eat. And if you're ill, you may need a particular medication. Those types of exceptions notwithstanding, what *must* you buy right now? For most of us, the honest answer is nothing.

However, if we were to go into a store, *any* store, odds are we would feel the need to purchase something. Perhaps an item whose very existence we were unaware of yesterday would become, in the blink of an eye, a necessity. But if we were to buy it and cart it home, what would happen? We'd have one more object to worry about, one more thing to take care of. What might have seemed to be a spontaneous, liberating action—that impulse purchase—would result in yet one more thread tying our soul to our possessions.

Do I own my possessions, or do my possessions own me?

I CONSIDER THE LONG-RANGE IMPLICATIONS OF
EVERY ITEM I'M TEMPTED TO PURCHASE.

Gender Differences

If aliens were to land on earth and observe humanity for any length of time, they might conclude that men and women are two different species who just happen to live in the same place. Cats and dogs, which *are* different species, often act more alike than do men and women.

And it isn't just actions. Men and women *think* differently. In fact, new scientific evidence verifies what most of us have known all along: men and women use their brains in different ways. Little wonder that we have so much difficulty getting along at times!

Even though Mary, the Mother of God, had special graces, she was still a woman; and Jesus, though he was God incarnate, was still a man; and Joseph, though he was a *good* man, was still a man. Which means that there had to have been times when Joseph and Jesus didn't have a clue what Mary was thinking, and vice versa. In fact, there must have been times when Mary headed out to her mother's or her sister's, leaving Joseph and Jesus shaking their heads and wondering, *What's going on here?*

The fact that God created men and women to be different doesn't mean that one or the other gender is superior. In fact, God is clear that men and women are complementary, neither having an inherent advantage over the other. In the poetic language of Genesis,

God created man in his image;
in the divine image he created him;
male and female he created them.

In what ways do I see all people as being
created in the image of God?

I CELEBRATE MY BEING, REJOICING THAT I'M
CREATED IN THE DIVINE IMAGE.

Doubt

St. Augustine once said that a thousand doubts do not make a single disbelief. When dealing with spiritual matters, we can doubt much, but if we're earnestly seeking the truth, we won't fall into disbelief. That doesn't mean, however, that we'll always agree.

Many people hold beliefs about Mary that others doubt. For instance, Catholics hold that Mary was ever-virgin and consequently never had any children besides Jesus. Other Christians maintain that the mention of Jesus' brothers and sisters in the Gospels is proof that Mary and Joseph *did* have other children. Catholics argue in turn that the terms *brother* and *sister* can refer to any close relative and maintain that Jesus' brothers and sisters were really cousins or even stepsiblings (assuming Joseph might have been married before).

While wars have been fought for less, our ruminating over such points is a bit like medieval monks speculating about how many angels could dance on the head of a pin. Rather than concentrating on areas of disagreement, why not focus on areas of agreement? For instance, all Christians agree that Mary was a virgin when she gave birth to Jesus, that Jesus was willing to start his public ministry in response to her request for more wine, and that Mary never forsake Jesus, following him even to the foot of his cross.

There are more than enough things to disagree about in this world. Let's not make Mary one of them.

How do I behave when I know I'm right?
Do I try to argue others into my point of view?

IF I MUST DISAGREE WITH SOMEONE, I DO IT AGREEABLY.

The Presentation of the Lord

According to Mosaic law, the firstborn son of a Jewish couple had to be brought to the Temple of Jerusalem and redeemed by the payment of five shekels (about $1.50). In addition, after the birth of a boy every woman had to offer a lamb (if she was well-to-do) or two turtledoves (if she was poor) for her own purification. Mary was no exception. She and Joseph dutifully traveled to Jerusalem to make the necessary offerings.

The fact that Mary and Joseph offered two doves instead of a lamb has historically been taken as evidence of their poverty—which indeed may be the case. But we can't be sure. Because the time-frame for the events surrounding the birth of Christ is a little shaky, we don't know exactly when the Wise Men arrived. If the Magi had already visited the family by the time of the Presentation, Mary and Joseph could have used some of their gold or traded some of their spices to buy a lamb.

If they *did* have the resources, why might Mary and Joseph nonetheless have opted for the "poorer" offering? Maybe because Mary wasn't only holy but smart. She knew that it wasn't necessary to spend extra money for a lamb when two doves would be perfectly adequate. Besides, if she had shelled out for the lamb, the Roman tax collectors would have been nosing around asking questions and demanding more than their share of the wealth. Being a bright woman, she kept a low profile by obeying the letter of the law—to the letter.

While Mary is always held up as an example of holiness, she can be a model of "street smarts" as well. The fact that she focused her sight on God doesn't mean she wasn't aware of the need to live wisely on earth.

Do I believe that worldly wisdom and heavenly grace are incompatible? Do I think that I have to choose between heaven and earth?

I USE MY GOD-GIVEN INTELLIGENCE TO MAKE
THE BEST OF LIFE HERE ON EARTH.

Diet

Ever wonder what sorts of foods Mary, Joseph, and Jesus would have eaten?

Their first meal of the day, taken between nine and noon, would generally have consisted of bread, fruits, and cheese. The bread would have been made of wheat or barley. The fruits would have included raisins, pomegranates, figs, and olives. The Book of Acts mentions that Jesus, as an adult, once prepared a breakfast for his followers that featured fresh fish cooked on an open fire.

The more substantial principal meal, eaten in the evening, would have included vegetables, such as beans flavored with oil and garlic, lentils, cucumbers, onions, and greens (including watercress, endive, and lettuce), more fruit, butter, goat's milk, wine, and (on special occasions) a meat such as lamb.

The diet of the Holy Family was a lot like the diet recommended for heart health today—heavy on the fruits and veggies, light on the meats and fats. Not that Mary, Jesus, and Joseph would have had much choice. They wouldn't have been able to afford to set a table laden with meats, cheeses, and rich dishes.

Ironically, today it's hard to afford the simple fare they took for granted. A breakfast of freshly baked stone-ground-wheat bread, pomegranates, figs, and olives would be a great deal more costly than a bowl of sugared cereal.

It takes determined effort to eat a health-promoting diet in today's culture. It's so much easier to slide into a fast-food mentality. However, we owe it to ourselves—and to our Creator—to take care of the bodies we were given by eating the proper foods in the proper amounts.

Do I ever overeat? Do I eat the wrong foods even when I know better?

I EAT HEALTH-PROMOTING FOODS IN MODERATE
QUANTITIES SO THAT MY BODY HAS THE FUEL IT NEEDS
TO COMPLETE THE TASKS GOD HAS GIVEN ME.

Blame

When Joseph and Mary finally found Jesus in the Temple, it seems unlikely that they were totally calm and unruffled. After all, their son had been lost for three days in their equivalent of New York City. They had to have been panic-stricken. Mary must have imagined that Jesus had been taken into slavery like his ancestor Joseph—or worse, was lying dead in some back alley. Never mind that an angel had told her twelve years before that Jesus was to be the Messiah; she was his mother, and mothers worry about their children.

When she finally caught up with him, she probably didn't talk in soft, level tones. It doesn't take much to hear a certain edge to her words: "Son, why have you done this to us? Your father and I have been looking for you with great anxiety." She probably was caught between being relieved to find him alive and well and being rightly angry that he had put them through so much worry.

However, Scripture doesn't record her placing blame. She didn't blame Jesus for staying behind (though she might have been tempted to). She didn't blame Joseph for not paying close enough attention (though she might have been tempted to). And she didn't blame herself for not checking up on Jesus (though she might have been tempted to). Instead, she took her son home, where he "was obedient to them."

Blame is never constructive. It rips our self-esteem and ruins our discernment. Whenever we're in a stressful situation, we should try to remain calm, as Mary did, rather than try to affix blame—and then we should make sure that the same thing never happens again!

Do I blame myself for things that aren't my fault?
Do I try to assign blame to others in order to make
myself feel better about difficult situations?

TODAY I WON'T BLAME ANYONE, INCLUDING MYSELF, FOR ANYTHING.

Blessings in Disguise

Have you ever experienced something that you were sure was a disaster, only to discover later that the disaster was a proverbial "blessing in disguise"? Perhaps you failed to get a job you really wanted at a company that soon went messily bankrupt, for example.

The problem with blessings in disguise is that they *are* in disguise. We can't be sure whether something is a genuine disaster or a hidden blessing until later—sometimes much, much later.

That's why hindsight is always twenty-twenty. It's easy to look *back* and see God's hand at work in our lives; but at the time things are happening, we generally don't have a clue how they're going to turn out.

Mary must have wondered about many of the circumstances of her life: becoming pregnant before she was married, having her baby in a stable, being forced to flee to Egypt in the middle of the night, waiting for thirty years for her son to do whatever it was he was supposed to do, watching him die on a cross. She might have had glimpses of the divine plan as she went along, but she couldn't have been absolutely certain ahead of time whether any given event was a plain disaster or a hidden blessing.

Like all of us, she had to hope and trust that God would bring good things out of her pain. She was able to do so because, although she didn't know the future, she did know God. Can we say the same thing?

How does it make me feel to realize that Mary
had to live by faith like the rest of us?

1 BELIEVE THAT GOD WILL WORK THINGS FOR GOOD IN MY LIFE,
EVEN WHEN 1'M UNCERTAIN OF THE OUTCOME.

Messages

God continually sends each one of us messages. Sometimes the messages are rather obscure; at other times they're very clear. Mary got several directives by heaven-to-earth angel service—sort of a celestial FedEx! Even in modern times, visionaries such as St. Bernadette Soubirous and the children of Fatima receive God's messages quite directly, in the form of appearances from Mary.

God's communication isn't limited to visionaries and seers, however. God gives each of us messages every day. Our job is to keep our hearts open to recognize them. Mary's angel-delivered messages were among the most direct communication God has ever undertaken, but her angelic pipeline wasn't always open. With a few rare exceptions, she had to rely on the ordinary means of divine communication— prayer, study, and the wisdom of other people—just like the rest of us.

If you want to experience God's messages in your life, the first step is to realize that God will communicate in the form you can most readily accept. Perhaps you respond best to listening to other people. If so, God will allow you to enter into situations with people who are able to convey the messages you need to receive. Or perhaps you're the kind of person who reacts best to private reflection and contemplation. If so, God will use those personality traits to direct your life in the ways that are best for you.

No matter what particular methods God uses to communicate with you, one thing is certain: God's love for you is so intense, so pervasive, and so all-encompassing that God will never let you go message-less.

How do I receive messages from God? If I don't think I do
receive messages, is it because I'm either consciously
or subconsciously blocking God's attempts
to communicate with me?

I OPEN MYSELF TO THE MESSAGES GOD HAS FOR ME TODAY.

Midlife Crisis

Ever wonder if Mary had a midlife crisis?

That possibility isn't as shocking as it might first appear.

Think how she must have felt when Jesus was, say, about twenty-eight years old. Definitely a mature man by Jewish standards, he was showing no signs of either coming into his own as the Messiah or getting married and having a family. It must have begun to dawn on Mary that she probably wasn't going to have any grandchildren; her friends and relatives were probably nagging, "When is that nice son of yours going to find a girl and settle down?"; she wasn't seeing any signs that the promised kingdom of God was just over the horizon; Joseph was dead; and she was getting older. Might she not have wondered, just for a moment, *What if I was wrong about that angel? What if it was all just a dream?*

Building the morning fire for the ten-millionth time, did she harbor a secret wish to visit Egypt just one more time? To see the palaces and statues of Pharaoh? To mingle in the Egyptian marketplace, where goods from a thousand lands were assembled, instead of traipsing through the dingy little market in the village square? We'll never know. But if Mary felt a little restless, it's okay. Feeling restless at midlife isn't a problem; it's what we do with the restlessness that matters.

Mary seems to have transformed any midlife restlessness she felt into continuing her son's work by being a mentor and spiritual guide for those in the fledgling Christian community. As she had throughout her entire life, she focused on how she could serve others rather than on what she might get for herself.

How am I using any restlessness in my life to
transform myself and those around me?

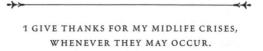

I GIVE THANKS FOR MY MIDLIFE CRISES,
WHENEVER THEY MAY OCCUR.

Humility

When it comes to pride and humility, we often get conflicting messages:

> *Take pride in your accomplishments, but don't toot your own horn.*
> *Pride goeth before a fall, but the squeaky wheel gets the grease.*

Are we supposed to be proud or humble?

Actually, we're supposed to be both. That's one of the paradoxes of the divine plan. The key to comprehending the paradox lies in understanding the difference between true and false humility.

False humility pretends to deny the worth of an accomplishment, all the while fishing for a compliment. Say, for instance, that you've just done what you know is an outstanding job on a project at work. When your boss tells you that you've done a great job, you lower your eyes and say meekly, "It was nothing." Well, both you and your boss know it wasn't "nothing"; indeed, you both know it was a major accomplishment. By exercising false humility instead of taking realistic pride, you denigrate the value of the work . . . and your part in it.

On the other hand, true humility acknowledges the value of an accomplishment but doesn't take undue credit. Mary's great prayer, the Magnificat, is a powerful example of true humility. In that prayer, Mary recognizes that "from now on all ages will call me blessed." She doesn't hem and haw with comments such as, "No, no, don't say anything about me"; rather, she expresses the truth of her place in history in a way that gives glory to God: "The Mighty One has done great things for me, and holy is his name."

May we follow Mary's example of true humility and acknowledge our accomplishments, while recognizing the One from whom all blessings flow.

> *How do I handle compliments? Do I feel that I have to make*
> *self-deprecating remarks when someone compliments me?*

I ACCEPT COMPLIMENTS AS FREELY AS I GIVE THEM.

No Longer an Option

The folk artist Mary Englebreit painted a picture showing a little guy heading down the left side of a forked road. The sign for his fork reads, "Your Life." The sign on the other side, the road not taken, reads, "No Longer an Option." Above the whole scene are the words, "Don't Look Back."

Mary Englebreit's painting vividly portrays one of the hard realities of life. We like to think that nothing is permanent, that we always get a second chance, but that simply isn't true. Once we make a particular decision, like it or not certain paths are closed forever.

Take Mary, for instance. Once she said yes to the angel, other paths were "no longer an option." She couldn't live as did Anna, the daughter of Phanuel, who "never left the temple, but worshipped night and day with fasting and prayer." She was destined to become the mother of Jesus, with all the joys and sorrows that would entail.

We assume that Mary never focused on the road not taken—but then she had the benefit of an angel's guidance. For many of us, the temptation to look back is always present. We stare at the paths we could have taken and kick ourselves for having made what we consider (with the clarity of twenty-twenty hindsight) to have been "wrong" choices.

If you regret certain past decisions and choices, spend a little time evaluating them, ask God for forgiveness if that's appropriate, and then get on with life. It's not necessary to tell yourself to "get a life," because you already have one. You just have to start living it, leaving regrets at the side of the road where they belong.

Do I spend time wishing things could be different?
Do I feel trapped by choices I've made in the past?

I REALIZE THAT I MADE THE BEST CHOICES I COULD GIVEN
THE INFORMATION AND WISDOM I HAD AT THE TIME.

Titles

Mystical Rose
Seat of Wisdom
House of Gold
Ark of the Covenant
Tower of David

While these historical titles for Mary are lyrical and awe-inspiring, some of them sound a bit odd to modern ears. Calling Mary Tower of David, for example, doesn't mean much to most of us today.

So what new titles could we give Mary? What could we call her that might be more relevant to those of us who live in the modern era? How about these:

> Courage of Single Moms. (Mary wasn't married when she became pregnant.)
> Determination of Widows. (Joseph died long before she did.)
> Understander of the Displaced. (The Holy Family were refugees in Egypt.)
> Woman of Assertion. (She didn't mince words at the wedding feast at Cana.)
> Working Mother. (*All* mothers are working mothers!)
> Help of the Worried. (She admitted when she found Jesus in the Temple that she'd been worried.)
> Hope for the Mothers of Teenagers. (After that little Temple incident, Jesus did eventually grow in "grace and wisdom.")
> Champion of Slightly Pushy Mothers. (At Cana she "urged" Jesus to perform a miracle.)
> Vindication of the Criticized. (The neighbors at Nazareth thought that Jesus was crazy.)

What other titles for Mary can you add to the list?

Do I see Mary as a role model for modern women? Why or why not?

¶ GIVE THANKS FOR ALL THE ROLE MODELS IN MY LIFE.

Our Lady of Lourdes

On this day in 1854 in Lourdes, a fourteen-year-old peasant girl, Bernadette Soubirous, had the first of what would turn out to be eighteen visions of Mary. In the nearly 150 years since, that quiet French grotto has become one of the world's premier places of pilgrimage, with thousands arriving every year, hoping and praying for a cure in its waters.

While Lourdes is the site of one of the most famous of Mary's appearances, people in numerous places around the world have had visions of a similar nature. For many, Mary's modern appearances are a source of enormous grace and comfort. For others—those who would talk of Mary's *alleged* appearances—belief in such signs smacks of superstition. The two sides find little common ground. Those who believe that Mary is appearing today are incredulous that anyone *wouldn't* believe. Those on the other side are equally incredulous that anyone *could* believe.

The real question in all this isn't whether or not Mary is appearing but what good her appearances bring forth. As Jesus told his disciples, "Every good tree bears good fruit, but the bad tree bears bad fruit." If belief in the words of prophecy that Mary is supposed to have spoken creates a change of heart, a return to the ways of God, then who are we—any of us—to say that the appearance wasn't real? As Mary herself is claimed to have said at Medjugorje, "From the very beginning, I have been conveying the message of God to the world. It is a great pity not to believe in it. Faith is a vital element, but one cannot compel a person to believe."

> *Is it important to me to believe that Mary is appearing today?*
> *What "fruit" does my belief (or disbelief) produce in my life?*

I LIVE AN EXAMINED LIFE, BRINGING FORTH THE BEST
FRUIT I'M CAPABLE OF BEARING.

Transparent Lives

One indisputable fact about Mary is that you can't look at her without seeing Jesus. No place in Scripture does Mary draw attention to herself; she always points the way to her son. It's as if her life were a transparent veil through which we're compelled to see Jesus and his message of love, forgiveness, and salvation.

In her transparency, Mary gives us a clear example of how we should live our own lives. From the Annunciation to the foot of the cross, Mary is always showing us Christ. Like Mary, we're each called to live in such a way that Christ is visible through all our actions.

There's a great irony in living that kind of a transparent life: the more we reveal Christ, the more we become unique individuals. Mary isn't lost or overshadowed by her revelation of her son. On the contrary, she's glorified by it. In the same way, the more we strive to bring the message of Christ to the world, the more we become the unique individuals we were created to be.

It's another example of the great mystery of the universe. To find life, you must lose it; to be seen, you must become transparent.

Is my life transparent? Can people see through me to Jesus?
In what ways can I make Jesus come alive in my life today?

¶ LIVE CANDIDLY, OPENLY, AND TRANSPARENTLY.

Prayer

Jesus said to his disciples,

> When you pray, say: Father, hallowed be your name, your kingdom come. Give us each day our daily bread and forgive us our sins for we ourselves forgive everyone in debt to us, and do not subject us to the final test.

In the nearly two thousand years since Jesus taught the prayer we call the Our Father to his disciples, Christians have adopted those words as their own, praying to God the Father, asking for both daily bread and daily forgiveness.

Since all Jesus' disciples knew the prayer, and since Mary spent a great deal of time in the company of the disciples both before and after her son's death and resurrection, the question arises, Did Mary pray the Our Father?

It seems likely she must have.

Because we're so accustomed to thinking of Mary in her glorified state as the Mother of God, we may forget that she doesn't have a relationship with Jesus only; she also has a relationship with God the Father—the same Father Jesus prayed to and taught his disciples (including his mother!) to pray to.

What's so remarkable about Mary's relationship with God is that it's the exact same relationship each one of us can have. Just as Mary is the daughter of the Father, we're daughters and sons of that same Father. God loves Mary, but God also loves each one of us. In the Father's sight, each and every child is precious and worthy.

> *Do I believe that I'm worthy of God's love?*
> *Do I treat myself as if I'm a child of God?*

I TREAT MYSELF WITH THE LOVE AND RESPECT A
BELOVED CHILD OF GOD DESERVES.

Criticism

Nazareth was a no-account town. People who came from Nazareth were no-account folks.

When the soon-to-be-disciple Nathanael first heard about a prophet and miracle worker from that town, he commented, "Can anything good come from Nazareth?"

Even the people of Nazareth doubted the likelihood of anyone important coming from their area. When talking of Jesus, they asked derogatorily, "Is he not the carpenter, the son of Mary, and the brother of James and Joses and Judas and Simon? And are not his sisters here with us?"

Such comments must have stung Mary. Criticism hurts—especially when it's in regard to our family. We want people to like us, to think well of us, to accept us. When people don't, we often feel wounded.

Mary's reaction to the criticism of her neighbors is unrecorded. We don't know if she went home and said to Joseph, "Did you hear what they were saying about Jesus in the marketplace?" We don't know if she went to Jesus himself and asked, "What are you going to do about the rumors people are spreading?" We don't know if she merely kept her thoughts in her heart, as she did so many other things.

How we handle criticism is a measure of our own self-esteem. If we have enough confidence, the words of others can't destroy us. They may *wound* us, to be sure, but the injuries aren't fatal. If the criticism is valid, it can prompt us to consider self-improvement. If it's invalid, we can dismiss it. In either case, we don't become incapacitated by the comments of others, because what others think of us doesn't matter. Ultimately the only thing that matters is what God thinks of us.

How do I handle the criticism of others?
Would my family and friends describe me as overly sensitive?

I KNOW GOD LOVES ME AS I AM, SO I AM NOT
DEVASTATED BY CRITICISM.

Passion

While not everyone needs passion, we all need *a* passion—something that makes us feel alive, authentic, "real." Maybe your passion is ballroom dancing, or silkscreening, or hang-gliding. It doesn't matter *what* your passion is. What matters is that you *have* a passion.

Brother David Steindl-Rast wrote in *The Music of Silence,*

> Someone will say, "I come alive when I listen to music," or "I come to life when I garden," or "I come alive when I play golf." Wherever we come alive, that is the area in which we are spiritual. And then we can say, "I know at least how one is spiritual in that area."

Mary had to have had a passion. Maybe it was pressing wildflowers or carding the whitest wool she could find for a tunic. Perhaps it was singing in the hills. We don't know what her passion was, but we know she had to have had one.

How do we know Mary had a passion? It's simple: passionless people aren't only unspiritual, they're boring; and Mary was anything but unspiritual and boring. Even in the brief descriptions of her found in the Gospels, she emerges as a woman of great holiness, determination, and—yes—passion.

Moreover, in her appearances throughout the world, Mary vibrantly demonstrates her current, compelling passion.

And what is that, you might ask?

Why nothing less than the salvation of all of humanity through the works of her son Jesus.

What is my passion? If I don't have a passion at the moment, what's something I'm interested in exploring?

I CELEBRATE MY PASSION WITH MY WHOLE BEING.

Routine

As much as we might fight it, most of us function more productively with some kind of routine in our lives. Consider what it's like to have a day off in the middle of the week. Doesn't the next day feel like Monday, no matter what day it really is?

One reason we do better with a routine is because routine provides structure. When we have parts of our life on automatic pilot, we don't have to continually reassess our place and position. In fact, a routine often gives us the freedom to focus our attention on other, more creative aspects of our lives.

Because of the time and place she lived, Mary had to have had a routine. With only oil lamps to brighten the dark, for instance, her bedtime would have come soon after the sun went down. Because the market was open only on certain days, she had to shop on an imposed schedule. We have more options than Mary did to be without a rigid routine, despite our ongoing work and family obligations. Just for fun, imagine what your ideal day would be like. Plan the activities you'd like to incorporate into your routine, such as physical exercise and spiritual reading. Once you've outlined your day, ask yourself how you could make that day a reality—and then *do* it!

*How do I feel about the routine in my life? Is it a routine that
I've consciously chosen or a routine that's been forced on me?
What positive changes can I make in my routine?*

I LIVE ACCORDING TO THE ROUTINE THAT BEST SUITS ME.

Self-Forgiveness

We all make mistakes.

We make mistakes because we don't have enough information, because we act on old models of behavior learned in childhood, because we make wrong assumptions.

We make mistakes because we're human, and to err is human.

In order to get beyond our mistakes, we need to do two things: first, we need to acknowledge our mistakes; second, we need to forgive ourselves.

Forgiving self is harder than forgiving others. It's relatively easy to be magnanimous in extending forgiveness to someone else, especially if that someone has asked for our forgiveness. But our own mistakes continue to rankle and irritate, permeating our souls like toxic chemicals in a landfill. Dumping more dirt on top only puts off the inevitable. We have to uncover the mistakes, recognize them for the corrosive materials they are, and dispose of them properly through self-forgiveness.

It's all too easy to assume that Mary never made a mistake and therefore never needed to forgive herself. But a mistake isn't the same thing as a sin. Traditional Marian theology teaches that Mary never committed a sin, but it doesn't say anything about making a mistake. In fact, the story of the finding of Jesus in the Temple proves otherwise. Mary made a mistake in not knowing where Jesus was when the caravan headed back to Nazareth. Because of her mistake, she and Joseph spent three anxious days searching for their son. But her mistake wasn't a *sin*.

Mary had to forgive herself for her mistake, just as we must forgive ourselves for our mistakes.

Do I treat my own mistakes more harshly than
I treat the mistakes of others?

I ACCEPT THE HEALING BALM OF SELF-FORGIVENESS.

Nothing Is Impossible

In one of her appearances at Medjugorje, Mary is supposed to have said, "In prayer you will find the solution for every situation, even if it is unsolvable."

Those words echo the words of the angel Gabriel at the Annunciation ("for nothing will be impossible for God") as well as Jesus' own words to his disciples about the way to salvation ("For human beings this is impossible, but for God all things are possible").

All things are possible with God. Nothing, absolutely *nothing*, is impossible for God. If we really believed Gabriel's words to Mary and Jesus' words to his disciples, we could and would transform our lives. But we *don't* believe that all things are possible, because we, with our limited vision, can't see a way to make our dreams happen. We can't envision how what seems impossible could actually occur.

But God has unlimited resources. God can make a virgin fecund, and God can find a way to give us the desires of our heart—if only we're willing to believe that nothing is impossible when we turn it over to God.

Is there some change in my life that I want to happen but believe is impossible? Have I asked God to work the impossible for me? Do I believe that God really can do all things?

I BELIEVE THAT GOD WILL DO THE IMPOSSIBLE FOR ME
IF I MAKE MY REQUESTS KNOWN.

Hurt Feelings

Standing outside, [Jesus' mother and brothers]
sent word to him and called him.
A crowd seated around him told him, "Your mother and your
brothers [and sisters] are outside asking for you."
But he said to them in reply, "Who are
my mother and brothers?"
And looking around at those seated in the circle he said, "Here
are my mother and my brothers. [For] whoever does the will of
God is my brother and sister and mother."

MARK 3:32–35

Were Mary's feelings hurt when Jesus said that anyone who did the will of God was his brother and sister and mother? Did she feel a little miffed that he wasn't willing to acknowledge publicly her special place in his life?

It's easy to assume that since Jesus couldn't sin, he couldn't do anything to hurt someone's feelings. That's not only circuitous logic; it's also just plain wrong. Hurting someone's feelings isn't the same thing as sinning. Unless Jesus set out deliberately to offend his mother (which he obviously didn't do), he wasn't responsible for her feelings. Jesus was simply speaking the truth, and sometimes the truth hurts.

So were Mary's feelings hurt? Maybe, for a moment—but then, because she was a woman of exceptional wisdom and insight, she must have realized the truth of Jesus' statement and let that truth set her free of hurt feelings.

Are my feelings hurt often? Am I too sensitive to criticism?
What do I do when my feelings are hurt?

WHEN I'M TOLD THE TRUTH, I DON'T TAKE OFFENSE; RATHER,
I ACCEPT THE INSTRUCTION I'M BEING GIVEN.

Ordinary Life

The home of Mary, Joseph, and Jesus was probably made of mud-bricks on a limestone foundation. A raised platform would have been used for sleeping and eating, with the rest of the house providing storage for grain and livestock. The flat roof would have been used for additional storage as well as offering a comfortable retreat for entertaining, dining, and sleeping.

As part of her regular household duties, Mary would have kept their small home clean. Did she ever have to tell Jesus to wipe his feet because she had just swept the hearth and he was tracking in mud? Did she ever sigh when Joseph absentmindedly shook sawdust on the sleeping mats? Did she ever wish for a self-cleaning home?

We tend to think that to be holy is to be elevated above the ordinariness of housework. But it's precisely in the ordinary that we discover our real selves.

In their book *Spiritual Literacy,* Frederic and Mary Ann Brussat encourage us to "look to see the significance of seemingly ordinary and insignificant events. . . . Some of the most rewarding spiritual journeys are those we take on our own block."

Mary's floor wasn't swept by angels, but in sweeping the floor and building the fire and emptying the chamber pots, Mary sanctified her home. We can do the same, whether we live alone or with many others. It's by the work of our hands that we create holy places and holy people.

Do I see all work as part of my spiritual journey? Do I think
that some tasks and occupations are more "spiritual" than others?

I SEE THE SPIRITUAL IN ALL THAT I DO.

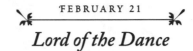

Lord of the Dance

If you've ever danced the rumba or the tango or the waltz, you know that the term *leading* is a bit of a misnomer. A "lead" doesn't so much force his partner to follow as simply dance his own patterned steps. His partner then has two choices—to dance her part or to stop the dance altogether.

Our relationship with God, the Lord of the Dance, is like a ballroom dance. God takes the lead, dancing the steps of divine love; and when we're in a state of grace, we, the followers, respond with our own matching steps. When we're out of sync—in the condition theologians call a state of sin—we fumble and possibly even cause the dance to stop. God may continue to lead, but we no longer follow.

The drama of the Annunciation shows us how the divine dance is supposed to be performed. God took the initiative, inviting Mary to the dance floor. ("The angel Gabriel was sent from God to a town of Galilee called Nazareth, to a virgin [named] Mary.") After God explained the rhythm of the dance ("You will conceive in your womb and bear a son, and you shall name him Jesus"), Mary had her chance to respond. She extended her hand and stepped onto the floor. ("Behold, I am the handmaid of the Lord. May it be done to me according to your word.") At that moment, the heavens rejoiced and the dance began.

Am I willing to let God take the lead in my life?
Do I try to lead God, or do I let God lead me?

I SING TO GOD, PLAY MUSIC TO GOD'S NAME, BUILD A ROAD FOR THE RIDER OF THE CLOUDS, REJOICE, AND DANCE BEFORE GOD.

Names

We refer to the mother of Jesus by the English name Mary, but her name may more correctly be translated Miriam. Various meanings are given to the name Miriam, or Mary. Bitterness, richness, and royal incense are among them.

When we consider Mary's life, we see that all three labels are appropriate. She certainly experienced the bitter sorrow of her son's death and the richness of his healing and teaching while she lived on earth. Now, in heaven, she's honored as the Queen Mother, worthy of royal incense.

What does your name mean? Have you ever looked it up? Sometimes when we learn the meaning of a person's name long after we've gotten to know the person, the name seems to have been divinely inspired. A Matthew really is a "gift of God," perhaps, or a Linda really is a "beauty." A Jennifer exudes all the qualities of a "fine lady," or a Kevin's life is marked by "kindness."

If you could choose any name, what name would you choose? Just for fun, try giving yourself a pseudonym. Write it down. Think of yourself as your new name. Does a different name change the way you feel about yourself and your abilities?

Whatever your name, always remember that God calls each of us individually, by name. It's up to us to listen for the call and to recognize our name when it's spoken.

Have I ever heard God call my name?

1 LISTEN FOR GOD'S CALL, AND 1 RESPOND WHEN
1 HEAR GOD SPEAK MY NAME.

Parents

Obviously Jesus and Mary had a fairly normal parent-child relationship. As evidence, consider the moment when Mary and Joseph finally located Jesus in the Temple of Jerusalem.

They came around a corner and saw Jesus talking with teachers of the law. They were so relieved that they didn't know whether to hug him or scold him. Either way, they realized that they were in the Temple and needed to maintain a certain decorum.

Nonetheless, the strain in Mary's voice transcends the centuries: "Jesus, my son, what are you doing here? Why have you put your father and me through all this? Don't you know that we've been looking *everywhere* [one can imagine Mary's voice getting a little higher at this point] for you? We thought you were with your cousins in the caravan, but when we camped the first night you weren't there. Do you have some explanation for your behavior?"

And Jesus answered with the same bewilderment that characterizes most teens: "What's the big deal? Didn't you know that I'd be here in the Temple, in my Father's house?"

One suspects that Mary said something like, "No, we didn't have a *clue* where you were. If we'd known, we wouldn't have spent three days looking."

Then she undoubtedly excused herself from the teachers, who, if they weren't already astonished at Jesus and his wisdom, were now totally flabbergasted by his mother.

The trip back to Nazareth probably wasn't much fun for any of them, but it's a comfort to know that all mothers and all sons have the same sorts of struggles—even if the mother is Mary and the son is Jesus.

> *If I have children, how do I get along with them?*
> *How do I get along with my own parents?*

1 KNOW THAT GOD, MY LOVING PARENT,
NEVER MAKES MISTAKES WITH MY LIFE.

Stars

We look to the heavens and see, in the words of the late Carl Sagan, "billions and billions of stars." Those points of light in the heavens represent mystery, even for scientists. Astronomers can discuss the stars in terms of their composition, their size, their temperature, and other precise calculations of science, but still their mystery remains.

The stars themselves generate many questions: What's really out there? Are there other worlds with other life forms? How do we fit into the whole of creation? How does God relate to the universe?

Despite our scientific understanding of the stars, only the hardest of hearts isn't captivated by wonder when we gaze upon the bowl of heaven strewn with twinkling lights.

We live in a world infused with spiritual wonder. Mary's appearances in places such as Fatima and Lourdes (as well as dozens of other locales around the globe) are part of that spiritual wonder. Rigorous investigation of seers and visionaries who report having seen Mary, scrupulous examination of the physical evidence (such as crying statues), and eyewitness accounts—all the trappings of science— may discredit some of the fraudulent claims, but they can do little to *verify* Mary's appearances. Those appearances, like the glory of the stars, aren't something that can be dissected; rather, they are something that inspires spiritual awe and amazement.

When was the last time I felt true wonder
at the glory of the universe?

I KNOW THAT THE WORLD IS FILLED WITH WONDER, AND I KNOW THAT I HAVE MY PLACE WITHIN THAT WONDER.

Timing

One thing Mary's life teaches us is that God's ways aren't our ways and God's timing isn't our timing. It's highly unlikely that Mary would have chosen to give birth in a stable, miles away from her mother and other relatives. And yet that was the place God chose. When we find ourselves wondering why certain things happen the way they do, it helps to recall the words of David's son, Qoheleth—words that Mary herself certainly would have known and prayed as part of her Temple education:

> There is an appointed time for everything,
> and a time for every affair under the heavens.
> A time to be born, and a time to die;
> a time to plant, and a time to uproot the plant.
> A time to kill, and a time to heal;
> a time to tear down, and a time to build.
> A time to weep, and a time to laugh;
> a time to mourn, and a time to dance.
> A time to scatter stones, and a time to gather them;
> a time to embrace, and a time to be far from embraces.
> A time to seek, and a time to lose;
> a time to keep, and a time to cast away.
> A time to rend, and a time to sew;
> a time to be silent, and a time to speak.
> A time to love, and a time to hate;
> a time of war, and a time of peace.

Do I trust God's timing for my life?

I BELIEVE THAT ALL THINGS HAPPEN AT THEIR RIGHT TIMES.

Visionaries

Who has Mary appeared to?

Juan Diego was a poor Aztec peasant.

Bernadette Soubirous was a sickly girl from a disrespectable family.

Lucia, Francisco, and Jacinta were young, uneducated Portuguese shepherds.

Mary seldom shows herself to the rich, the powerful, or the influential. She chooses instead the most unlikely people of all. Generally (but not always), visionaries are young, because the young aren't as jaded and cynical as their elders and therefore aren't as likely to dismiss Mary's apparition as the result of too much spicy food the day before.

One of the more interesting facts about visionaries is that their outward lives don't change all that much after their visions. They continue to be "real" people, with real likes and dislikes, despite having seen and talked with Mary. Their prayer life becomes more intense, certainly, but it doesn't usually become radically different. Visionaries may attend Mass more frequently, pray the Rosary more often, and spend more time in reading the Scriptures and in prayer after their vision, but the spiritual paths they walk are ones we all can travel.

Those who have seen Mary teach us two important lessons. First, genuine faith doesn't change who we are; it enhances it. Second, even when we experience a great miracle, we still have to find faith every day through the ordinary means of prayer and devotion.

What would I do if I had a vision of Mary?
Do I wish or hope that I could be present when Mary appears?

Winter

For never-resting time leads summer on
To hideous winter and confounds him there,
Sap check'd with frost and lusty leaves quite gone,
Beauty o'ersnow'd and bareness everywhere.

SHAKESPEARE, SONNET 5

Even in those climes where the sun shines all year round, winter is equated with snow and cold and "bareness everywhere." In Galilee, where Mary lived, snow would have been unlikely, but Mary might well have seen some on the mountaintops. At the very least, she would have been familiar with references such as this one from Psalm 147: "Thus snow is spread like wool, frost is scattered like ash."

No matter that Mary probably never made a snowball. It's certain she still experienced winter.

We *all* do. Winter isn't just Nordic blasts and "beauty o'ersnow'd"; it encompasses the cold emptiness that comes over all of us. Mary, being human, had to have had moments when, like St. Augustine, she prayed, "God of life, there are days when the burdens we carry chafe our shoulders and wear us down; when the road seems dreary and endless, the skies gray and threatening; when our lives have no music in them and our hearts are lonely, and our souls have lost their courage. Flood the path with light, we beseech you; turn our eyes to where the skies are full of promise."

In the winter of our soul, let us, along with Mary and St. Augustine, always "turn our eyes to where the skies are full of promise."

Do I ever feel weighed down by the burdens of life?
Do I feel as if I'm trapped in endless winter?

I KNOW THAT FOR EVERY WINTER THERE'S A SPRING.

Grandparents

An ancient writing called the *Nativity of Mary* (sometimes referred to as the *Protoevangelium of James*) claims to provide details of Mary's own birth and childhood. While never accepted as sacred Scripture, the *Nativity* has greatly influenced many of the traditions surrounding Mary.

According to this writing, Mary's parents were named Anna and Joachim. Whether or not those were their actual names isn't important. What *is* important is that they were Jesus' grandparents.

Our grandparents provide a tangible link with our own past. In them, we see where we came from, not just in a physical sense but in a spiritual sense as well. Grandparents can often convey essential life information, bridging the gap between the generations in a way parents can't.

We don't know, of course, what Anna and Joachim taught Jesus, or even if they were alive when Jesus was born. But assuming that they were alive, we can imagine that Joachim would have passed on some of the great stories of Scripture, explained the priestly rituals of the Jewish faith (since he's believed to have been a priest himself), and told Jesus what life was like in "the good old days" before the Roman occupation. Perhaps Anna fixed Jesus some special "grandmother" treats, entertained him while Mary went to the market, and listened to his hopes and dreams. In short, Anna and Joachim probably acted just the way grandparents should.

What role did your grandparents play in your life?

I GIVE THANKS FOR THE LEGACY OF MY ANCESTORS, INCLUDING GRANDPARENTS.

Roses

The rose is one of the most popular flowers in the world. More than thirteen thousand varieties have been identified, ranging from the elegant tea rose to the sprawling wild rose. For centuries, this fragrant flower has been the symbol of purity, fidelity, and love.

About the year 600 B.C.E., the famous Greek poet Sappho wrote these words:

> Would Jove appoint some flower to reign
> In matchless beauty on the plain
> The rose (most will agree)
> The rose, the Queen of Flowers should be.

Because of the rose's preeminent place in horticulture, it seems fitting that many of Mary's traditional titles incorporate the word *rose*. Among her most famous titles are Rose of Sharon, Mystical Rose, and Rose Ever-Blooming. Just as the rose is the Queen of Flowers, so Mary is the Queen of Heaven.

One way we can have a more concrete connection with Mary is to incorporate roses or rose fragrances in our everyday lives. Perhaps the next time you have an important decision to make, you might light a rose-scented candle and ask Mary to pray that you will have the necessary wisdom and insight. Or tuck a small bottle of rose-scented hand lotion in your drawer at work and think of Mary as you apply it during your daily routine.

How can I let Mary become a greater influence in my life?
In what ways can I bring some of the beauty of the
Rose of Heaven into my daily environment?

¶ TAKE TIME TO "SMELL THE ROSES."

The Sabbath

The Ten Commandments are listed in chapter 20 of the book of Exodus. Most admonitions get a single verse, but the commandment "Keep holy the Sabbath" gets four long, detailed verses.

Keeping the Sabbath was an essential element of Jewish law during Jesus' day. Since Jesus himself kept the Sabbath, it's unthinkable that his mother wouldn't have.

The Sabbath (or Shabbat) reminded Mary and Jesus—and by extension reminds all of us—of the promises God has made. It gives us, as it did them, a chance to distance ourselves from our everyday life and concerns as we evaluate what we're doing to bring about peace and justice in the world. It was, and still is, a day of rest for people and animals alike—a day set aside for restoration and renewal.

Today, with the busy lives most of us lead, we often have two days on the weekend for "rest." But all too often, we merely exchange one kind of busy-ness for another. We come back to work on Monday exhausted from our "time off."

This week why not "keep holy the Sabbath"? Set aside one day to break the ordinary routine. Take a walk. Spend some time in prayer. Fix a special food treat that requires slow preparation, such as home-baked bread. Nap. Read.

The options are limitless. The only criteria your Sabbath activities need meet are these: the activities must be outside your ordinary weekday routine, and they must give you pleasure. In choosing such activities, you will begin to understand that keeping the Sabbath holy really means keeping your heart turned toward God.

Can I "keep the Sabbath" this weekend?
What will I do to make the day holy?

I TAKE THE TIME GOD HAS ORDAINED FOR REST AND RENEWAL WITHOUT FEELING GUILTY.

Sacred Versus Scared

QUESTION: What's the difference between *sacred* and *scared*?
ANSWER: The position of the letters *a* and *c*.

Jokes aside, the concepts *sacred* and *scared* are closely related. The sacred may cause us to feel scared, since looking into the realm of the holy is to glimpse the reality that exists beyond our limited senses. It's little wonder, then, that almost every time an angel appears the first words are "Don't be afraid."

Mary's appearances, however, show us that the sacred need not be scary. Those who see Mary almost always comment on the light surrounding her—a light that's brighter than the sun, yet not harmful to gaze upon. Moreover, visionaries generally express a sense of great sadness when their visions stop—a sadness accompanied by an intense longing to see Mary once again.

Encountering the sacred—whether it's in a vision of Mary, through daily prayer, in the liturgical rituals of a church, or at a shrine—always creates a change in us; and change can be scary. It's much easier to stay in the status quo than it is to allow God to enter into our everyday reality and turn things upside down. Because once the sacred enters into one's life, things are guaranteed to be turned upside down.

Just ask Mary!

How has God entered into my life today? Do I see the presence of God as something sacred or something to be scared of?

I'M NOT SCARED OF THE SACRED.

Caravans

One of the timeless images of the desert is a caravan of camels and riders crossing the endless sand. Most caravans two centuries ago were made up of merchants transporting merchandise between centers of trade throughout the Middle East. But caravans weren't used exclusively by traders. Since the wilderness was fraught with danger, ordinary travelers often joined a caravan heading in the direction they wanted to go for protection against robbers and other hazards. While being in a group might not ensure safety, at least there was some comfort in numbers.

Joseph and Mary were part of such a caravan on their way back to Nazareth from Jerusalem when Jesus stayed behind in the Temple. The size of the group was indicated by Luke, who wrote, "Thinking that he was in the caravan, they journeyed for a day and looked for him among their relatives and acquaintances." The group had to have been fairly large for Mary and Joseph to have overlooked Jesus for an entire day. It was only when they began to look for him in earnest that they realized he was truly missing.

Isn't that the case with us sometimes? We don't know we're missing something until we start to look for it. In the case of spiritual matters, we can travel along in our caravan of life, watching out for the dangers of the road, and fail to realize that we're missing the most important element of our lives until we stop to evaluate the situation. Then, like Mary and Joseph, we may have to retrace our steps and search diligently to find that which we've lost. The good news, however, is that just as Mary and Joseph found Jesus in "his Father's house," so too can we find what we're looking for in *our* Father's house.

Have I neglected my spiritual side?
Do I let myself become distracted by the cares of life's journey?

Death

Did Mary die?

Sounds like a funny question, but it's one that's plagued theologians for centuries. The official title for the passing of Mary from this world to God is the Dormition, from the Latin *dormire*, "to sleep." Some scholars hold that Mary did not die but merely fell asleep, presumably waking up on her way to heaven. Others maintain that she actually died, as all living creatures must die. Even when Pope Pius XII solemnly defined the doctrine of the Assumption, which says that Mary was taken body and soul into heaven, he left the question open.

It seems as if those who would prefer to have Mary enter heaven without first dying want to accord her an unnecessary honor. Death isn't an evil to be avoided; rather, it's the passage to the next life. In many ways, death is like birth: both are natural processes surrounded by mystery, and both result in an entirely new dimension of life. Since Mary was born into this world in the natural, ordinary way, it seems likely that she would also be born into the next in the natural, ordinary way.

Moreover, Mary's entire life serves as a guide for us—a witness to the way of holiness possible for every human being. To think that Mary didn't experience death is to believe that she didn't fully experience life. While theologians can discuss the issue endlessly, for those of us who try to emulate Mary, the idea that she's our guide in all stages of life—including death—is a supreme comfort.

Do I fear death? Am I afraid of the pain of dying,
or am I afraid of death itself?

I LIVE MY LIFE IN SUCH A WAY THAT DEATH HAS NO STING.

Assertiveness

What's the difference between being aggressive and being assertive?

One dictionary consulted defines exhibiting *aggression* as "being self-assertive" and shows *assertion* as "being self-assertive." Talk about circuitous logic! In practical terms, however, to be called *aggressive* is an insult, while to be called *assertive* is a compliment. The adjective *aggressive* generally describes a pushy, antagonistic person. *Assertive,* on the other hand, indicates someone who's definite and clear-minded without being hostile.

Mary was often assertive but never aggressive. Just look at the way she treated the servants at the wedding feast at Cana. "Do whatever he tells you," she ordered. And look at the way she dealt with her son on that same occasion. "They have no wine," she told Jesus pointedly. When Jesus answered, "Woman, how does your concern affect me? My hour has not yet come," she was undaunted. She knew that he would do what she'd asked.

Standing up for your rights, defending your interests, even stating your desires—are signs of a healthy self-esteem. Yet religion has sometimes been used to convince women that they should be doormats, submissive to the point of nonexistence. Mary, the model for women, was hardly a doormat. So why should women—indeed, why should *anyone*—try to become something Mary herself wasn't? If Mary could be assertive without being aggressive, so can all of us.

Am I afraid that I'll come across as being aggressive if I speak
my mind? Do I think that being submissive is
somehow more holy than being assertive?

I'M ASSERTIVE BUT NEVER AGGRESSIVE.

Safety Zone

A classic Far Side cartoon shows a little bird in a huge cage on a tropical island. Outside the unlatched cage, flamingos are feeding and palm trees are swaying in the breeze. The caption reads, "Winning the lottery had changed his life, but at times Chico still felt strangely unfulfilled."

Chico was trapped in his safety zone. Even though he could have left the cage at any time, he chose to remain within the comfortable, familiar boundaries.

Sometimes we're like Chico. Even though God has given us the resources we need to be liberated in the Spirit, we prefer to be safe rather than fly free.

Safety feels *comfortable*. It allows us to remain within the status quo, not rocking any boats and not taking any risks. But unless we're willing to leave our safety zone, we can't change or grow. And any living creature that doesn't grow dies.

Mary's actions demonstrate the absolute necessity of leaving the comfort zone in order to grow. It would have been much "safer" for her to tell the angel to hie back to heaven, but she stepped out of not only her own comfort zone but that of her culture as well, to say, "Let it be done to me according to your will." In doing so, Mary not only became fulfilled personally, but she allowed God's plan to be fulfilled for all humanity.

Am I willing to take risks in order to grow?
Do I miss out on life because I'm afraid
to leave my comfort zone?

I REALIZE THAT ALL GROWTH REQUIRES THE WILLINGNESS
TO STEP OUT OF MY COMFORT ZONE.

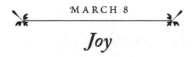

Joy

I can wade grief
Whole pools of it
I'm used to that
But the least push of joy
Breaks up my feet
EMILY DICKINSON

Like Emily Dickinson, many of us practice wading grief until we become so good at it that we trip and fall when a speck of joy comes along.

While Mary's life is proof that all of us must drink from the cup of sorrow, her life also offers encouragement that we can drink from the goblet of joy as well.

At least seven joys of Mary have been commemorated: the Annunciation, the Visitation, the Birth of Jesus, the Adoration of the Magi, the Finding in the Temple, the Resurrection, and the Assumption. While these are the *big* joyful events of Mary's life, she undoubtedly had other, smaller joys.

Turning out a perfect loaf of bread, watching the hills around Nazareth burst into spring flower, smelling the air after a morning rain—Mary must have rejoiced in these simple pleasures as well.

In order to appreciate the joy in our lives, we must first look for it. Concentrate on all the pushes of joy that occur in the course of your day, rather than looking for all the pools of grief.

What gives me the most joy?
In what ways can I become a source of joy for others?

I'M FILLED WITH JOIE DE VIVRE.

Handmaid of the Lord

Mary's comment "Behold, I am the handmaid of the Lord. May it be done to me according to your word" sounds a bit odd to our modern ears. After all, we don't have handmaids anymore. In fact, most of us wouldn't know what to do with a handmaid if we were given one. The closest we can come is a servant—but then most of us don't have servants either.

Which brings us to another issue: Why does Mary call herself a handmaid or servant? In a culture where servants had very few rights, why would Mary choose to put herself in that position?

To understand Mary's response, we must first understand that to be a handmaid or a servant isn't the same thing as to be a slave. A slave has no rights whatsoever. A slave's every action belongs to the master. A slave cannot, *dare* not, make individual decisions or choices. A slave is property. A servant, on the other hand, isn't *owned* by a master. A servant remains a person, not an item on a ledger sheet. A servant chooses to serve; he or she isn't forced into service.

It's important to understand that distinction. Mary was willing to become God's servant, but she never became God's slave. She chose to cooperate with God's request; she wasn't forced into it.

Through her actions, Mary demonstrates that God desires us to serve willingly and freely. God doesn't want—and has never wanted—slaves. God desires instead to have willing servants.

What choices am I facing in my life right now?
Do I trust that God has given me all I need
to make wise decisions?

I CHOOSE TO DO GOD'S WILL, NOT BECAUSE I *HAVE* TO
BUT BECAUSE I *WANT* TO.

Sleep Happens

Have you ever been so tired that you literally couldn't keep your eyes open? Perhaps driving late at night you've had to roll down all the windows, turn the radio as high as it would go, and hope that you could make it to the nearest rest stop without an accident. Or maybe, in studying for a final exam, you've been surprised (somewhere between one sentence and the next) to find your head on the table.

The human body can go without sleep for only so long. Eventually the autonomic processes take over, the conscious brain shuts down, and sleep happens. If a person is prevented from falling asleep for a long enough period of time, mental and emotional breakdown occurs. The fact is that humans were created with the need to sleep.

Although we don't have a record of any particular time when Mary slept, we know that Joseph slept and we know that Jesus slept.

One possible origin of the word *sleep* is the German *schlaff,* which mean "loose." Given that derivation, *to sleep* means to loosen the bonds of worry and care and trust that despite appearances, God is still in control of the world. As Edward Hays noted in *Pray All Ways,* "[Sleep] is an expression that we are able to allow the Divine Mystery to take over in the midst of troubles and deadlines."

Do I ever think of sleep as a waste of time?
Conversely, do I ever sleep my life away?

I ALLOW MYSELF THE REST I NEED WHEN I NEED IT.

Wind

All these devoted themselves with one accord to prayer, together with some women, and Mary the mother of Jesus, and his brothers. . . . When the time for Pentecost was fulfilled, they were all in one place together. And suddenly there came from the sky a noise like a strong driving wind, and it filled the entire house in which they were. Then there appeared to them tongues as of fire, which parted and came to rest on each one of them. And they were all filled with the holy Spirit.

ACTS 1:14, 2:1–4

It seems fitting that the Spirit of God would first come to Mary and the apostles in the form of wind. All other forces of nature can be mitigated or controlled to some degree. Rain can be diverted through dams and floodgates. Snow can be shoveled or melted. Fire can be contained or extinguished. But wind? Not for naught the saying "free as the wind." We stand powerless before the forces of a hurricane, a tornado, or a gale. We can do nothing except wait, for the wind will do what the wind will do.

But the wind isn't always a driving, destructive force; it can also be a lover's kiss on a dew-covered daisy, a will-o'-the-wisp on an early spring night, the soft, still voice in the treetops.

Like the ever-changing wind, God comes to us under many guises. Sometimes God blows full force into our lives; at other times God comes with only the faintest rustle as herald. Just as the wind is never completely still in the world, so too God is never completely absent from our lives.

How has God come into my life recently—full-force gale or gentle, wafting breeze?

I TURN MY FACE TO THE WIND, AND THERE I FIND GOD.

Proper Sacrifices

In the time before Christ, the Jewish people offered blood sacrifices. An unblemished male animal was ceremonially killed and its blood sprinkled about the altar. The carcass was then placed on the altar and ignited, becoming completely consumed by the flames.

Mary and Joseph were following the letter of the law when they offered the sacrifice of two doves in the Temple forty days after the birth of Jesus. It's reasonable to assume that during Jesus' lifetime, he, Mary, and Joseph also made other burnt offerings at the Temple.

Since we no longer make blood sacrifices, what does God want from us?

A proper sacrifice to God is one that creates and restores, not one that tears down and destroys.

All too often, we think that God wants us to offer up our individuality, to become something other than who we are, but that's not what God desires at all. God wants the exact opposite: God wants us to sacrifice those things that keep us from becoming unique individuals.

God doesn't call us to sacrifice ourselves to an abusive relationship, for example. God doesn't ask us to sacrifice our talents or abilities in order to attempt to make someone else feel better. God *does* ask us to sacrifice our selfish desires and wishes in order to become more loving and giving. God *does* desire that we sacrifice our greedy natures so that we can share more freely.

God still wants sacrifices, but only those that change our hearts—not those that destroy our spirits.

Have I sacrificed something that God didn't want?
Could the inappropriateness of my sacrifice be
one of the reasons God didn't seem
to honor that sacrifice?

I OFFER MYSELF AS A LIVING SACRIFICE TO GOD.

Sappiness

Why are many portraits of Mary so sappy? Check out any collection of paintings of Mary, and you'll see a plethora of doe-eyed teens with cover-girl lashes and rosy cheeks—girls who obviously do nothing but gaze heavenward all day long.

Why do we insist on portraying Mary as a simpering soul? Do we believe that sappiness is the same as holiness?

Mary was about as far from being a simpering sap as any woman could be. In fact, she was a very gutsy girl. Take her reaction when she discovered that she was pregnant. Did she fuss around wondering how to break the news to Joseph? Did she maunder about in a heavenly daze? No. She packed her bags and headed to her cousin's house. She did what she had to do and let the chips fall where they may. If Joseph hadn't wanted to marry her when she returned, she apparently was determined to have the baby and make her own way.

When she asked Jesus to change water into wine many years later, she definitely wasn't mealymouthed.

When she defied the Roman guards to stand at the foot of her son's cross, she most definitely wasn't a pious wimp.

In looking to Mary as a model for women, let's not denigrate her strength in a misguided attempt to praise her holiness.

Do I find it easier to relate to Mary as a docile, reserved woman or a strong, independent thinker?

1 RECOGNIZE THAT HOLINESS AND STRENGTH ARE COMPATIBLE, NOT CONTRADICTORY.

Unexpected Gifts

Though frankincense isn't something we purchase at department-store fragrance counters, this sweet, gumlike substance from trees that grow in South Arabia, Ethiopia, Somalia, and India was used as perfume in Mary's time. Because of its additional use in ritual offerings, the gift of frankincense from the Wise Men is said to symbolize Christ's future priestly role.

In looking back, we can see the symbolism, but it's highly unlikely that Mary got the connection when the caravan of camels and astrologers from the East showed up at her doorstep. After the guests left, she (being a good Jewish housewife) undoubtedly viewed the frankincense, as well as the gold and myrrh, as a hedge against bad times. Whatever Mary did with the frankincense, we can be certain that she put it to good use. Such an unexpected gift would have made a valuable trade item—in fact, it may very well have paid for the trip to Egypt when the Holy Family had to flee Herod's wrath.

Like Mary, we receive unexpected gifts all the time. Most of them aren't monetarily valuable, but they're spiritually or emotionally invaluable. A particularly glorious sunset. A kind word from a stranger. A kiss from a baby. The world is literally filled with gifts for our taking. We just have to hold out our hands and let them fall into our lives.

What gifts have I been given today? Have I remembered to give thanks for all the good things I've received?

TODAY I'LL LOOK FOR AT LEAST ONE GIFT
THAT GOD WANTS TO GIVE ME.

Holy Ground

Places where Mary is believed to have appeared have an almost magical lure. People flock to Lourdes, Fatima, and Medjugorje by the thousands just to be able to say they've stood on holy ground. But it doesn't take an extraordinary religious event to consecrate a place. Anywhere you encounter God in a profound way, anywhere old ways of thinking give way to new means of loving, anywhere the ordinary yields to mystery—that's sacred space.

The places where Mary has appeared are holy not only because Mary has appeared there—although that's a factor—but also because of the faith and devotion of the pilgrims who have visited them. When you enter a church that's been in continual use for years, you may experience some of that same holiness. In an almost tangible way, the prayers of the thousands who've been there before you have transformed a mere building into holy ground.

In order to grow spiritually, we must all find "holy ground" in our lives—places where we can rest our cheek on the chest of God, where we can be totally and fully present to the Divine. Your place may be alongside a wild mountain stream; mine may be in a sunlit corner of a walk-up flat. The exact location doesn't matter. What *does* matter is that we carve out a piece of sacred space to call our own.

Where is my "holy ground"?
If I don't have such a place, where do I feel the closest to God?
Can this location become my sacred space?

I CREATE SACRED SPACE BOTH WITHIN MY SOUL
AND WITHIN MY ENVIRONMENT.

Recreation

Somehow it seems that Jesus must have been a somber little kid. Just as in Byzantine icons he's pictured as a miniature adult on Mary's lap, we tend to think of him as always being basically a grown-up. Maybe it's because he was a spiritual prodigy. Whatever the reason, it's hard to imagine Jesus doing anything besides praying or perhaps helping Mary and Joseph.

But like kids everywhere, kids in Jesus' day made time for play; and Jesus was a real kid. It's likely that he and his friends would have played with simple toys—perhaps wooden ones fashioned by Joseph. He would have explored the caves and crevices in the hills above his home. He might have practiced using a sling or spear. Perhaps he sang and danced with his friends, and occasionally (in modern parlance) just "hung out."

We can free our images of Mary and Jesus from stiff stereotypes by picturing Mary playing patty-cake with a six-month-old Jesus. Or seeing Mary give her inquisitive toddler a piece of broken pottery to keep him out of her hair as she prepared the daily bread or carded wool. Or envisioning an adolescent Jesus wrestling with his pals or running races (and not necessarily winning!).

If such images startle or surprise you, remember that recreation is really re-creation. When we don't take time to play, something vital in our souls begins to wither and die. To be fully alive, to be fully human, we must take time to re-create ourselves through playful recreation. As Ralph Waldo Emerson said, "It is a happy talent to know how to play."

Does the idea of Jesus' playing seem scandalous to me?
How do I play in my life?
Do I need to find a better balance between work and play?

I ALLOW MYSELF TO RE-CREATE DAILY.

Separation

One of the great ironies of being a parent is this: if you do your job well, you end up alone. That's because the goal of parenting is a healthy separation of child and parent. It's only when you do your job poorly and separation doesn't occur that you have someone hanging around for the rest of your life.

Even more ironic, if you do your job well and your children separate, they turn into the kind of people you'd like to have stay with you. If you don't do your job well and they stay put, they turn into the kind of people you'd prefer would leave.

Mary allowed Jesus to separate. She let him lead his own life. She clearly was deeply involved in his life and ministry, up to and including his death, but she let him do it his way, even when his way led to the cross.

It isn't easy to learn to let go of our children and permit them to find their own way. They're bound to make mistakes. They're bound to make decisions we don't like. They're bound to get hurt. Yet if we don't allow those we love to separate, we not only stifle their growth, we stifle our own growth as well. "To everything there is a season," said the son of the great King David. In parenting, as in much of life, we need to be aware of whether we're in the season of holding on or the season of letting go—and act accordingly.

Do I try to manage the lives of those I love?
Do I have trouble letting go?

I GIVE THOSE I LOVE THE FREEDOM TO BECOME INDIVIDUALS.

Common Sense

Mary is praised for many virtues, but one of her more underrated qualities is her uncommon common sense.

Take her reply to the angel Gabriel, for instance. Put in modern jargon, it went something like this: "How could I be pregnant when I've never had sex?"

Now that's definitely a commonsense question. Most people, when faced with an angel, wouldn't have the presence of mind to ask such a down-to-earth—and blunt—question. (Most people probably wouldn't discuss sex with an angel either, but that's another point.)

Common sense is such a, well, *common* virtue that we often overlook its value. It is, however, what allows us to get through an average day with a minimum of mishap.

The bad news is that not everyone is born with common sense. The good news is that we all can learn to develop it. If you haven't been blessed with an innate measure of common sense, the next time you find yourself in a mess, think about someone you know who has more than his or her share. Ask yourself what that person would do. Ignore your own tendencies and do what your role model would do, even if it feels uncomfortable. You may never end up being a paragon of common sense, but at least you can learn enough to come in out of the rain if you aren't carrying an umbrella.

Have I ever been told that I lack common sense?
Do I use the common sense I've been given?

I TRUST THAT I CAN DEVELOP THE VIRTUES I LACK.

Joseph the Carpenter

We know that Joseph was a carpenter. One Gospel account tells us that Jesus followed in his father's footsteps: the crowds ask, "Is he not the carpenter, the son of Mary, and the brother of James and Joses and Judas and Simon?"

Most paintings that depict Jesus and Joseph in the workshop show them making ox yokes, stools, and household items. But Joseph was probably more of a contractor than he was a craftsman.

The word used for someone in his profession is *tekton*, which conveys the idea of a person with a wide range of building skills, including skills in working with masonry and wood. That term also indicates a person with expertise in architectural design. Far more than a simple woodcarver, a *tekton* would have been a supervisor and leader of other less skilled workers. Given that the Romans were pouring an enormous amount of money into construction sites in Jerusalem, Tiberias, Sopphoris, and Caesarea Maritima, it's likely that Joseph and Jesus traveled as far as today's Lebanon or even Egypt on building projects, some of which may have lasted months. During those months, Mary may have stayed at home, visited relatives, or accompanied her husband and son to the job site. In any event, Jesus, Joseph, and Mary probably didn't lead nearly as sheltered or isolated a life as we tend to think.

How does it change my view of Joseph to think of him as a contractor/architect rather than a woodcarver? How does it influence my image of Mary?

I DON'T ALLOW PEOPLE'S PROFESSIONS TO INFLUENCE MY JUDGMENT OF THEM AS PERSONS.

Magic and Superstition

Where belief in Mary is concerned, the boundary between faith and superstition is sometimes gossamer thin. People who seldom pray may hang Rosary beads on their rear-view mirror as a talisman. People who never set foot in church may be afraid to leave the house without wearing their Miraculous Medal. People who scoff at psychics may devour everything they can find about the unrevealed Third Secret of Fatima.

The idea that there's someone out there (or up there) who has an influence on future events can be rather comforting—especially if she's on our side. And Mary always is.

However, if we think that we can somehow command Mary to do our bidding through the use of objects or incantations disguised as prayers, we're sliding perilously close to believing in magic.

Mary is not, and never has been, a magic worker. Although many miracles have been attributed to her intercession, she doesn't perform miracles of her own accord. All she has and all she is rest on God. Like each of us, Mary is wholly dependent on God. "She was fully aware of the greatness of her mission; but at the same time she recognized herself to be and remained 'a lowly servant,' attributing all glory to God the Savior," observed Pope John Paul II in *Insegnamenti* on March 19, 1982.

We most certainly can and should ask for Mary's help, but we must realize that we obtain her intercession through faith, not superstition.

When I ask Mary for help, do I secretly think that
I'm somehow "getting around God"?

WHEN I NEED HELP, I ASK MARY TO PRAY FOR ME.

Just the Facts

What do we really know about Mary?

The historical facts can be summarized in a few lines:

A young Jewish girl named Miriam (or Mary) is visited by an angel, who asks her if she would be willing to be the mother of God's son. She answers yes. A few months later, she and her husband, a carpenter named Joseph, travel from their hometown to the village of Bethlehem, where she gives birth to her son in a stable because the local inn is filled. They name the baby Yeshua—in Greek, Jesus—and use a manger for a crib. The boy grows up to be a charismatic teacher and preacher with an extraordinary gift for inspiring followers. He is eventually arrested as a threat to Rome and executed for treason. She goes to live with his closest friend.

Mary's life is an object lesson in nonjudgment. If we were to attempt to evaluate her life using only these historical facts, we would have to conclude that she was an insignificant blip on the radar of history. Dozens of other women have lived more dramatic and seemingly more influential lives. Yet behind the sketchy facts of Mary's life lies the great drama of Christianity.

Judging another's life decisions is always treacherous. Even when we think that we have all the facts, we probably don't. And the factual information that we *do* have we process through our own mental filter.

If we want to become spiritually mature, we must learn to accept others and their lives without judgment. In doing so, we not only allow others the chance to become whole, we allow ourselves the opportunity to become whole with them.

Am I a judgmental person? Can I accept other people and their decisions without adding my own mental two cents?

1 DON'T JUDGE, LEST 1 BE JUDGED.

What Really Counts?

What really matters in life?

Spiritual masters from all traditions agree that the essence of life lies not in having but in being, not in receiving but in giving, not in holding on but in letting go.

When we reach the point in our spiritual development where we can understand this truth—not just intellectually but within the deepest recesses of our heart—we can begin to be as thankful for our adversities as we are for our blessings.

Adversities allow us to strip away self-deceit in order to see that true wealth has nothing to do with possessions. All that really counts is love. The person who loves and is loved has everything.

Mary understood this principle from her earliest youth. If she hadn't, she couldn't have made the choices she did. In saying yes not just to love but to Love itself, she opened herself to enormous blessings—but also to enormous adversities and sorrows.

There's no sorrow that Mary hasn't experienced. She's lived through—triumphed over—all the pains of our mortal existence. She knows what it's like to be everything from an unwed mother to a widow, from the mother of an acclaimed hero to the mother of an accused criminal. She's suffered poverty, experienced monetary wealth from the gifts of the Magi, traveled abroad, remained at home, and been a refugee, a homebody, a nobody, and a queen.

When we find ourselves battered by the adversities of life, Mary offers us encouragement and succor by her example. As Gabriel of St. Mary Magdalene noted, "The Blessed Virgin Mary has, before us, trodden the straight and narrow path which leads to sanctity; before us she has carried the cross, before us she has known the ascents of the spirit through suffering."

Do I rail against adversity or accept it as part
of my spiritual training ground?

I KNOW THAT EVERYTHING THAT HAPPENS TO ME
CONTRIBUTES TO MY SPIRITUAL MATURITY.

Obedience

Can you imagine God—omniscient, all-powerful, and eternal—being obedient to you? That's what happened to Mary and Joseph. The Creator of the universe went down with them and came to Nazareth and was obedient to them. He went to bed when they told him to, picked up his clothes, swept the shop, fed the animals—in short, he did what they asked.

While it's mind-boggling to think that God would become obedient to a mere creation, obedience isn't a one-way street. Those who give orders have as much responsibility as those who carry them out. Jesus could be obedient to Mary and Joseph because they didn't ask him to do anything unfair or unjust. He could obey because they gave orders worthy of obedience.

We're never called to be obedient to evil or injustice. Accused war criminals from Nazi Germany who tried to defend their atrocities by saying that they were merely obeying orders weren't pardoned. If orders and rules are unjust or immoral, we're duty-bound to change them, not to blindly obey.

If you're in a position of authority, either at work or in your family, consider your authority a sacred trust. Use your power sparingly, honorably, honestly—so that your orders may be worthy of obedience.

To whom am I obedient? Who has to obey me?

I DON'T ASK OF OTHERS WHAT I'M NOT WILLING TO DO MYSELF.

Dancing

The apocryphal *Nativity of Mary,* sometimes called the *Protoevangelium of James,* is an ancient book telling of Mary's birth and childhood. While never accepted as Scripture, it contains some lovely passages about Mary. One such passage reads, "[T]he Lord God put grace upon her and she danced for joy with her feet, and the whole house of Israel loved her."

To dance for joy—what a wonderful image! So often what passes for dancing in our culture is rhythmic shuffling, only more or less to a beat. But to *really* dance is to escape the bounds of earth for a moment and become suspended in flight. There's nothing else on earth like it. Mary dancing for joy is a glorious image indeed.

Dancing is the spontaneous reaction of children to delight. When we become adults, we often squelch our spontaneity and assume a pose of reserved appreciation. But God isn't impressed with reserve. God longs for us to join in the dance of creation that began in the fullness of time and continues through eternity.

So today dance your way to wholeness, dance your way to joy—with Mary, dance your way to God!

Do I think that dancing is something done only by trained artists on the stage? Could I dance right now? Why or why not?

1 LET THE LORD OF THE DANCE LEAD ME IN THE WALTZ OF CREATION.

The Annunciation

We tend to think of the Feast of the Annunciation as one of Mary's special days, but in fact the correct title of the celebration is the Annunciation of the Lord. When Gabriel appeared to Mary, he announced the impending birth of the Messiah, not Mary's forthcoming pregnancy.

This distinction may seem slight, but it's significant. The central message isn't about Mary; rather, it's about the person who will be born to her, and about his mission. As the Scriptures say, "He will be great and will be called Son of the Most High, and the Lord God will give him the throne of David his father, and he will rule over the house of Jacob forever, and of his kingdom there will be no end."

Mary's importance and influence lie not in her own actions but in the fact that she made possible the birth of Jesus. She's honored for what she allowed to happen through her, not for what she herself has done.

Such thinking doesn't diminish Mary's importance; instead, it puts it in its proper perspective. When we view a magnificent bronze, we focus on the artist and the finished work of art, not on the wax mold. The mold is essential, certainly, but it's the final product that commands our attention.

The same is true of Mary. As St. Augustine said, "Mary is the living mold of God." While we owe Mary our respect and admiration, it's her son to whom we owe our adoration.

How can I let God use me as a mold?
What would I like my lasting legacy to be?

I GIVE THANKS THAT MARY'S WILLINGNESS TO BE A MOLD
MADE POSSIBLE THE BIRTH OF JESUS.

Ordinary Folks

Mary and Joseph are often said to have lived in poverty, but that seems to insult both of them. As a trained craftsman, Joseph should have been able to earn a decent living. If he didn't do so, then he was either unskilled or lazy. Neither of these options is very flattering to him. Moreover, if they really were all that poor, Mary obviously didn't do a very good job of emulating the ideal woman set out in Proverbs 31—the woman who plants vineyards, makes successful business deals, and takes care of her husband and children. If Mary and Joseph really were destitute, then God chose two incompetents to raise Jesus. Not a very likely scenario.

In truth, poverty is relative. In Mary and Joseph's time, no middle class existed. A person was either rich or poor. Since Mary and Joseph weren't wealthy, they were poor by default. But that doesn't mean that they were destitute beggars at the city gates. It means simply that they were average, ordinary folks.

Our culture doesn't like the ordinary. All our advertising tells us that in order to be valuable, we have to "step out of the ordinary." We have to "make our mark," "be unique," "stand out from the crowd." Realistically, though, few of us will achieve either fame or notoriety. We live ordinary lives. By the world's standards, we'll never be a big success.

Mary and Joseph's lives give us a different perspective. They show us that the world's standards aren't God's standards. By the world's standards, Mary and Joseph are nobodies. By God's standards, they're superstars. Which standards do you choose to meet?

How do I feel when I think of myself as "ordinary"?
How do I feel when I think of Mary as "ordinary" too?

1 USE GOD'S STANDARDS, NOT THE STANDARDS OF THE WORLD.

Change

We change our hair color, our clothing styles, our jobs, our houses, and our cars, but despite all our external changes, we remain the same within. The French have a proverb that summarizes the situation: "The more things change, the more they stay the same."

If we want to effect real change, we can't just move surface items around. We have to shift our mental and spiritual tectonic plates. We have to alter the foundations of our worldview.

Because authentic change is so difficult, most of us are content with making surface modifications. But nothing of value happens until we're willing to shift the continents of our closely held beliefs and cherished prejudices.

Mary can help us when we're ready to undertake real change. She's there as model, guide, and nurturer as we strive to break free from old patterns to facilitate life-giving change in our selves and in our relationships. All we have to do is ask for her help.

As Catholics have prayed for years in the *Memorare*, "Remember, most gracious Virgin Mary, that never was it known that anyone who fled to your protection, implored your help or sought your intercession, was left unaided. . . . Mother of the Word Incarnate, despise not my petition, but in your mercy hear and answer me."

Have I ever asked Mary for help when I wanted
to make a change in my life? What happened?

I TRUST THAT I'LL RECEIVE THE STRENGTH AND GRACE TO MAKE
THE CHANGES I NEED TO MAKE AT THIS TIME IN MY LIFE.

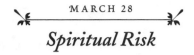

Spiritual Risk

Some people are natural-born risk-takers. They dive off cliffs, free-fall, bungee-jump, helicopter-ski, hang-glide—anything for an adrenaline rush. Others are more cautious, barely sticking their toes in the waters of life. Although cautious types tend to live longer, they also tend to lead more boring lives.

Fortunately, all of us, whether we're naturally risky or naturally cautious, can lead exciting spiritual lives, because spirituality always entails risk—the risk of seeing yourself for what you really are, the risk of having to make changes, the risk of altering your life.

Mary encourages us to take spiritual risks, because she above all other men and women knows that we *need* to risk in order to become whole. She tells us to "take courage," because she knows that without the willingness to risk, we can't change; and unless *we* change, the world can't change.

So how does one risk spiritually?

Spiritual risk begins with the willingness to become more open, more vulnerable. It means letting others peek over the walls of self-protection that we've built around our egos. It means allowing others to see our weaknesses as well as our strengths. It means being willing to be hurt. It means becoming open enough to let others share our sorrows, becoming free enough to experience deep intimacy, becoming trusting enough to let God absorb our pain.

Are you willing to take the risk?

When was the last time I let someone see the real me?
How do I feel when someone opens him- or
herself up to me?

I KNOW THAT WITH GOD SPIRITUAL RISKS AREN'T RISKY BUSINESS.

Roman Rule

The Romans created the last great worldwide civilization of ancient times. Beginning in present-day Italy, they spread their culture throughout the Mediterranean Basin and beyond. In the years 166–167 B.C.E., they moved into a little backwater country called Judea. Much to their surprise, the rural peasants of this country didn't roll over and become absorbed into the Roman culture. Instead, they remained steadfastly and defiantly Jewish, even after several centuries of military pressure.

This was the world into which Mary was born—a world occupied and dominated (but not destroyed) by Rome. Mary had to learn how to live her Jewish faith while surrounded by a culture that was indifferent at best and hostile at worst to her belief system.

Times aren't much different for committed believers today. Our culture tends to either mock or ignore spiritual matters. As an example, virtually no major character in any hit TV show attends religious services. News coverage of spiritual matters, if present at all, clusters around Christmas and Easter. Serious discussions of faith are generally relegated to obscure channels at odd hours of the night or to the back pages of newspapers and magazines.

Finding a way to integrate spirituality with everyday life in a culture that doesn't honor such activity is a challenge each of us must solve in his or her own way. When the task appears too daunting, remember that Mary faced a similar situation. Ask yourself what she would have done—or better yet, ask *her*.

Can people around me tell what I believe by my actions?
How do I make my spiritual life a part of my everyday life?

I LIVE MY FAITH EVEN WHEN IT IS DIFFICULT.

Permission

Remember when you were in kindergarten or elementary school? Before you could leave the classroom, you had to raise your hand and get permission. It didn't matter how urgent your need; you still had to wait until the teacher let you go.

Because our image of authority figures is based largely on our early role models, we sometimes think of God as the teacher and ourselves as the students, and we imagine that we have to ask God for permission before we can act.

Actually, it's just the opposite. God never enters into our lives without our permission. It's we who give God permission to act.

Mary's life shows how God ideally works with humanity. The question Mary faced—the question we all face—is whether or not we're willing to allow God to enter into our lives to act in our own best interest. The key here is *best interest*—a concept that encompasses not only what's best for us but what's best for all of those around us as well. Since we often don't know what's best, we have to be willing to trust that God knows—not an easy thing to do!

Ironically, when we finally give God permission to do what's best for us, we generally discover that God's best is more wonderful than anything we could have imagined.

Am I willing to trust God with my life?
How do I feel when I'm not totally in control?

I KNOW THAT GOD ALWAYS WORKS IN MY BEST INTEREST.

Orphans

At the death of her father, a forty-year-old woman tearfully said, "Now I'm an orphan." No matter how old we are, the loss of our parents makes us feel incredibly, overwhelmingly alone. We become orphans in a hostile world.

Just before the Crucifixion, Jesus promised his disciples, "I will not leave you orphans." Because his next statements talk about God the Father and the coming of the Holy Spirit, we usually assume that Jesus was talking about them. But on the cross, Jesus gave us a mother as well as a Father. He made sure that we had *two* parents to take care of us.

As we learn in the Gospel of John, "When Jesus saw his mother and the disciple there whom he loved, he said to his mother, 'Woman, behold, your son.' Then he said to the disciple, 'Behold, your mother.' And from that hour the disciple took her into his home."

Although John literally took Mary into his home, we can all spiritually bring Mary into our homes. In doing so, we truly welcome her as our mother.

Pope John Paul II, who has a particular devotion to Mary, made this observation in his encyclical Redemptoris Mater:

> *The Mother of Christ . . . is given as Mother to every single individual and all mankind. The man at the foot of the cross is John, "the disciple whom he loved." But it isn't he alone. Following tradition, [we] call Mary "the Mother of Christ and mother of mankind." . . . [S]he is "clearly the mother of the members of Christ."*

If you're longing for a mother's touch, a mother's love, Mary is waiting for your call.

What do I want from a mother?
Do I believe that Mary could be a mother to me?

IF MY MOTHER WRONGED ME, I FORGIVE HER. I NOW
OFFER HER MY ACCEPTANCE AND LOVE.

Let It Be

The Beatles' song "Let It Be" mentions Mother Mary coming in times of trouble. Whether or not the song refers to the Blessed Virgin Mary isn't important. What's important is that Mary, our divine mother, *does* come to us in times of trouble.

Sometimes people get the idea that Catholics pray *to* Mary for help in hard times and difficult situations. That's not the case. We pray to God alone, although we can—and should—ask Mary to pray *for* us.

The nature of our prayer relationship with Mary is best expressed in one of the most ancient prayers of Christianity: the Hail Mary. The first half combines Gabriel's announcement to Mary and Elizabeth's greeting: "Hail, Mary, full of grace. The Lord is with thee. Blessed art thou among women and blessed is the fruit of thy womb, Jesus."

The second half, which has been used almost since the beginning of Christianity, is a plea to Mary for help: "Holy Mary, Mother of God, pray for us sinners, now and at the hour of our death."

Just as we can ask other people for their prayers, so too can we ask Mary for her prayers. Of her gracious and generous response we can be assured. We must not, however, expect Mary to do something that God wouldn't do. Mary comes to us in times of trouble as confidante, comforter, and mother—not as omnipotent deity.

Do I pray to Mary, or do I ask Mary to pray for *and* with *me?*

I HONOR MARY, BUT I WORSHIP GOD ALONE.

Waiting

In *The Merchant of Venice,* Portia says, "My little body is a-weary of this great world" (act 1, scene 2). After Jesus' resurrection, Mary must also have felt a-weary of this great world. With Jesus having returned to heaven, her work on earth must have seemed complete. All that remained to her was to join her son—yet she was to continue living for some time. Although we don't know when she died, tradition holds that she lived at least several more years in Ephesus with the apostle John.

We grow so accustomed to thinking of Mary in her glorified state, sharing her son's vision for the world, we're tempted to forget she had to live without seeing Jesus in the flesh until her own death. Perhaps Jesus had given her a timetable of the future, but perhaps not. Maybe, like the rest of us, Mary had to wake up every day not knowing how much longer she would have to wait.

Waiting is one of the most difficult things we do. Waiting for a doctor's report, waiting for a baby to be born, waiting for a teen to come home at night, waiting in a hospital emergency room, waiting for a check, waiting . . . waiting . . . waiting. Few things make us feel more helpless or bring us closer to the brink of despair.

When we wait, we seldom can do much to speed things up. So the next time you have to wait, rather than spending the time fretting and worrying, look at your wait as an opportunity to let go of your expectations and let God handle the details.

Am I a patient "waiter," or do I get frustrated and angry
when I have to bide my time?

I DON'T BECOME FRAZZLED OVER UNEXPECTED DELAYS.

Candid Speech

What does it mean to be candid? It means being honest, certainly, but it means more than that. It means not hiding one's thoughts, not being evasive. It means speaking the truth with kindness and consideration. It means being true to yourself and others, without causing hurt or harm.

Our closest and most intimate relationships must be based on candid speech. Only when we let down our barriers and speak freely and frankly can we begin to share the most essential parts of our being.

Candid talk can't stop with friends and family, however. In order to develop spiritually, we must also learn to be candid with God. Telling God what lies in the deepest recesses of our hearts and minds is difficult, in part because it doesn't seem very "pious" to tell God what we're thinking when we aren't thinking "spiritual" thoughts. But do we really believe that if we don't tell God, God won't know? As Psalm 139 says, "Your eyes foresaw my actions; in your book all are written down; my days were shaped, before one came to be." It's only when we're candid with God that we can begin to experience God's presence fully in our lives.

Mary was most certainly candid with God. She knew God in human form, as the mother of God. What relationship could be more candid that that?

When I pray, do I use formulas, or do I pray from the heart?
Do I ever tell God exactly what I'm thinking,
even if it doesn't seem "holy" or "right"?

WHEN I PRAY, I TELL GOD WHAT'S ON MY HEART AND IN MY MIND,
NOT WHAT I THINK GOD WANTS TO HEAR.

Love Letters

Many people have a bundle of love letters tucked away at the back of a closet or the bottom of a cedar chest. Years after they were written, when the ink is faded and the paper yellowed, the letters remain, a lasting testimony to passion and desire.

Mary is God's love letter to the world.

Written on her heart and imprinted on her soul are God's longings for the human race. Sent as a symbol of God's great love for each one of us, she herself isn't Love, but she's the vessel by which Love was sent in human form into the world.

While Mary is God's great love letter, we're all intended to be part of God's loving message to the world. Mother Teresa of Calcutta once said, "I am a little pencil in the hand of a writing God who is sending a love letter to the world." If you can't imagine yourself in the same category as Mary or Mother Teresa, perhaps you can think of yourself as a piece of paper or an envelope or a stamp.

However you envision your role in God's eternal communication, always remember that you play a part in the celestial mail service that no one else can fill. After all, a letter without a stamp is as worthless as a stamp without a letter.

What is God trying to communicate through me?
How am I helping or hindering God's love message
to the world?

↑ BRING GOD'S LOVE TO ALL ↑ MEET.

Reality

"Does it hurt?" asked the Rabbit.
"Sometimes," said the Skin Horse, for he was always truth-
ful. "When you are Real you don't mind being hurt."

THE VELVETEEN RABBIT

Mary was a historically real person, but she was also, in the words of the Skin Horse, a Real person. Mary stands as an example of what each one of us is called to become. She's a real woman who allowed God to love her into Reality. Being Real isn't about our physical composition; it's about love. It's about becoming completely and fully human. It's about the willingness to be hurt.

Becoming Real doesn't happen overnight. It's a process—and more often than not a painful one. At the time of Jesus' presentation in the Temple, Simeon warned Mary, "You yourself a sword will pierce so that the thoughts of many hearts may be revealed." At the time, she could hardly have known what that would entail, but she did know that in order to become Real she would have to pay a heavy price.

We too have to pay for becoming Real. We have to be willing to open ourselves to others, to share their pain (and joy), to love even when we would rather hate, to forgive when we would rather bear a grudge, to give when we would rather take. We have to be willing to have our fur worn off and our joints loved loose. We have to be willing to become shabby and threadbare in the sight of the world. Once that happens, we become Real—and then, and only then, do we understand that Reality was worth whatever price we had to pay.

Who is the Realest person I know?
Am I afraid of the pain of becoming Real?

I'M WILLING TO LET GOD LOVE ME INTO REALITY
EVEN THOUGH IT MAY HURT.

Family

John's Gospel says that Jesus' mother and "his mother's sister . . . and Mary of Magdala" were standing together at the Crucifixion. Oddly, some traditional legends about Mary indicate that she was the only child of elderly parents. It's possible that the word *sister* in this passage refers to one of Joseph's sisters or to the wife of one of his brothers (that is, one of Mary's sisters-in-law), but the most likely explanation is that one of the women with Mary was her own flesh-and-blood sister.

But what about the other Mary, the one from Magdala? Mary Magdalene, as she's sometimes called, is often thought to be a reformed prostitute. All we really know about her, though, is her hometown and the fact that Jesus freed her from seven demons. Nothing in Scripture says she was a woman of the streets.

Ultimately, it doesn't matter who she was. Standing there, at the cross, she became a part of Jesus' family by fulfilling the words, "Whoever does the will of my heavenly Father is my brother, and sister, and mother."

Mary Magdalene found the family she needed in Mary and Jesus. If your family isn't able to give you the strength and support you need, consider Mary Magdalene. Like her, you can create the family you want and need through your choice of spiritually compatible friends and companions.

What do I want from my family?
Where do I find the most support?
How can I become family to someone in need?

1 RECOGNIZE THAT AS A CHILD OF GOD 1'M PART
OF THE FAMILY OF HUMANITY.

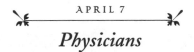

Physicians

While she would have been most familiar with herbalists and midwives, Mary apparently developed a friendship with at least one physician—Dr. Luke, the author of the Gospel of Luke. In his Gospel, Dr. Luke recorded a number of details about the Annunciation, the Visitation to Elizabeth, Jesus' birth, and other events—details that could have come only from Mary. Who else, for instance, would have mentioned such intimate details as the fact that Jesus was wrapped in swaddling cloths and laid in a manger? Who else could have known that Mary kept her puzzlement over the strange things surrounding her son's birth "in her heart."

Dr. Luke must have had a kindly bedside manner, because he was able to get Mary to talk about events surrounding Jesus' early life in a way none of the other New Testament writers could. It's nice to imagine the two of them sharing a cup of tea, talking about Mary's arthritis, and reflecting on Jesus' youth.

Dr. Luke's account points out that medicine is as much art as it is science. The ability to empathize, to draw out the hidden aspects of our lives, is part of the art. Often the difference between a competent physician and a beloved doctor lies more in the art than in the science.

If you have a beloved doctor, take a few minutes to express your appreciation the next time you see him or her. Mary's friend Dr. Luke would approve.

Have I ever told my doctor how much I appreciate him or her?

I GIVE THANKS FOR THE MEDICAL PROFESSIONALS IN MY LIFE.

APRIL 8

The Miracle of Childbirth

Anyone who has borne a child knows that childbirth is painful, difficult, and messy. It's no wonder that some spiritual writers in the early years of the Church claimed that Mary was spared the normal process when she gave birth to Jesus. Some have suggested that Jesus sprang forth from her womb in a sort of bloodless cesarean section. Still others opted for a more normal entrance but suggested that Mary would have felt no pain or discomfort during labor and delivery.

While it may seem "holier" to spare Mary the pain of birth, what's so awful about doing things the natural way? Jesus was conceived miraculously, it's true, but why would his birth have required divine intervention as well? Childbirth is miraculous enough as it is. Why would God want to make that miracle doubly miraculous?

Although we know a great deal about birth, scientists have only begun to realize that in some ways the rigors of the birth process help prepare a child for life outside the womb. In fact, the birth process may indeed mirror the death process, by which we pass into a new life. If Jesus went through an ordinary death, why shouldn't he have gone through an ordinary birth? And why shouldn't Mary have had the extraordinary experience of becoming a mother in the ordinary way?

What do I consider a miracle?
Do I believe that the ordinary can be miraculous?

1 RECOGNIZE THAT SOME ORDINARY EXPERIENCES
ARE REALLY MIRACLES.

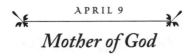

Mother of God

To Catholics, Mary's traditional title of honor Mother of God has a comforting familiarity born from centuries of use. But to non-Catholic ears, it sounds positively heretical. How can God, who always was and always will be, have a mother? Doesn't the title imply that Mary existed before God?

If that was what Catholics meant when they called Mary the Mother of God, it would indeed be heretical. But the title Mother of God should more accurately be "Mother of Jesus, who is the Son of God." God, the Eternal One, can't have a mother. Jesus, on the other hand, needed a human mother in order to become fully human.

As Rev. John Randall writes in *Mary: Pathway to Fruitfulness:*

> She taught him to speak and delighted in his first words. He learned her accent, her intonation, her idiomatic expressions. She taught him the names of flowers and insects, the words of psalms. Through her, God the Father loved and comforted his Son when he was hurt by bruises or cut by rejection or loneliness. She looked down smiling with pleasure at this child she loved, until one day she found herself looking up into his face. He had grown up.

She was, for all eternity, his mother. And ours.

Do I think of Mary as my mother?
If I believe that Mary is my mother, do I consider
Jesus my brother?

I'M THANKFUL FOR ALL WHO HAVE ACTED AS MOTHERS TO ME.

Receiving Messages

NASA has sent message probes into outer space with the hope that if there's extraterrestrial life out there somewhere, it will receive the messages and contact earth. As far as we know, no aliens have taken NASA up on its offer. But that doesn't mean we aren't being continually sent heavenly messages.

Every minute of every hour of every day, God contacts earth.

If it doesn't seem as if God is sending you any messages, remember that not every message is earthshakingly profound. Maybe today your message is as simple as, "You aren't alone," or "Things will be okay." Whatever the message is, you can be certain it will be exactly what you need to hear.

Another reason you may not seem to be getting any messages is that the messengers God chooses are among the most unlikely imaginable. A young Jewish girl from a little town in a faraway, insignificant country, for instance. Over the centuries, in her appearances on earth, Mary has brought God's messages of love, conversion, and hope to the entire world.

As you go through your days, look for the lesson, the instruction, the meaning in every person you meet. Virtually anyone can come with a message for you from God. The clerk at the grocery store. Your co-worker at the coffee machine. Your spouse. Your neighbor. The driver in the next car. Just keep your eyes and your ears open—you'll be amazed at what God is trying to tell you today and every day.

Do I look for God's messages in the people I come
into contact with every day?

1 LISTEN WHEN GOD TRIES TO GET MY ATTENTION.

Clothing

Many of us have a closet full of clothes, but nothing to wear. Mary wouldn't have had that problem, since she didn't have a closet—and even if she had, she would have had very little to put in it. In her day, women would have had one outfit for everyday wear and perhaps another, more fancy garment for special occasions—nothing approximating our extensive wardrobes.

Even though Mary wouldn't have had many outfits, she probably felt the need for something new every now and then. Maybe to celebrate Passover in Jerusalem. Perhaps for a special wedding, such as the one at Cana. At those times, Mary would have wanted to look her best, and that might have meant something new to wear.

There's nothing wrong with wanting to look our best. We just have to be careful that we don't confuse what's on the outside with what's on the inside. The most expensive designer fashions can cover a black and corrupt heart.

If you enjoy buying and wearing new clothes, you might consider adopting this rule: nothing new comes into the house unless something old goes to charity. That way you'll avoid the dual traps of accumulation and selfishness (not to mention being able to get new things without feeling guilty!).

Am I a clotheshorse? Do I judge people by what they wear?
Do I judge myself by what I wear?

I REALIZE THAT CLOTHES DON'T MAKE THE MAN OR THE WOMAN.

Songs

Alzheimer's is one of the cruelest of all diseases. It not only reduces sufferers to a state of helpless dependence, it also strips them of their memories. The disease so scrambles their memory storage-banks that they "remember" things that never happened while forgetting such essentials as the names of their children (or even the fact that they have children).

Oddly, however, many Alzheimer patients can clearly remember songs from their childhood. A group of otherwise withdrawn and unresponsive patients may come alive when they hear favorite melodies from long ago.

It's not surprising, really. A song can often draw us back to the past, allowing the years to evaporate for a brief moment. Hearing "America the Beautiful" might transport you back to your fourth-grade class, where you sang that song every day after recess. Or a popular melody from your high school days might drop you back into tenth grade, when you had your first "real" romance.

Although we don't know what songs Mary might have sung to Jesus as he was growing up, we *can* surmise that she sang to him. It's a rare mother who doesn't sing to her baby, for music is one of the ways we not only demonstrate our love but add beauty to our environment.

Rather than flipping on the radio today and listening to whatever the DJ dictates, take some time to choose music that reflects your mood. Put on a CD (buy a new one if necessary) and really listen to it. Let the music sink deep into your spirit—and while it's doing so, let it create a memory that can never be erased.

Do I use music to enhance my life or to drown
out the sounds of silence?

I CHOOSE THE MUSIC I LISTEN TO WITH CARE.

Work

The proverb "A woman's work is never done" is obviously true for Mary. Even in heaven, she doesn't get to rest. Over the centuries, she has reappeared throughout the world, spreading her son's message. Her work will be done only when Jesus' work is completed. And since Jesus said that the angels themselves don't know when that will be, Mary may still have a lot more work to do.

None of us really knows when our work will be finished. Sometimes we don't even know what our real work is. We may think that our work is to run a company or raise a family (or a thousand and one other things), but those jobs may not be what God thinks our work is. God judges our work by very different standards than we do. For instance, we may not think stopping to help someone figure out which grocery-store aisle the waxed paper is on is any big deal; but in the eternal scheme of things, the kind word we utter to that confused stranger may make an enormous difference. For all we know, that stranger is considering suicide, and our stopping may offer proof that life is worth living. Since we can't know the ultimate outcome of our actions, it's best to act as if everything we do is our "real" work.

What have I done recently that made a difference
in someone's life?

I DO MY BEST AT ALL TIMES AND LET GOD SORT OUT THE DETAILS.

Intimacy

In *A Tree Full of Angels*, Macrina Wiederkehr writes, "The heart cannot live without intimacy. We all need special people in our lives to whom we can show our souls."

As much as we need food, water, and sleep, we also need intimate relationships. Unfortunately, intimacy is often equated with sexual expression, but intimacy isn't the same thing as sex. Indeed, the most profound intimacy often occurs without sex—a mother with her child, for instance, or close friends whose relationship has survived distance and absence.

In the Catholic tradition, Mary and Joseph are believed to have lived celibate lives during their marriage, thus enabling Mary to remain "ever-virgin." Despite the lack of a sexual union, no one has ever suggested that Mary and Joseph didn't share an intimate relationship. Cardinal Léon Josephy Suenens writes, "This side of her life is not a game of make-believe, but an engagement fully lived out. . . ."

In a world saturated with sex and sexual images, nonphysical intimate relationships aren't always valued. But the closeness that comes with sharing hopes, dreams, fears, ideals, frustrations, joys, and sorrows—in short, with sharing the stuff of life—is the only intimacy that lasts forever.

Don't enter into such a relationship lightly. It may be a direct link to heaven.

Who are my closest friends?
How do I nurture our relationships?

1 APPRECIATE THE DIFFERENCE BETWEEN INTIMACY AND SEXUALITY.

Taxes

Benjamin Franklin once wrote in a letter to a friend, "But in this world nothing can be said to be certain except death and taxes." Undoubtedly Mary would have agreed—at least about the taxes part. The ultimate reason she and Joseph had to travel when she was pregnant (and the reason she ended up giving birth in a stable) was to fulfill the prophecy that said the Messiah would be born in Bethlehem—but the immediate reason was that the Roman governor of Syria was conducting a census. Three guesses why he wanted to know who lived where and owned what. If you guessed "to levy taxes," proceed directly to "Go!"

No one likes to pay taxes, especially when it seems that the government is doing a poor job of using the money. Yet our money isn't really our own. It's a sign of the greater community we share. In paying our taxes, we're reminded that we're responsible for each other; we're affirming that as a community we need to have schools, roads, police and fire protection, public transportation, medical care for the poor, and housing for the displaced.

When we resent paying our fair share of taxes, we are, in one sense, resenting those less fortunate than ourselves. Those who, perhaps, have had to give birth all alone in a strange town in a dank and dirty stable.

Am I honest in calculating my taxes?
Do I resent having to pay taxes?

I GIVE TO CAESAR THAT WHICH IS CAESAR'S AND
TO GOD THAT WHICH IS GOD'S.

Earthiness

One of the archetypal figures in literature is the Earth Mother. The embodiment of caring, nurturing, and sustaining, she's both earthy and spiritual. The fairy godmother in *Cinderella* is an Earth Mother. So is Princess Leia of the *Star Wars* trilogy. And so is the Blessed Virgin.

The difference, of course, is that fairy godmothers and Princess Leia are fictional characters, whereas Mary is a real woman. Like fictional Earth Mothers, however, Mary combines a deeply spiritual nature with a practical, earthy side.

It's easy for us to recognize the spiritual nature of Mary, because it's been emphasized since the beginning of Christendom. The other side may be more difficult to see, having not been "promoted." But it's there.

Mary couldn't have been the ephemeral creature we see in statues, too dainty to help a sheep birth a lamb and too refined to clean out a stable. She couldn't have been the fey figure portrayed in art, whose hands never bore the marks of labor and whose brow never beaded with sweat.

Mary lived in a time and place where hard physical work was the norm. As part of her daily routine, she would have had to cook, clean, spin, and sew—all by hand. In addition, she would have known what it was like to work with the soil, planting seeds and harvesting crops as well as helping her husband with his labors. She would have known all the harsh, gritty aspects of life—and death—in an agrarian culture. She certainly would have spent time in prayer, but her work would also have been her prayer.

When we're tempted to think that certain duties are "beneath us," let's remember that Mary, "blessed among all women," lived with her heart in heaven but with her feet squarely planted on terra firma.

Do I try to get out of work that I think is lowly or unrewarding?
Do I believe that some jobs are inherently more noble
than others?

I VALUE ALL HONEST LABOR.

Confidence

Among Mary's many titles, you probably won't read Woman of Confidence, yet Mary had to have been a supremely confident woman. After all, confidence can be defined as "firm trust"; and if nothing else, Mary had firm trust—not in her own abilities but in God's abilities. Because she trusted God to take care of her no matter what, she was able to bear a son through the power of the Holy Spirit. If *that* isn't confidence, then nothing is!

It's difficult to have absolute confidence in another person (or even in yourself) because of the fallibility of human nature. However, it's possible to have complete confidence in God. God didn't let Mary down, and God won't let any of us down either.

Why, then, does it so often seem as if God doesn't answer our prayers?

The easy reply is that God *always* answers prayers; it's just that sometimes the answer is no. But such a simplistic answer begs the question.

While we can never completely understand, one reason our prayers sometimes seem to go unanswered is that we become too attached to a *specific* answer. When we don't get the response we seek, it feels as if our prayer has been ignored.

Mary had complete confidence in God because she didn't have any preconceived notions of how God would act; she was willing merely to trust that God *would* act. Likewise, when we're confident that God *will* act on our behalf, we begin to see that God always *does* act in our best interest.

When I pray, do I tell God what I'd like the answer to be, or am I willing to pray without trying to dictate God's response?

1 HAVE CONFIDENCE THAT GOD ANSWERS MY PRAYERS.

Fiat!

In some translations of Luke's Gospel, when Gabriel asks Mary if she's willing to become the mother of the Savior, she answers, *"Fiat!"*

More than a mere yes, her response means, "Let it be! Let it happen!" It's a *resounding* yes—and not just to the question of the moment but to the adventure of life, with all its ups and downs, ins and outs, pains and joys.

Mary's response—*"Fiat!"*—should be ours as well. We're all called to live life to the fullest, not to go around like servants in a fantasy castle waiting for some distant moment when a prince will arrive to awaken the imprisoned princess with a kiss (and in the process wake everyone else up as well).

The time for waiting is over. The prince has *already* arrived. The princess is *already* awake. It's time to rouse ourselves from the dreamworld and start living!

Today observe your surroundings through freshly awakened senses. Look at the street you live on as if you've never seen it before. Drink your morning coffee as if it were the first cup you've ever tasted. Listen to the chirp of birds as if you've never heard birdsong before. Run your hand along the line of your cheek as if you've never felt a jawbone before. Breathe in the morning air as if this were your first breath. Make *"Fiat!"* your response to all of creation.

Do I ever feel as if I'm sleepwalking through life?
When have I felt the most alive, the most awake?

FIAT! YES! LET IT BE!

Spiritual Bouquet

Mary is called by many flowery names—not just eloquent words but the names of actual flowers, such as the rose and the lily. Even the name of her great prayer, the Rosary, is derived from the word *rose.*

A traditional Catholic practice in years past was to create a spiritual bouquet—a collection of spiritual gifts, such as a promise to pray a certain number of Rosaries, to make a brief visit to church, or to read certain prayers aloud for another person's intentions. This garland of promises was printed on a decorated card and presented on a special occasion (such as Easter, Christmas, or Mother's Day). Intended to bless both the giver and the receiver, it was a way of letting loved ones know you were thinking about and praying for them and their intentions.

Try creating a spiritual bouquet for someone important in your life. Unlike the old-fashioned spiritual bouquet, yours doesn't have to consist of Rosaries or set prayers. Instead, you could promise to wish someone happiness every time you think of him or her this week. Or you could vow to remember the recipient with positive thoughts every morning when you brush your teeth. Or you might agree to say a special prayer every day at noon to help that person with a special need, such as quitting smoking or starting an exercise program.

While many spiritual actions are best kept secret, a spiritual bouquet is one that needs to be shared. In letting other people know that you treasure them enough to keep them in your heart and mind, you not only build them up, but you strengthen yourself as well.

Why not start creating a spiritual floral arrangement for someone right now?

Am I afraid that people will think I'm too "religious" if I say that I'll pray for them? Do I think that I should keep my religion to myself?

I'LL GIVE AWAY A SPIRITUAL BOUQUET TODAY.

Cousin Connection

The Gospels tell us that Mary's kinswoman Elizabeth named her son John. John would thus be Mary's nephew and Jesus' cousin. Since they were close in age, they probably had a number of things in common. Then again, maybe not. John might have been a rather peculiar child, since he grew up to be a rather peculiar adult, living in the desert, eating honey and locusts, and wearing skins for clothing. Jesus, on the other hand, must have been a fairly ordinary child (that little Temple incident notwithstanding), since no one could believe that he was the Messiah when he finally began his teaching.

Cousins are odd relatives. Some are almost as close as siblings, while others are so distant they wouldn't recognize each other if they met on the street. Although in our culture we use the same word to mean the children of our father's siblings and the children of our mother's siblings, cousins on one side of the family often seem more like "real" relatives than cousins on the other. If you have equally good relations with both sides of your family, consider yourself doubly blessed!

This might be a good time to do a little investigating into your family tree. Ask your oldest living relatives on both sides what they know about the family, and write down their observations. Their memories may be invaluable in the future. If nothing else, you may gain some insight into where you came from—and maybe even where you're going!

Do I know my cousins?
Am I closer to cousins on one side of the family than the other?

I REALIZE THAT I'M PART OF AN EXTENDED FAMILY.

Myrrh

One of the gifts of the Wise Men, myrrh was worth a king's ransom. Indeed, it was used in the burial ritual of kings. Obtained from the sap of a shrublike plant, it was used as incense as well as perfume. In fact, the erotic poem "The Song of Solomon" alludes several times to the desirability and value of myrrh.

Did Mary wonder when she received such a gift? In retrospect, we understand its significance, pointing as it does to both Jesus' kingly status and his impending death. Since Mary had to ponder several other things surrounding Jesus' birth, it seems unlikely that she would have immediately understood the cosmic significance of the gift. Possibly, having only the faintest glimmer of realization that this baby in her arms would have to die in order to reign as the King of Creation, she thought that the Magi were generous eccentrics.

Sometimes, like Mary, we get hints that whatever is happening to us is of vast importance, but we don't get the whole picture. We know that we need to pay attention, but we really aren't sure what we're paying attention to—or why. All we have is the feeling that something big is waiting down the road and the sense that we need to be ready.

At those times, we need to be like Mary, graciously accepting what's offered to us while expecting that the significance will be revealed in due time.

> *Do I want to know the whole story at the very beginning?*
> *Am I willing to wait and let things unfold in God's time?*

I ACCEPT EACH DAY AND ITS GIFTS AS THEY COME.

Gratitude

Next time you're driving or riding in a car, try this experiment. First concentrate on everything red in your field of vision. At first you may not see much, but within seconds red objects will pop up everywhere. Next concentrate on blue. Suddenly all the red objects will seem to vanish, leaving the world dominated by blue. The same will be true for every color you think of. You'll see what you look for.

This same principle holds true in life. If you look for the good, you'll find it. Conversely, if you look for the sad or the bad, you'll find that. That's why it's so important to develop an "attitude of gratitude." The more gratitude you express, the more reasons you'll have to feel grateful.

Mary's great prayer—known as the Magnificat or the Canticle of Mary—shows that she had a finely developed attitude of gratitude. From the opening line ("My soul proclaims the greatness of the Lord") to the ending verse ("He has helped Israel his servant, remembering his mercy, according to his promise to our fathers, to Abraham and to his descendants forever"), Mary's entire prayer is one of thankfulness to God. She not only expresses her appreciation for God's work in her own life, but she recalls God's grace to the entire nation of Israel.

An attitude of gratitude is something we can all develop. Let Mary's lifestyle of gratitude become ours as well.

Do I see my glass as half full or half empty?
What am I grateful for right now?

TODAY 1 LOOK FOR ALL THE GOOD THINGS IN MY LIFE.

Happiness

Like dew on morning petals, happiness can't be captured or kept. Although you can recall past times of happiness and look forward to being happy in the future, happiness itself can be *experienced* only in the present.

What makes us truly happy? Usually it's not material possessions—things such as a new house or an exciting vacation. While these can make us feel exhilarated or rejuvenated, the happiness they bring is short-lived and elusive. The only happiness that accompanies us throughout our life-journey is that which comes from developing loving relationships with others—particularly with God.

The mere presence of God brings us unexplainable happiness. Like a breath of fresh air or a cooling breeze, it blows through our lives, changing everything and nothing at the same time. No wonder mystics and prophets have had such a hard time explaining it!

Visionaries report experiencing the same inexplicable feelings of happiness when Mary appears. And it's no wonder. She of all people is closest to Jesus. She carries within her being his spirit and message. When Mary appears, God is undeniably with her; and where God is, so is true happiness.

Abraham Lincoln once said that people are about as happy as they make up their minds to be. If you lack happiness, ask Mary to pray that you'll be filled with the Spirit of God. Ask her to help you feel the touch of God in your life today. Then make up your mind to be happy.

Do I really want to be happy?
Have I ever secretly enjoyed being miserable?

I KNOW THAT MY HAPPINESS DOESN'T DEPEND
ON EXTERNAL CIRCUMSTANCES.

Crucifixion

And they crucified him.

LUKE 23:33

Crucifixion wasn't a Roman invention, but by the time of Jesus' death, the Romans had perfected the technique. After being scourged, the condemned man carried his cross to the place of execution. He was then completely stripped of his garments (unless local custom forbade it), made to lie on the ground, and bound (with rope or nails) by wrists and feet to the wood.

Death on a cross almost never occurred due to blood loss. The wounds in the wrists and feet, while agonizing, didn't sever any major blood vessels. Crucifixion victims died of asphyxiation instead.

The greatest agony of crucifixion occurred from the almost constant sensation of suffocation. To speak, as Christ did from his cross, would have taken an enormous toll, because it required the victim to push up against the nails in his feet and hold that position for as long as it took to complete the communication.

Christ spoke seven times from his cross—a remarkable feat. One of those seven utterances was to make sure that his mother would be cared for after his death. He gave her to his friend John—and he gave John to her. Moreover, he gave her to us to be our mother as well.

May St. Gemma Galgani's prayer become our prayer: "You are my heavenly mother. You will be toward me like any mother toward her children. . . . O my Mother, do not forsake me! My dearest Mother, do not abandon me!"

Am I willing to share my family with others?
Do I make sure that my family is cared for
when I can't be with them?

LOVING OTHERS IS EASY, BECAUSE I KNOW THAT I'M LOVED.

The Holy Spirit

*All these devoted themselves with one accord to prayer, together
with some women, and Mary the mother of Jesus, and his
brothers. . . . When the time for Pentecost was fulfilled,
they were all in one place together. . . .
And they were all filled with the Holy Spirit.*

ACTS 1:14, 2:1, 4

Apparently Mary received the Holy Spirit along with the apostles on
that first Pentecost. Because Mary is so closely linked with God,
some people treat her as if she herself were divine. But Mary isn't a
goddess. She was and is one of God's creations. She has no power, no
grandeur, no glory save that which God has given her. As St. Maximilian Kolbe, who was executed at Auschwitz, put it, "Of herself,
Mary is nothing, even as all other creatures are; but by God's gift she
is the most perfect of creatures."

Being a creature—albeit a perfect one—Mary could still benefit
from receiving the gifts of the Holy Spirit (although she undoubtedly
didn't need them nearly as much as the rest of us). The sevenfold gifts
that filled Mary at Pentecost—wisdom, understanding, counsel, fortitude, knowledge, piety, and fear of the Lord—can fill us as well, giving us the strength and courage we need to faithfully carry out our
life's work.

*Which gift of the Holy Spirit do I need to develop most in my life?
Which gift comes the most naturally to me?*

DIVINE WISDOM IS MY DAILY GUIDE.

Approval

Contrary to what some people think, no one, not even devout Catholics, must believe Mary has ever appeared, even in "approved" apparitions such as Lourdes and Fatima. Approval simply means that, after stringent investigation, the Church has examined the apparition and can find nothing false. In other words, approval merely states people are free to believe Mary has appeared, not that they must believe.

For some people, church approval is essential. They won't even accept the possibility that Mary could be appearing until church officials have given their okay. For other people, church approval is superfluous. They are willing to believe that Mary is appearing even after church officials have publicly declaimed a vision.

Seeking approval from others is a little like trying to convince people one way or the other about Mary's appearances. People will either believe or not believe Mary has appeared. People will approve or not approve of us and our behavior. The key to self-approval is much like the key to judging Mary's appearances. If Mary's appearances really come from God, they will bear "good fruit." Hearts will be softened, lives will be changed, souls will be saved. If our lives bear "good fruit," others will be encouraged, comforted, and inspired, at which point it no longer matters who does or doesn't approve of us!

Do I want everyone to approve of me and my choices?

I ACCEPT THE FACT I CAN'T PLEASE ALL OF THE
PEOPLE ALL OF THE TIME.

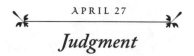

Judgment

After the Resurrection, it would have been very easy for Mary to return to Nazareth and tell all those judgmental neighbors, "See, I *told* you he was the Messiah!" but she didn't. Instead, she provided us with an outstanding example of nonjudgmentalism.

One of the cardinal rules of spiritual maturity is this: "Judge not, lest you be judged." Put another way, "That which goes around, comes around."

So often we discover that the things we've been the most judgmental about are the very things we ourselves end up having to face. If, for instance, we've been critical of a friend's divorce, we may ultimately find ourselves struggling through a separation, wanting desperately to cry out and be understood.

The only way not to be judged is not to judge. Being nonjudgmental doesn't mean abandoning standards and ethics, of course. But while we don't have to pretend that every action is acceptable and all decisions are correct, neither can we set ourselves up as judge and jury for the world.

In traditional Catholic teaching, Mary is always viewed as our help, our intercessor, our comforter in times of trouble. She's the one we go to when we need a mother's arms. She helps everyone who comes to her. As the great Marian prayer, the *Memorare*, says, "Never was it known that anyone who fled to your protection . . . was left unaided." Mary—who has more right to judge than anyone else in the world—never judges. Likewise, we must never judge one another.

Do I ever pay undue attention to other people's business?
Do I find it easy or difficult to be nonjudgmental?

I LET PEOPLE LIVE THEIR OWN LIVES.

Lost and Found

All of us have had the experience of losing something valuable. Maybe it was our keys or our wallet. The stages of loss are the same whatever the object. First panic when we realize something is missing. Then desperate searching. Next a heartsick feeling of loss, coupled with a desperate hope that the missing object will somehow turn up.

Mary knows what it's like to lose something, although in her case it was a some*one*—Jesus, who stayed behind in the Temple when he was twelve years old. Imagine her utter panic when she realized that he wasn't with the other boys in the caravan. Consider her desperate searching, then her heartsickness as she and Joseph began to retrace their steps. What thoughts must have been going through her mind? Not only had she lost her own son, she had lost the Son of the Most High as well.

But Mary also knows what it's like to find that which has been lost. After three impossibly frantic days, she and Joseph finally located Jesus in the Temple. Two thousand years later, we can still sense her great relief and joy.

Because Mary knows what it's like both to lose and to find her son, her role now is to help all of us find him. Since she knows what it's like to search diligently, she encourages us in our search, letting us know that at the end we will find him not in the Temple of Jerusalem but in the temple of our own souls.

What have I searched the most diligently for in my life?
Have I found what I was looking for, or am I still on my quest?

1 KNOW THAT 1'LL FIND WHAT 1 WANT MOST FROM LIFE.

Passover

Passover is the great Jewish festival of freedom and deliverance, commemorating the Jews' exodus from Egypt. When God made it known that he was going to punish the Egyptians, the Jews marked their doorposts with the blood of unblemished lambs. That night, the Angel of Death "passed over" their homes, sparing them from death.

We know that the Holy Family celebrated Passover, because they were in Jerusalem for the feast when Jesus lingered behind in the Temple. And we know that the night before he died, Jesus celebrated the feast with his disciples. Although Mary isn't mentioned in the Gospel accounts of that last Passover, perhaps she was there, in another room with the other women.

Listening to Jesus talk, sensing his growing agitation, watching Judas depart abruptly, did Mary have a mother's sense that something was about to happen? Did she pray for a miracle? Did she beg that once more God would "pass over" and spare Jesus? We know that Jesus himself asked to be spared; it seems likely that his mother would have made the same request.

How often do we pray out of desperation? How often do we reach out in utter despair to God? How often do we ask to be "passed over" from trials and tribulations?

The answer Jesus received—and the answer Mary would have received also—is the same message we receive. We may not be miraculously saved, but we're guaranteed the strength to go through with the trial. That alone is answer enough.

What trial am I facing right now that I would
like to be "passed over" from?

I KNOW THAT GOD WILL GIVE ME THE STRENGTH TO FACE
EVERY CHALLENGE THAT COMES MY WAY.

Star of the Sea

Of all the designations given Mary, one of the most popular is Star of the Sea. From St. Bernard to Pope John Paul II, holy men and women throughout the centuries have praised Mary under this title.

But what does Star of the Sea mean?

Embodied in those few words is profound spiritual insight. Mary herself isn't the end of our journey; rather, she's the way we come to understand our deepest spiritual needs and longings. She's a light in the stormy seas of life, a beacon in the raging hurricanes of trouble. Her response to God and her example of faith-filled living are an inspiration to all who seek to know and understand the truth. St. Thomas put it best when he said, "Even as sailors are guided into port by means of a star, so Christians are guided toward Heaven by means of Mary."

If you find yourself struggling to keep a heavenward course, pray these words Pope John Paul II spoke in Rome on June 14, 1979: "I entrust you all to Mary most holy, our Mother in heaven, the Star of the Sea of our life: pray to her every day, you children! Give your hand to Mary most holy, so that she may lead you to receive Jesus in a holy way."

What areas of my life seem the most storm-ravaged?
Where can I find a "safe harbor"?

I SET MY SIGHTS ON NOTHING LESS THAN HEAVEN ITSELF.

Deception

It's bad enough to try to fool others, but self-deception is the cruelest delusion of all. To try to convince ourselves that we're something or someone we aren't is worse than living a lie: it's denying what we really are.

All of us were born with unique gifts and talents. Each of us has something we can do better than anyone else in the world. For some, the talent is obvious. The late Carl Sagan, for instance, could present scientific thought in a way that fascinated the average reader or TV viewer. For most of us, however, our gifts aren't so public; they may be apparent only to those people within our intimate circles.

Nonetheless, if we try to convince ourselves that either (a) we don't possess any gifts or (b) we possess gifts that we don't really have, we end up being unable to effectively use the talents we do have.

Mary is an example of a woman who knows herself and her weaknesses ("his handmaid's lowliness"), but she also knows her strengths ("all ages will call me blessed"). She knows what she can't do—and what she can.

As we grow in spiritual wisdom, let us ask God to help us strip away the mask of self-deceit—to pray, in the words of the poet Robert Burns, "O wad some Pow'r the giftie gie us to see oursels as others see us! It wad frae mony a blunder free us, and follish notion."

*Have I ever analyzed my gifts and talents honestly and
realistically? What do I see as my greatest strengths?
My greatest weaknesses?*

I ACCEPT MY UNIQUENESS.

Wholly Holy

All the great religions of the world agree on one point: we're called to become wholly holy. How holiness is defined naturally differs. The Hindu concept of Nirvana isn't the same as the Christian vision of heaven, for instance. Yet beneath the differences is a common goal—for humanity to mend its brokenness.

This call to healing wholeness isn't limited to the spiritual side of existence. We're called to become whole in body as well as spirit. Unfortunately, all too often we emphasize one aspect of our being to the neglect of others. We work on our career, for example, while neglecting our relationships. We work on our soul while neglecting our body.

Because Christianity's focus has been on the next life for much of its history, we tend to forget that finding the right balance between heaven and earth is a primary goal of Christian teaching. Mary, in being assumed to heaven body and soul, clearly shows that wholeness is God's goal for each of us. If the spiritual side were the only thing that is important, Mary wouldn't have needed her body until the end of time. Yet God allows her to be whole in heaven in order to show us that the physical and spiritual can't be divided. We become wholly holy through the proper use of our bodies. It's only through the physical that we can come to truly understand the spiritual.

Why this should be is mystery. That it *is* is reality.

*Which do I spend more time developing: my spiritual side or
my physical body? How can I achieve a better balance
in order to become wholly holy?*

I DON'T OVEREMPHASIZE EITHER THE SPIRITUAL OR
THE PHYSICAL, BUT GIVE TIME TO BOTH.

Essence

One of the most telling scenes in Mary's life takes place at a wedding feast in the town of Cana.

During a wedding celebration in those days—a get-together that could last for up to two weeks—the host was expected to provide food and drink for the guests. At this Cana wedding, someone miscalculates, and the wine runs out on the third day—a major social faux pas.

It's not clear why Mary is aware of this difficulty, but in any event, she points out the problem to Jesus, fully expecting that (despite the fact that his "time had not yet come") he'll take care of it.

The quintessence of Mary is revealed in this story. Mary is deeply concerned about the little things of life: she's concerned about purely secular issues, such as wine at parties, and she's concerned about the feelings of a bride and groom. Coupled with that concern is utter trust that her son will do what she asks, that he'll take care of things. On this occasion, Mary shows her complete faith in approaching Jesus about even the most minor details of life. In dealing with the waiters and servers, she also reveals her assertive confidence.

If you want Mary to help you with the problems of life, if you want to understand why the saints have always turned to Mary in times of need, if you want to know what Mary is really like, read the story of the wedding at Cana (John 2:1–11).

Do I believe that Mary will help me with "nonspiritual"
problems, or do I believe that she cares about
spiritual issues only?

I BELIEVE THAT MARY CARES ABOUT ALL ASPECTS OF LIFE.

The Dark Side

In the *Star Wars* trilogy, Obi-wan Kenobi warns young Luke Skywalker of the dangers of the dark side of the Force. The dark side has already seduced Luke's father, turning him into that paragon of evil, Darth Vader, and Obi-wan desperately tries to keep Luke from suffering the same fate.

This modern myth reiterates a timeless truth: we all can be corrupted. Within each of us lurks a dark side, prowling like a ravenous beast, waiting for the chance to pounce and devour.

All of us except Mary, that is.

Catholic theology teaches that Mary was conceived in her mother's womb without a dark side. She *could* have sinned, but she didn't—not because she was incapable of sin, as was Jesus, but rather because she wasn't drawn to sin the same way the rest of us are.

Such grace may make Mary seem so far above the rest of us that we haven't got a chance of following in her footsteps. However, Mary's Immaculate Conception, as it is called, was the result of God's grace operating to the fullest in her life. God offers each of us that same grace. We may be born with a dark side, but God gives us the chance to have our shadow-nature obliterated through the workings of the Holy Spirit—the same Holy Spirit that descended on Mary and the apostles at Pentecost.

Mary was given certain privileges, elevated above us, not so that we can never hope to go where she's gone but so that she can show us how to travel life's roadways.

Do I recognize my own dark side?
Have I asked Mary to pray that I can vanquish my evil desires?

I ACCEPT THE FACT I HAVE A DARK SIDE, BUT I REFUSE
TO LET IT TRIUMPH OVER ME.

Worry

Despite the fact that Jesus told his followers time and again not to worry, even his mother apparently worried when he was lost in the Temple. (What mother wouldn't have?) "Son, why have you done this to us? Your father and I have been looking for you with great anxiety."

Although worry is a normal human response to difficulty, a life marked by worry is an ill-spent life. One of our greatest challenges is to learn how to overcome worry. The solution is both impossibly simple and frustratingly complex: to overcome worry we must learn to trust that God knows best.

Learning to trust God isn't easy. The task is complicated by our childhood, our image of God, and our own weaknesses. If we haven't experienced trust on a human level, with people we can see, how can we trust God, whom we *can't* see?

The only way to learn to trust God is to *just do it* (in the words of Nike's famous advertising slogan). We can't think about trusting God. We can't analyze the steps to trusting God. We can't do a flow chart on the pluses and minuses of trusting God. We have to *just do it!*

Start small. Begin by trusting that God will take care of a minor problem—finding a parking space or a lost earring. Gradually, as you begin to see that God does take an active interest in the details of your life, you'll be able to trust more and more.

Is it going to be easy? No. Is it going to be worth it? Indubitably!

Do I really believe that God has my best interest in mind?

JUST FOR TODAY, I WON'T WORRY.

Virtues

In classic reflections on Mary, writers often mention that she lived in a very limited geographic area and wasn't exposed to the "great world," remaining a humble maid in a small village.

Well what about that trek to Egypt to escape King Herod's wrath?

Egypt was one of the great cosmopolitan centers of the world. Since Joseph was a carpenter and would have been working during the sojourn to earn a livelihood, the Holy Family wouldn't have been living in the sticks. In order for Joseph to find work, they would have had to live in a population center. Furthermore, getting to Egypt would have required passing over a fair amount of new and different territory.

No, Mary wasn't a mere homebody. She was better traveled and more experienced in the ways of the world than most of her Nazareth neighbors. She had seen people and places her friends and relatives could only imagine. She wasn't a small-town girl who'd never made it to the big city.

When we look at Mary, we have to be careful not to rationalize her virtues by falsifying the facts of her life. Mary was undoubtedly humble and modest; however, she had those virtues not because she hadn't been exposed to a wealth of opportunities but because she was inherently humble and modest. The virtues we admire in Mary aren't there because she was limited in experience but because she was *un*-limited in what really matters—love.

Have I ever thought about what Mary's life in Egypt
must have been like? Can I imagine it?

1 KNOW THAT 1 CAN GROW IN VIRTUE NO MATTER
WHERE 1 AM OR WHAT 1 DO.

Loneliness

Despite our plethora of worldly goods, Americans are, in the words of Mother Teresa of Calcutta, the poorest group of people on earth. The poverty and hunger Mother Teresa speaks of can't be purchased away with a trip through Mall of the Americas. They can't be banished by unlimited credit on a VISA gold card or chased away by a winning lottery ticket. The poverty and hunger Mother Teresa refers to are a poverty of the spirit, a hunger of the soul, a profound loneliness.

All around us people are starving for a kind word, a loving touch, a word of prayer. Behind the doors of expensive homes, families are literally dying from lack of love.

Scientific studies have shown that a single cell placed in a petri dish will just sit there and eventually self-destruct. However, two or three cells, even if they are placed in opposite corners of the petri dish, will begin to multiply and grow. The lesson is clear. A single cell, even when given all the material it needs to survive, can't. It dies of loneliness. But two or more cells, even when they aren't contiguous, will not only live, they will flourish.

In like manner, human beings were not created to live in isolation. When we shut ourselves behind the doors of our homes and cars and offices, we become like single cells in a petri dish—literally dying of loneliness.

Mary continually reinforces this truth in her appearances. Over and over she tells us, in the words of her son, we are all branches of the same vine, parts of the same body. We need each other, Mary says, and the sooner we learn that lesson the better off we will be.

Am I lonely?
Do I expect others to contact me, or do I reach out to others?

I KNOW THAT TO HAVE A FRIEND I MUST FIRST BE A FRIEND.

Compliments

Because Mary has been so revered over the years, it's hard to imagine that anyone would ever criticize her. But it's not true. Her neighbors in Nazareth were very critical. Even if they didn't criticize her directly, they criticized her son and, as every mother knows, it hurts more to have your children criticized than to be criticized yourself.

Mary's neighbors didn't like the idea Jesus was able to preach and teach with authority or he could heal the sick. If he hadn't been preaching and teaching and healing, you can bet they would have found something else to criticize. It's just human nature. At the same time, when Jesus was doing what they wanted him to do, the neighbors were equally quick to offer their compliments. In one sense, he couldn't win for losing!

One thing we learn as we grow wiser is that we can't please all the people all the time. And there's no point trying. What elicits compliments from one person may well elicit criticism from another. Learning to take both compliments and criticism with the same detachment is a first step toward true interior freedom. In truth, we must all ultimately learn to live our lives, not with the intent of being complimented by others, but with the intent of being complimented by God. What kind of action does God compliment? The prophet Isaiah gives us a clue: "This, rather, is the fasting that I wish: releasing those bound unjustly, untying the thongs of the yoke; Setting free the oppressed, breaking every yoke; Sharing your bread with the hungry, sheltering the oppressed and the homeless; Clothing the naked when you see them, and not turning your back on your own."

How do I react when I am criticized?
How do I react when I am complimented?

I TAKE BOTH CRITICISM AND COMPLIMENTS WITH
THE PROVERBIAL GRAIN OF SALT.

Multifaceted Character

The Catholic Church has set aside numerous days during the year to honor Mary. In addition to the major feasts (such as the Immaculate Conception and the Assumption), every Saturday, as well as the entire months of May and October, is under Mary's patronage.

What's particularly interesting about Marian days and seasons is that each reflects a particular aspect of Mary's character. For instance, October is devoted to Mary, Queen of the Rosary, while May is devoted to Mary, Queen of Heaven.

Over the ages, each generation has taken some aspect of Mary and adopted it as her ultimate persona. Mary has alternately been seen as the humble, submissive maiden who meekly acquiesced to God's will and the strong, independent woman who insisted that her son do something about the wine situation at the wedding feast at Cana. She has been viewed as the imperial Queen of Heaven and the gentle, docile mother. These varied aspects of her character are so different that it sometimes seems as if she's more than one person.

But she isn't. She's a single, complex woman who exhibits various aspects of her character depending on the situation she finds herself in. To limit her to a single facet—such as submissiveness or independence—is to minimize the whole person. And if Mary teaches us anything, it's that wholeness is the closest thing to holiness that we can experience.

Am I a whole person? What aspects of my character
do I tend to over- or underemphasize?

I SEE MARY AS A WOMAN OF MANY FACETS.

Motives

When Jesus was being condemned as a traitor and sentenced to death by crucifixion, his disciples hightailed it out of the area. Peter, the leader of the twelve, denied Jesus three times and then was nowhere to be seen at Golgotha. We know that the disciple John was lurking somewhere in the crowd, because Jesus called to him from the cross, but apparently the only people who really stuck by Jesus to the bitter end were his mother Mary, her sister, and Mary Magdalene—who, if she wasn't a reformed prostitute, had been demon-possessed.

Mary was there because—well, what mother would *not* be present when her beloved son was dying? It's impossible to imagine Mary staying away.

Why Mary's sister was there is a bit more puzzling. She could have been present because of her devotion to Jesus, but it's just as reasonable to assume that she was present because of her devotion to her sister. We'll never know her motives this side of heaven.

Mary Magdalene's motives, on the other hand, are utterly clear. She was there because she loved Jesus totally, completely, passionately. She loved him so much that she couldn't bear to be separated from him, returning afterwards even to his tomb.

Sometimes people's behavior doesn't make sense to us. We shake our heads at their actions, wondering whatever has possessed them to behave the way they do. If, however, we could step inside their heads and fully comprehend their motives, we would learn that most people don't act merely on whim; they behave in a manner consistent with their operating premises.

Mary Magdalene's operating premise was love. What's yours?

What's the most important thing in the world to me?

MY ACTIONS ARE CONSISTENT WITH MY BELIEFS.

Most Blessed Among Women

When Elizabeth saw Mary coming up the road to her house, she called out, "Most blessed are you among women!" Notice that she didn't say, "Blessed are you among women"; rather, she called Mary "*most* blessed." The greeting rightly indicates Mary's status, but it also carries meaning for all other women. If Mary is *most* blessed, then other women are also blessed. They may not be as blessed as Mary, but they're blessed nonetheless.

Do you feel blessed? If you don't, perhaps it's because you haven't been counting your blessings. One way to begin to recognize the blessings in your life is to make a blessings list. Some people choose to record blessings on a particular day every week; others make a master blessings list, adding to it as ideas arise; still others set a certain number of blessings—say, one hundred—and keep track until they reach that number.

No matter how you choose to set up your list, outlining everything that blesses you is bound to be a blessing in and of itself. You'll begin to see blessings that you hadn't recognized before. You'll begin to realize that everything—even adversity—can be a blessing.

The more you count your blessings, the more blessings you'll have to count. What are you waiting for? Why not start counting right now?

Has a difficult or sad situation ever turned out to be
a blessing to me in the end? When was the last time
I counted my blessings?

I KNOW THAT I'M BLESSED BEYOND MEASURE.

Talent

When we talk about talent, we're usually referring to a particular skill or gift. We might say, for example, that a person has a talent for playing the piano or for ice skating. Many parents today watch their young children intently, trying to determine what latent talents lurk in their offspring. If they spy a particular gift—say, for gymnastics or soccer—they immediately have visions of college scholarships and product endorsements. If a talent is there, it must be developed, these parents urge—no matter that their child has no interest in being an Olympic gymnast or a World Cup soccer player.

Mary had to have seen numerous talents in her son—human as well as divine. She must have recognized, as the years went by, that Jesus could have been anything he wanted. Yet for thirty years he was a simple carpenter.

Caryll Houselander writes, "Other mothers, seeing such singular gifts as Christ must have had, . . . would surely have fretted if such a son had not shown more ambition, had not made a name for himself, why [should he] be a humble carpenter?"

For Mary, the fact that Jesus "was about his Father's work" was sufficient. She didn't have to plan his life for him; she was able to let him develop in his own way and in his own time.

Would that we who are parents could do the same thing for our children!

If I have children, do I try to plan their lives for them?
How active do I think parents should be
in shaping their children's futures?

I'M WILLING TO KEEP MY HANDS OFF OTHER PEOPLE'S LIVES.

Humor

Did Mary have a sense of humor? It's hard to say, since the Gospel writers didn't see fit to mention anything one way or the other. Delving into the realm of pure speculation, however, we can surmise that Mary *must* have had a sense of humor since God wouldn't have wanted Jesus raised by a sour, dour person. Yet we sometimes get the notion that piety requires solemnity; we think that holiness is synonymous with seriousness, while levity is the mark of spiritual immaturity.

Many of the greatest saints had a rollicking sense of humor. St. Philip Neri's two favorite books were the Bible and a joke book. St. Don Bosco was well known for his practical jokes. St. Teresa of Avila, one of only two women doctors of the Catholic Church, is known to have prayed, "From sullen saints deliver me, O Lord." Blessed Pier Frassatti, who died of polio at age twenty-four, said that joy is the serious business of heaven.

Seeing the humor in any situation is one of life's greatest graces. It enables us to break out of our self-centeredness and see that much of life really is funny. Moreover, it allows us to see that much of what we do really is funny.

Of course, none of this proves anything about Mary's sense of humor. But in the absence of evidence, it's nice to think that she probably did have a good sense of humor.

Do I have a good sense of humor? Am I able to laugh at myself?

I DON'T TAKE MYSELF TOO SERIOUSLY.

I Love You

"I love you." Those are the most powerful words anyone can speak. To say "I love you" is to enter forever into a relationship with another person. While we're inclined to think that love and sex are synonymous, they aren't. We can be passionately in love with someone and never become sexually involved.

In the Catholic tradition, Mary is believed to have been a perpetual virgin. She and Joseph are said never to have had marital relations. However, even though they didn't express their love physically, Mary and Joseph must have been in love with each other—if for no other reason than that God wouldn't have chosen to have his son grow up in a household where the parents were at odds with one another.

While we're not accustomed to thinking of love without sexual involvement, inspiring examples of chaste love exist among the saints. Consider St. Francis de Sales and St. Jane Frances de Chantal, for example. Jane was a widow and mother of six children, and Francis was her spiritual director. The dearest of friends, they spent hours together discussing theology and spiritual issues. In one of his letters, Francis wrote these words to Jane: "It seems to be that God has given me to you. I am assured of this more keenly as each hour passes."

If we limit ourselves to thinking that we can love only romantically, we cut ourselves off from experiencing the truly life-transforming power of love.

When was the last time I said, "I love you"?
Have I ever told my closest friends how much they mean to me?

1 EXPRESS MY LOVE, BOTH IN ACTIONS AND IN WORDS.

Intercession

In 1988, cardiologist Randolph Byrd published a ten-month study of 393 patients. Half of the patients had been prayed for; the other half hadn't. The results of the study were astonishing. The prayed-for patients (who hadn't known they were being prayed for) required fewer antibiotics, suffered less congestive heart failure, and experienced fewer cardiac arrests.

The conclusion: intercessory prayer works.

In some fashion, our prayers touch God in a way that can miraculously (but not magically) release healing for others. The scientific evidence is compelling: prayer does make a difference. As remarkable as it seems, we can intercede ("go between") another person's needs and God, asking God to act on that person's behalf.

That's exactly what Mary does for us when we ask for her prayers. The major difference between Mary's intercession and ours, however, is that Mary (because she's in heaven) knows God's will more clearly. She doesn't have to ask with the "blind faith" we must employ. Thus we can go with confidence to Mary, trusting that she'll take to God only those requests that are best for us and for others.

Is there something I want right now that I'm willing
to entrust to Mary's intercession?

I PRAY FOR THOSE WHO ASK FOR MY PRAYERS.

Journaling

Keeping a journal requires commitment, dedication, and persistence. In addition, it requires personal honesty. In order for a journal to be more than a logbook of daily activities, we have to banish the critic—the "watcher" who sits on our shoulder and judges our work. We must be willing to expose our deepest feelings and emotions.

Journaling is a little like donating blood drop by drop. The process doesn't seem all that painful at the time, but when we look back, we realize just how much of our life energy has been poured out on the pages.

If we're honest in our journals, we reveal the truth to ourselves even when—maybe *especially* when—we don't want to recognize it. In the pages of our journals, we expose ourselves to ourselves. That's one of the reasons rereading a journal can be both enlightening and painful. With the clarity of hindsight, we can see not only where we went but where we should have gone.

Every day, Mary writes her journal on the hearts of those who follow her son. She keeps track of her love for humanity, her desire for grace and redemption in the lives of those who listen to her words of wisdom and attempt to live them in their lives. Over and over, she says the same thing she said at that wedding feast so long ago: "Do whatever he tells you." Mary may be writing the words on our hearts, but it's up to us to read them aloud.

Am I willing to "do whatever he tells me"?
Do I know what Jesus is telling me to do at this moment?

I'M WILLING TO LET GOD SHOW ME WHAT I SHOULD DO TODAY.

Dragons

A great sign appeared in the sky, a woman clothed with the sun,
with the moon under her feet, and on her head a crown of
twelve stars. She was with child and wailed aloud in pain as
she labored to give birth. Then another sign appeared in the sky;
it was a huge red dragon, with seven heads and ten horns, and
on its heads were seven diadems. Its tail swept away a third
of the stars in the sky and hurled them down to the earth.
Then the dragon stood before the woman about to give birth,
to devour her child when she gave birth.

REVELATION 12:1–4

The woman who faces the dragon in Revelation is traditionally believed to be Mary. Her child is Jesus, and the dragon is identified as Satan. While the imagery in the last book of the Bible is metaphorical and poetic, the sense of impending evil is real.

Every age has its dragons. From the Black Plague to AIDS, from Attila the Hun to Hitler, from the Ice Age to the Atomic Age, dragons wait to devour us. In the late 300s, St. Gregory Nazianzus penned words that resonate in our souls some sixteen hundred years later: "Alas, dear Christ, the Dragon is here again. Alas, he is here: terror has seized me, and fear."

It's only natural, given all the lurking dragons, for us to be seized by terror. Yet the message that Mary brings is not one of fear, but one of love. Mary tells us that despite appearances, we have nothing to fear, for in the words of Scripture, "There is no fear in love, but perfect love drives out fear." If you love, you need not be afraid of dragons, says Mary.

What am I most afraid of?
What dragon is breathing fire in my life right now?

I CHOOSE LOVE OVER FEAR THIS DAY.

Mary's Month

The composer of the famous song "April in Paris" was once asked why he thought April in Paris was so wonderful, when in fact it was often rather cold and nasty. He replied that he knew Paris in May was much nicer, but May didn't work as well in the lyrics.

May is Mary's month. It's only fitting that one of the loveliest months of the year be given to the Flower of Heaven.

A favorite old-time Catholic custom during this month is to make a "May altar." As devotions go, this one is a study in simplicity. A statue of Mary is placed in an honored spot, and fresh flowers are put in front of it. Everything else is optional. Some people pray the Rosary daily before the statue. Others say a quick prayer every time they pass. Still others content themselves with remembering to change the flowers when they wilt.

The point of the May altar isn't to add one more thing to an already busy schedule, and it certainly isn't to turn Mary into a quasi-goddess with a cult following. No, the point is to remind us that Mary stands as a model of encouragement, comfort, inspiration, and faith. It's also to help us remember that Mary isn't only the mother of Jesus; she's our mother as well. As Pope Paul VI once said, "Let us think about the indescribable good fortune of being able to call her Mother, of being related to her. . . . [W]e share the child's habit of turning to his mother at every moment and telling her everything."

This May, let's turn to our mother in our needs, confident that she'll listen to us with a mother's ear.

Do I think of Mary as my mother or just as the Mother of God?

WHEN I NEED A MOTHER'S LOVE, I TURN TO MARY.

The "Real" Mary

In the Gospels, no one ever says a simple hello to Mary. The angel Gabriel greets her with, "Hail, favored one!" Her kinswoman Elizabeth says, "Most blessed are you among women." Even Jesus, meeting up with her at Cana, says, "Woman, how does your concern affect me?"

Somehow it seems fitting that Mary's greetings are so unusual. After all, she's unique among women.

Who is this Mary? What do we believe about her?

We know, based strictly on biblical information, that she was a virgin who lived in Nazareth. She was betrothed to a carpenter named Joseph. Because of a census ordered by the governor of Syria, she had to travel while pregnant to Bethlehem, where she gave birth to her firstborn son. She lived for a time in Egypt with her family. Her son Jesus, who grew up to be a preacher and teacher, was executed as a traitor to Rome. She ended up living with one of her son's friends—a man named John.

Considering the fact that all Christians have the same basic biblical information, the spectrum of feeling about Mary is rather amazing. From some Catholics (who've elevated affection for her almost to the point of Mary-olatry) to some Protestants (who've demoted her to a very minor character in the story of Jesus), Mary has generated virtually every feeling possible.

But who is Mary, really? What *should* our feelings about her be? What lessons does she have to teach us? These aren't questions someone else can answer for us. We must seek the answers ourselves, by reading the passages about Mary in Scripture, by reading what others have written about her, and by asking Mary herself to come into our lives in a real and profound way. Then, and only then, can we come to understand who Mary is and what role she should play in our lives.

Where on the spectrum of feeling about Mary do I fall?
Is Mary important to me?

I SEEK THE TRUTH, NO MATTER WHERE MY SEARCH LEADS ME.

Dreams

When Mary was to receive a message from God, she was visited by an angel. When Joseph needed divine guidance, he got a dream. While it may seem that Mary's deliveries came express while Joseph was stuck with parcel post, most of us, if we're honest, would rather get a message in a dream than by angel express.

Dreams are safer than angels—not to mention more socially acceptable. After all, you can talk about a dream you had last night. The minute you start discussing celestial visitors, however, people begin to back away.

Dreams are one of our most valuable sources of inner knowledge. Dreams often reveal our inner conflicts and our deepest longings, as well as solutions to our current problems. The difficulty with dreams, though, is that the message frequently comes cloaked in symbolism and imagery.

Consider the woman who dreamed several nights in a row about dropping her watch. Finally she realized that her dream was trying to tell her she was losing time by continuing to stay in a dead-end relationship. It was only after she had deciphered the symbols that she stopped having the dream.

Although books on dream symbols are available, you're your own best guide to your dreams. If you want to know what messages your dreams are sending you, keep a notebook by your bed and first thing in the morning write down any dreams you remember. Look for patterns, repeated images, and recurring themes. Ask yourself what the dreams seem to be saying. Eventually the message will be clear.

Oh, and while you're at it, you might ask Joseph for his help. He's had quite a bit of experience in deciphering dreams!

What messages have I received through my dreams?
Are my dreams trying to tell me something right now?

I'M AWAKE TO THE POSSIBILITY OF LIFE-CHANGING MESSAGES
COMING TO ME THROUGH MY DREAMS.

Heartache

To become a parent is to experience heartache. That's as certain as dirty diapers and sleepless nights. It has nothing to do with how terrific your kids are. Even the best kids cause their parents heartache at some time.

Jesus was no exception. Mary and Joseph were heartsick when he was lost after their trip to Jerusalem. Any parent would be—a twelve-year-old missing, God (literally) knows where. Panic doesn't even begin to describe Mary and Joseph's feelings before they tracked down Jesus at the Temple.

But that episode was just a prelude to the heartache Mary felt at the Crucifixion. There was her little boy (*every* man remains a little boy to his mother, no matter how old he is), wounded and suffering. She knew he hadn't done anything wrong, but that knowledge didn't matter. There was no court of appeals. No second trial. No clemency. Just the cross.

Mary's understanding of what it means to suffer makes her not just a role model but a source of great comfort. You can always tell if someone's efforts at comforting come from personal experience or if they come from mere extrapolation from the facts. It's only when a person has experienced the depths of pain that he or she can truly comfort another.

Mary's comfort comes from her own ruptured heart. She uses her broken heart to give us solace. Like her, we can take our own broken hearts and use them to comfort those around us. We can let our pain absorb some of the pain of others' lives. The irony is that in doing so, we don't increase our own pain; on the contrary, we diminish it, for sorrow is always reduced when it's poured into more than one heart.

Who needs my comfort today?
Am I willing to let my pain be used as solace for others?

I BELIEVE THAT SORROW SHARED IS SORROW DIVIDED.

Gate of Heaven

Gate of Heaven is another one of Mary's traditional titles. This doesn't mean, however, that she's decoupaged on St. Peter's Pearly Portal. Instead, the title refers to Mary's role as a way through which we can enter into a relationship with her son.

Protestants and Catholics often disagree on this point. Protestants, arguing that we can go directly to God, claim that there's no need to go through Mary. This is, of course, absolutely true. However, a story told by St. Louis de Montfort helps clarify Mary's role in Catholic teaching. St. Louis tells of a poor farmer who had only a worm-riddled apple to present to the king as rental for his farm. The farmer knew that his apple was imperfect, unfit for royalty. The farmer took the apple to the queen, who was his friend, and asked her to give it to the king. The queen, out of love for the farmer, cut the bad spots out of the apple, put it on a golden serving dish, and surrounded it with flowers. The king, seeing the apple in such a lovely setting, was delighted to accept it as full payment for the farm.

In similar fashion, we can take our needs and desires, however tarnished and flawed they may be, to Mary, asking her to present them to her son on our behalf. Just as the king wouldn't reject the apple from his queen, so too Jesus won't turn away our requests when they're presented by Mary.

Can we go to God directly with our requests? Of course. Do we always have to? Not as long as we have Mary as our friend.

If I could be granted one request, what would it be?
Have I asked Mary to take my request to God on my behalf?

I DESIRE TO HAVE MARY AS MY FRIEND.

Queen of Peace

Before he was taken up to heaven, Jesus told his followers he was leaving them the gift of peace.

What does *peace* mean in this context? Not merely the lack of conflict, for the absence of active hostility (or "war in masquerade," as John Dryden called it) can be a cover-up for enormous stress. Consider the uneasy truces that exist in various parts of the world today, for example. But *peace* doesn't mean total agreement either. Put two people in a relationship, and unless one is a complete doormat, they'll have their disagreements.

So what does Jesus mean by *peace,* and why is Mary often called the Queen of Peace?

Peace embodies such qualities as harmony, accord, goodwill, silence, tranquillity, serenity, relaxation, contentment, and stillness. It's an oasis for the soul, a state of being in which we sense the fundamental harmony underlying creation. It's what we long for, what we were created for.

Mary is called the Queen of Peace because she came the closest of all creatures to living in the perfection God originally created. Uncorrupted by the tendency toward sin during her years on earth, she was able to experience unity with God in an unprecedented manner. Unlike us, she didn't simply get *glimpses* of serenity and harmony; she was *infused* with them.

Of course, she still experienced moments of sorrow, frustration, and sadness. She wouldn't have been human if she hadn't. But God's transcendental love lifted her above the pain.

When we find ourselves caught in the turmoil of life, we need only remember that Mary was able to live in peace because she brought Peace into the world. Because Peace reigns, we too are able to live in peace.

When have I felt the most at peace?
What can I do today to create an "oasis" for my soul?

1 DON'T LET THE PASSING AFFAIRS OF THE WORLD
DISTURB MY INNER HARMONY.

Duty

Duty. What a boring word. It conjures up really dull images of really dull people doing really dull jobs. And when people say, "Duty before pleasure," they often mean, "Duty *instead* of pleasure."

But duty needn't mean drudgery. Mary did her duty, yet she clearly found time to attend wedding parties and check out the wine supply. Jesus did his duty, yet he obviously wasn't dull or his enemies wouldn't have branded him a glutton and a drunkard.

Basically, our duty is to do what we're called to do at any given moment. A doctor's duty is to care for the sick. A writer's duty is to produce words. A parent's duty is to rear children. All duty is serious, but not all duty is solemn. A comedian's duty, for instance, is to make people laugh.

When we're doing our true duty—the duty our hearts call us to—we're filled with joy. We feel energized and creative, no matter whether we're auditing tax reports or painting a masterpiece. It's only when we try to do the duty that others impose on us that duty becomes drudgery.

Mary shows us clearly what it means to define our own duty. If she'd asked her friends and relatives what she should have done after the angel Gabriel's appearance, she might have been told that her duty was to become Joseph's wife and leave saving the world to someone else. If she'd asked the wine steward at Cana if it was her duty to get more wine, he would undoubtedly have told her to mind her own business. Yet Mary knew what her real duty was—and in doing her duty, she found her joy.

If you're feeling weighted down and depressed, could it be because you're allowing others to define your duty for you?

What's my duty right now? Does my duty bring me joy?
If not, am I certain it's really my duty?

I ALWAYS DO MY DUTY—MY *REAL* DUTY.

Free Will

If people were creating a world, most of us would vote to dispense with free will. After all, free will just complicates things. It allows people to make bad decisions, to do harm and hurt, to destroy their own lives and the lives of others. A world without free will, where everyone was kind and loving and *had* to do the right thing, would be much nicer. But it would be superficial. If we had no choice but to love everyone and everything, then love would have little value.

God couldn't create such a world. A place where people have to be good and kind and loving is populated by robots, and God didn't want robots. God wanted children, and children come packaged with free will.

Even those closest to God have free will. Mary freely chose to say yes to Gabriel. Jesus freely chose to say yes to Calvary.

Free will is God's greatest gift to us. It's what makes us human. More than the ability to create tools, more than language, more than fire, more than anything else that anthropologists see as separating us from the other primates, free will is our birthright. We alone of all the animals have the ability to choose right from wrong. We can (and often do) choose the wrong—St. Paul, in his letter to the Romans, said, "I do not do the good I want, but I do the evil I do not want"—but we can also choose the good. The ability to see the right thing—and choose it, despite our natural inclinations—is what enables us to freely love God and enables God to freely love us.

Do I allow others to exercise their own free will?

I GIVE THANKS FOR MY FREE WILL.

Ecumenism

While the Blessed Virgin Mary is an important part of Catholic teaching and tradition, she isn't the sole possession of Catholics. She's mentioned forty-two times in the Koran, she was seen and honored by many Muslims in an appearance at Zeitoun, Egypt, and she's beginning to be discussed seriously in Protestant theological circles.

Despite having been a barrier to unity among Christians for centuries, Mary has recently become a bridge to ecumenism. Although many differences remain, centering on such Catholic teachings as the Immaculate Conception and the Assumption, both Protestants and Catholics agree on Mary's essential role as the *Theotokos,* or Mother of God. In that one area at least, Mary is, in the words of Martin Luther, "raised above the whole of humankind."

Certainly Mary herself seeks the unity of all believers, as Charles Dickson, a Protestant pastor, points out in *A Protestant Pastor Looks at Mary.*

> The agony that a mother experiences when her children are squabbling and fighting among themselves may be a fair analogy to describe the agony the Blessed Virgin Mary must experience amidst the quarrels dividing the disciples of her Son. In view of this it is not surprising that the bishop of Osnabrück in Germany has suggested that Mary be regarded as the "patroness" of ecumenism, the rallying point where Christians of all varieties may find unity, common goals and mutual love.

No matter what we may believe about Mary, we must never let our personal beliefs become a point of contention.

Am I willing to let others believe what they want about Mary?
Do I actively seek to establish good relations
with those outside my own faith?

1 GIVE OTHERS THE FREEDOM OF BELIEF
THAT 1 WANT THEM TO GIVE ME.

Humanity Versus Divinity

Mary is a stumbling block for many non-Catholics, because the honor she's accorded seems to border on adoration. Many non-Catholics rightly assert that she's sometimes given praise so lofty that it sounds as if it should go to God alone. Even some Catholics have trouble with prayers such as St. Thomas Aquinas's: "Virgin, full of goodness, Mother of mercy, I entrust to you my body and soul, my thoughts, my actions, my life and my death."

It's not Mary's fault that she's burdened with such lofty phrases. She's been given accolades such as "co-redemptrix" by men and women trying to express an inexpressible concept—the unique position Mary has as the Mother of God and the mother of humanity.

However, we must never lose sight of the fact that Mary was a *human* woman. As Pope Paul VI wrote, "Our Lady is dependent upon Christ for all she possesses." It's true that she was chosen to be the mother of the Savior, and that honor alone is enough to accord her our highest praise. Indeed, it's precisely because of that honor that so many men and women have resorted to hyperbole.

However, if you can't bring yourself to use gushing, flowery phrases to praise Mary, that's fine. To honor her as the Mother of God is enough, for in that praise is contained the greatest glory given to any human.

Do I have trouble relating to Mary as a real human being, or do I have more trouble relating to her as the Queen of Heaven?

I GIVE MARY THE HONOR SHE'S DUE.

Spontaneity

Are you a spur-of-the moment kind of person or a detailed planner? Do you like to have your route marked out on a map, or do you like to take whatever road happens along?

It's hard to tell which category Mary would have fallen into, but given that she was willing to say yes to an angel with very little hesitation, dash off with haste to see Elizabeth, and pack up and head off to Egypt on the strength of Joseph's dream, it seems likely that she had at least a little spontaneous streak somewhere in her makeup.

When was the last time *you* did something completely and totally spontaneous? Have you *ever* done anything genuinely spontaneous? If not, perhaps now's the time. You don't have to do anything as radical as catching the next plane to Vienna; you can step into spontaneity with something as small as buying a particularly luscious-looking apple the next time you pass a fruit stand or giving someone you care about a hug—just because you feel like it.

Spontaneity adds sparkle to life. It's champagne bubbles, babies' giggles, kittens' purrs, puppies' wiggles, lovers' kisses. Without spontaneity, daily life becomes, well, *daily*. What's more, allowing a bit of spontaneity into your life gives God room to bestow some unexpected blessings. If you fail to allow spontaneity its place, you may be missing out on more than you think!

*If I could do anything I wanted right now, what would I do?
What's stopping me?*

I'M OPEN TO THE CELEBRATION OF LIFE.

End Times

In the past century, Mary has appeared more times than in all the rest of the centuries combined. In her alleged visitations at Medjugorje, she's said to have announced that these will be her last appearances on earth. Virtually all visionaries have been given secret messages relating to the final chapter in history. The Third Secret of Fatima, as yet unrevealed, is widely believed to contain information about the end of the world.

Do Mary's appearances signal the end times? Many people claim that they do, pointing to the urgency in Mary's messages as a sign that we have very little time left. But the fact remains that we don't know how close we are to the end. We may be only a day away from the apocalypse, but Scripture says that to God a day is like a thousand years and a thousand years is like a day.

Mary's messages are urgent, to be sure, but they're no more urgent than those of Jesus. Nothing Mary has ever said is new or different from the original message of her son: repent, dedicate your lives to God, pray, fast, hope.

Because Mary doesn't add any new information to the basic Gospel message, we have nothing to fear from her appearances. However, we do need to heed her warnings. As she herself said to Lucinta at Fatima, "It is necessary that they amend their lives and ask pardon for their sins."

If today were your last day on earth, what would you do?
If you knew you had only a month more to live,
what would you change?

I LIVE EACH DAY AS IF IT WERE MY LAST.

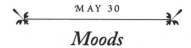

Moods

We all have moods. Without moods we would be like Data in the TV series *Star Trek—The Next Generation,* incapable of experiencing emotion. But Data so longed to experience human feeling that he had a computer chip implanted to allow him to feel emotion. Having done so, he learned a cardinal lesson: we can't have emotions without having moods.

There is, however, a big difference between having moods and being moody.

Moods are milestones on the road to spiritual growth. Some of the moods we all experience include amazement, puzzlement, determination, sadness, anxiety, happiness, nervousness, joy, and excitement. Since moods are merely states of mind, they don't necessarily require action on our part. We need to recognize them, however, and attempt to figure out what they're trying to tell us about our lives and relationships.

Being moody, on the other hand, is a signal that we have soul-work to do. It tells us that our spiritual compass isn't set on heaven. It warns us that we're being drawn down dangerous paths of self-indulgence, self-centeredness, and selfishness.

We know very little about Mary's moods. We know that she was "troubled" when Gabriel visited and "anxious" when Jesus was missing in the Temple, but not much else. We can assume, however, that she felt the full range of human emotions (and their accompanying moods).

However, one thing we know for certain is that Mary was never moody, for her spiritual compass was always pointed heavenward.

Have I ever been called moody?

1 ACCEPT MY MOODS, BUT 1 STRIVE NEVER TO BE MOODY.

The Visitation to Elizabeth

Immediately after Mary learned that she was to become the mother of the Savior, she headed for the hill country to visit her kinswoman Elizabeth, who the angel Gabriel had said was also pregnant. Why would Mary undertake such a journey in the early stages of her own pregnancy, when—if she was like most women—she was feeling queasy and miserable?

Some people think that it was because she wanted to help her kinswoman, and her concern probably played a role. After all, Elizabeth was elderly by the standards of the day—pregnant "in her old age"—and Mary could definitely have been of assistance. But surely there were other women who could have aided Elizabeth during her last few months of pregnancy.

Maybe Mary's decision to visit Elizabeth was prompted as much by natural human curiosity as it was by her desire to serve. Maybe she wanted to be absolutely, positively sure that what the angel had told her was true. If Elizabeth were pregnant, then Mary would have proof positive that what she was feeling really was the Messiah growing in her womb, and not just her imagination.

How often we think that if we had Mary's faith we'd be able to believe with ease. But faith and the need for verification aren't incompatible. It would take nothing away from Mary's profound acceptance of God's miraculous working in her life if she wanted a little concrete proof. After all, the truth can always withstand rigorous investigation.

Do I ever feel guilty when I long for evidence of God's working
in my life? Do I ever think my natural human
doubt is a sign of disbelief?

I ALLOW MYSELF TO ASK GOD FOR VERIFICATION AND DIRECTION
WHEN I'M FEELING DOUBTFUL OR DISTRUSTFUL.

Summer Rain

The difference between winter rain and summer rain is almost as great as the difference between winter and summer themselves. Winter rain is destructive; summer rain is refreshing. Winter rain pummels; summer rain soothes. Winter rain is take; summer rain is give.

The essence of summer rain is felt most profoundly after the clouds have passed: everything takes on new clarity, and the earth feels renewed. It's as if life had been given a new start.

In a world all too often battered by wintry storms, Mary's appearances are like summer rain. She comes with messages of love, bringing hope and encouragement to all who will listen. Those who experience her presence are gently washed by her compassion. But Mary's real gift, like summer rain, is seen only after her vision has faded into memory.

If we heed the messages she brings, our existence takes on new clarity. As we begin to understand her universal messages of love, forgiveness, and repentance, they can literally change our lives.

Exactly what does Mary ask? In all her appearances, in every word she's ever uttered, in every message she's ever sent, she says the same thing: "Love!" Love your neighbor, love your family, love those who hate you, love those whom you would rather hate. Above all, says Mary, love your God.

It's one of the great truths of creation that once we're filled with love of and for God, we begin to see all other living creatures through God's eyes. Once that happens, we're not only better able to love everyone and everything, we're virtually *compelled* to do so.

Am I currently experiencing storms in my life?
Am I ever responsible for creating storms in other people's lives?

INTO EVERY LIFE A LITTLE RAIN MUST FALL.
I WELCOME THE RAIN IN MY LIFE.

Morning Star

When the planet Venus is visible in the early dawn, it's known as the morning star. (When it's visible at dusk, it's called the evening star, but that's just a celestial quirk.) Ancient peoples, not understanding planetary orbit, thought that Venus's appearances and disappearances resulted from actions of the gods.

The planet Venus was believed to be under the control of Venus, the goddess of love, possibly because the morning star is one of the brightest and loveliest of heavenly bodies. Somehow it seems appropriate that Mary is often called the Morning Star. Venus, the first star, represents Mary, the first person to believe that the Messiah was to be born, the first to experience the miracle of Jesus, the first to join Jesus in body and soul.

The very words *Morning Star* have a poetic ring. Their compactness reflects the essential poetry of Mary's life. While Mary is the ultimate stanza in God's creative poem of humanity, we're all verses. Have you ever thought about what your verse says—not what others think your verse should say, but what you know God has written on the depths of your soul?

Often, because of the pressures of life and the insistence of others, we tuck our soul-verses away (much as Emily Dickinson sheltered her poetry during her lifetime). We pretend that the verses others have assigned us are the verses we would have written for ourselves. But that may not be the case. In order to take our rightful place in the song-poem that is the universe, we must first learn what our stanza should say and then begin to write it on our hearts and incorporate it into our lives, as Mary did in becoming the Morning Star.

Am I doing what I want to with my life?
If I could do anything or be anyone, what would I do or be?

I'M A UNIQUE CREATION.

Failure

Imagine the scene back in Nazareth after Jesus' trial and crucifixion. Since news—especially bad news—travels fast, Mary's neighbors would probably have soon heard that Jesus had been arrested for treason against Rome and put to death. The gossips would undoubtedly have had a bad case of tongue-burn from all the red-hot remarks they'd shared: "Did you hear that Mary's son was arrested? And *crucified?* I knew all along that he'd come to a bad end. He was always a strange one. This just proves it!"

To those in Mary's world, Jesus would have been considered a failure—and by virtue of association, his mother would have been thought a failure as well. After all, if your son is executed by the government, you must have done something wrong in rearing him!

How quick we are to judge success and failure by worldly standards. If someone achieves wealth, power, and status, we call him or her a success. Someone in a dead-end job with no retirement and no future we brand a failure.

But God's standards for success and failure are quite different from ours. Consider the single mother who works two minimum-wage jobs to feed and clothe her children. The dad who turns down a big promotion because it would mean spending too much time away from his family. The executive who opts out of the corporate climb in order to become a priest or minister. In the world's performance evaluation, such people are considered losers. In God's review, however, they're the real winners. Let's never forget that in Jesus' case, after the failure of the Crucifixion came the triumph of the Resurrection!

Who is the most successful person I know?
What do I consider the greatest success in my own life?

¶ USE GOD'S STANDARDS IN EVALUATING MY LIFE.

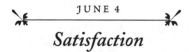

Satisfaction

Everyone has his or her own idea of what constitutes complete satisfaction. Maybe it involves a creative endeavor, such as writing a poem or painting a watercolor. Perhaps it's something more objective, such as painting a room or weeding the garden. Or maybe it has to do with the broader vision, such as raising a family or achieving a professional goal.

Feelings of satisfaction come to us most easily when we like what we're doing. Unfortunately, most of us don't get to do exactly what we want all the time. In fact, we have to do things we'd rather not do much of the time. In the face of that necessity, is it possible to experience satisfaction not just once in a while but all the time?

While Mary hasn't spoken of satisfaction in her various appearances, and the Gospel accounts make no mention of it, we can be certain that she was satisfied with her life because she so obviously followed this simple rule: if you can't do what you like, then like what you do. Mary probably had plans for her life that were interrupted by Gabriel. Yet it's clear that once her new direction was set, she embraced her life fully and joyfully. We too may have life-plans that are interrupted by people and events outside our control. But we, like Mary, always have the option of liking what we do, no matter what that may be.

Am I doing what I like? Do I like what I do?

1 CHOOSE TO LIKE WHAT 1 DO (AT LEAST MOST OF THE TIME!).

Immaculate Heart

In two places in his Gospel, Luke talks about Mary keeping certain events and memories "in her heart." It's from these two references that devotion to the Immaculate Heart of Mary has arisen.

Devotion to the Immaculate Heart arose during the Middle Ages, when religious symbolism and spiritual fervor were at their peak. St. Bernardino of Siena, sometimes called the Doctor of the Heart of Mary, reflected that in Mary's heart we can see seven burning furnaces with seven flames representing the seven acts of love that are shown in the seven "words" of Mary in the Gospels. That devotion continued to gain followers over the centuries, until finally, in 1944, the Feast of the Immaculate Heart was made part of the universal calendar of the Catholic Church.

While many who love Mary find particular joy and inspiration in the devotion to the Immaculate Heart, it's not everyone's favorite way of viewing her. Non-Catholics, in particular, often find it baffling or off-putting (or both!).

However, devotion to the Immaculate Heart is one of the great treasures of Mary, because it shows us that Mary presents herself in ways that appeal to all types of personalities and people. Like the mother she is, Mary makes her love and her message accessible to us in whatever way we can best accept—be it as a humble maid in Nazareth or in the lofty theological tones of the Immaculate Heart.

*Do I tend to view life in one way only? Am I stuck in a rut
in my thinking about how Mary should be
presented in the world?*

1 CELEBRATE THE FACT THAT NOT EVERYONE THINKS
THE SAME WAY 1 DO.

Legacy

If Christians were called on to prove Mary's existence through archaeological evidence, it would be nigh on impossible. She didn't build a monument or have a plaque erected in her hometown. She didn't write anything. She lived and died obscurely, leaving barely a trace of physical evidence to prove that she existed. Yet her legacy has lived on through the centuries, both in the person of her son Jesus and in her example.

Most of us will leave very little (if any) evidence that archaeologists could use to prove our existence. Yet each of us, like Mary, will leave a legacy, not necessarily in offspring but in the way our lives have affected other people.

Our lives are like stones thrown into the lake of humanity. No stone, however small, can be tossed into the lake without causing some change. If the stone is large enough, it disturbs the entire surface and then creates a disruption on the bottom when it settles. But even the tiniest pebble, once its ripples have subsided, brings the lake that much closer to filling in, drying up, and becoming a meadow.

We may not think that what we do or say has much effect, but we never know. The time we spend listening to a friend who's in the throes of marital problems may feel like a large rock and yet have little or no lasting effect, while the tiny pebble of a kind word and a smile to a grocery-store clerk may become a turning point in that person's life.

Because we can't know how our actions may change the lives we touch, it's our responsibility (and our privilege) to live as if everything we do will have everlasting consequences.

How do I feel about myself today?
Do I see myself as an essential part of humanity?

I TREAT EVERYONE I MEET AS I WOULD LIKE TO BE TREATED MYSELF.

Festive Occasions

Why are weddings so universally popular? The obvious answer is that they're inherently joyous occasions, celebrating, as they do, optimism and hope for new life. But more than that, weddings are popular because they give us a legitimate reason to have a party.

Getting together with friends, laughing, eating, drinking, dancing, talking—these activities are the proverbial good times of life. And weddings provide us with a good reason to enjoy these activities!

It's ironic that so many religious celebrations in honor of Mary are more like funerals than weddings. (Indeed, the Rosary is said as part of most Catholic funerals.) It's ironic because the Gospel account that gives us the most vivid picture of Mary, not as a wife or a mother but as a woman, describes a wedding feast. Mary couldn't have been too staid and dull or she wouldn't have noticed—and, more important, cared about—the lack of wine at that wedding.

Because religion and spirituality deal with eternal issues, we tend to think of them as solemn, serious subjects. And they often are: indeed, reading most theology texts would convince you that religion is one of the driest, dullest topics on earth.

Actually, though, religion and spirituality should be joy rather than drudgery. Certainly the issues they deal with aren't to be taken lightly, but seeking God should be as much celebration as solemnity. If Mary could get her son to work his first miracle at a party, who are we to put a damper on life?

Do I tend to think of religion as serious business
to be done only in church on Sunday?

I KNOW WHEN TO BE SERIOUS AND WHEN TO BE PLAYFUL.

Empathy

In a classic *Star Trek* episode, Dr. McCoy finds himself in the company of a true "empath"—someone capable not only of sympathizing with another's plight but of actually feeling what the other person is feeling. In that episode, the empath ends up literally sharing Dr. McCoy's pain.

Wouldn't we all like that—knowing someone who wouldn't just sympathize with us but would actually share our struggles?

For many of us, Mary can become our empath. There's no struggle, no sorrow, that she hasn't experienced. Therefore, she can share our difficulties in a particular and personal way. However, we can't just dump our troubles on Mary and go waltzing off into the sunset. Once we've experienced the comfort that comes from knowing that our struggles are shared, we're obligated to take that understanding and use it for the benefit of others.

In one of the great mysteries of life, when we're willing not just to listen as someone talks about his or her pain but to let that person's pain become our pain as well, God allows us the privilege. If our desire is great, we can begin to truly feel what another is feeling.

While it's true that we can never become total empaths, we can come much closer than we might think. St. Don Bosco once prayed that he be given the illness that one of the boys in his school was suffering, because the boy had a lead part in a play. His request was granted, and St. Don Bosco immediately fell sicker than he'd been in some time. Later he jokingly remarked that if he'd known what it was going to be like, he might not have prayed so earnestly. So be careful when you offer to share another's burden: you might get more than you bargained for!

Am I willing to share the pain as well as the joy of those I love?

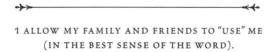

I ALLOW MY FAMILY AND FRIENDS TO "USE" ME
(IN THE BEST SENSE OF THE WORD).

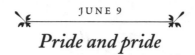

Pride and pride

Of the seven deadly sins, Pride has always been considered the most serious (the most deadly?). It was Pride that caused Satan to be cast out from heaven, and Pride has been the downfall of many in the history of humanity.

Because of all the warnings against the vice of Pride (with a capital *P*), many of us have difficulty with the virtue of pride (with a lowercase *p*). Pride is sinful, but pride is praiseworthy. Pride feels self-important, but pride expresses self-respect. The biggest difference, however, is that while you *have* Pride, you *feel* pride.

It's clear that Mary felt pride, but not an iota of Pride is evident in her life. Her response to Elizabeth is evidence of that: "My soul proclaims the greatness of the Lord; my spirit rejoices in God my savior. For he has looked upon his handmaid's lowliness; behold, from now on will all ages call me blessed. The Mighty One has done great things for me."

Mary understood that acknowledging accomplishments and status—even recognizing *special* status—isn't a problem as long as we understand these two points: (1) we're given gifts of accomplishment or status not because we're special in and of ourselves but because God has a special purpose for us, and (2) all the good things we have ultimately come from God.

If we can keep these two points in mind, we can take legitimate pride in our actions without falling into the fatal trap of Pride.

How do I react when someone gives me a compliment?
Can I accept praise as easily as I accept criticism?

I TAKE *pride* IN MY WORK, BUT I NEVER INDULGE IN
Pride IN MY ACCOMPLISHMENTS.

Forgiveness

"To err is human; to forgive, divine." This ancient aphorism contains an interesting underlying truth. When we choose to forgive those who have hurt us, we rise above our human nature to partake of God's own divine nature.

Little wonder that Mary tells us over and over to forgive.

Forgiveness doesn't come naturally to any of us, not even to Mary. She had to have felt white-hot waves of anger when she saw her son, bruised, beaten, and defiled, dying upon a Roman cross. As a mother, her first instinct must have been to lash out at those who'd dared to hurt her child. Yet Mary was able to forgive, just as her son was able to forgive, because she first acknowledged that a wrong had been done.

Sometimes we get the odd notion that we can forgive people without first acknowledging their guilt. However, we can't forgive someone for doing something that we refuse to recognize happened. For instance, let's say you were abused as a child. You can't forgive your abuser until you acknowledge that you were abused, that the abuser was in the wrong, and that the abuser deserves to be punished. If you don't acknowledge that something bad happened, what is there to forgive?

Because the acknowledgment of our wounds is so painful, we often try to leapfrog over that part of forgiveness directly into the good-feeling magnanimity of saying, "It's okay." However, the way things work in this world, we must first recognize that what happened to us isn't okay. Look at Jesus. He didn't try to gloss over his treatment. Only after acknowledging it as horrendous could he say, "Father forgive them for they know not what they do."

Is there someone I've tried to forgive but have been unable to?
Have I acknowledged (at least to myself) the nature of the
offense before attempting to grant forgiveness?

I FORGIVE THOSE WHO HAVE HURT ME
(BUT I ALSO RECOGNIZE WHEN I'VE BEEN HURT).

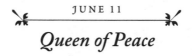

Queen of Peace

Pope Paul VI summarized a fundamental point about peace when he said, "If you want peace, work for justice." Peace is much more than just the mere cessation of fighting. It's a wholeness, a completeness, a fairness for all humanity. Indeed, we can't have peace without justice, for injustice is one of the major causes of war and strife.

When we call Mary the Queen of Peace, we're simultaneously calling her the Queen of Justice. One of Mary's unapproved but much respected appearances is in Medjugorje, in what used to be known as Yugoslavia—a part of the world ripped by political, religious, and ethnic strife, much of it caused by injustice. One of Mary's messages there was, "Love your Muslim brothers and sisters. Love your Serbian Orthodox brothers and sisters. Love those who govern you."

In an indirect way, Mary was saying the same thing as Pope Paul VI. If we love those around us, we'll find ourselves unable to make decisions that harm them. We'll choose options that eliminate injustice, and consequently we'll promote the cause of peace.

Promoting peace and justice doesn't require us to picket in front of government buildings or write letters to international organizations (although those responses are valid). Each of us can begin to work for peace and justice in our own homes, our own neighborhoods, our own cities. A good place to start is with an examination of our attitudes toward the poor. It isn't enough to have an intellectual concern for the less fortunate; we need to ask ourselves (1) what we're doing to help eliminate poverty in our city and (2) what more we could and should be doing.

We can spend our entire lives praying abstractly for peace, or we can work concretely for justice. The choice is ours.

What am I doing to promote justice in my part of the world?
What do I think Mary would do if she were living
in my city today?

BECAUSE I WANT PEACE, I WORK FOR JUSTICE.

Faith

The word *faith* is mentioned more than 250 times in the New Testament. It's precisely about the role of faith that Martin Luther began a discourse that would tear the Christian Church apart. Even today, Catholics and non-Catholics quibble over the distinction between salvation by faith alone and salvation by faith in conjunction with works.

Making the leap of faith required to believe in God can be difficult. After all, putting your future in the hands of an unseen God who makes promises about eternal life and happiness flies in the face of reason. Yet in order to let faith reign, we must let go of reason and step into the unknown. That's precisely what Mary did when she was confronted by Gabriel: she let go of reason; she let go of head-knowledge, which says that a child is the result of a sexual union between a man and a woman, that God doesn't come to ordinary people, and that miracles don't just happen. In letting go of reason, she enabled all of us to come to faith.

While faith is important, it's not as important as one of the other major virtues. As St. Paul said, "If I have all faith so as to move mountains but do not have love, I am nothing."

Mary most assuredly had faith. She had to have had enormous faith to believe Gabriel's message, to trust that God's promises were coming true through her. Her faith was God's great gift to her. Yet it's not her *faith* that draws us to her; rather, it's her love.

When you have trouble believing, remember that faith is a gift from God but love is a decision. If you can't believe, decide to love.

Do I ever envy people who seem to have more faith than I do?
How can I choose love today?

BECAUSE LOVE IS A DECISION, I CHOOSE TO LOVE.

Morning People

The world is divided into morning people and night people. For some reason, morning people generally claim inherent moral superiority by virtue of their waking up early. They seem to think (and don't deny it, you morning folks!) that just because their minds are alert at five A.M., they have some special connection to heaven that lie-abed folks don't have.

Morning people take Benjamin Franklin's poem as their creed:

> Cocks crow in the morn to tell us to rise,
> for he who lies late will never be wise.
> For early to bed and early to rise
> makes a man healthy, wealthy and wise.
> He that would thrive must rise at five.
> He that has thriven may lie in til seven,
> and he that will never thrive may lie in til eleven.

Obviously most of the people who've assigned titles to Mary have been morning people: she's known as the Morning Star, the Dawn of the New Creation, and the Star That Bore the Sun, for example. Despite these titles, however, we have no idea whether Mary was a lark or an owl. Perhaps it's time for night people to give Mary a few titles that resonate more loudly in the silent dark. How about Star of Midnight, Comfort of Sunset, or Mother of the Wee Hours? (Who knows: maybe Mary was a night person and would appreciate a few new references.)

> *Am I a lark or an owl? When do I do my best work?*
> *Do I ever try to make my family follow my schedule*
> *just because I prefer it?*

1 KNOW THAT VIRTUE DOESN'T DEPEND ON BIOLOGICAL RHYTHMS.

Reality

In attempting to explain the nature of the universe, scientists tell us that even what appears to be solid is actually an infinity of space. Between the atoms and particles and subatomic particles, nothing is as it appears, we're told. What we see is *not* what we get!

While science is just coming to that conclusion, spirituality has known it all along. Reality isn't what we can touch and smell and taste; reality is God. And God is nothing like what we imagine God to be. God isn't a bright light or a voice out of nowhere. God isn't a Superman in a celestial cape or an old white-bearded man sitting on a throne made of clouds somewhere "up there."

Although we don't know what God is like, Mary does. In her appearances throughout the centuries, she has come to earth to help us understand God's nature. She knew God as her human son on earth, and now she knows God in triune glory. Moreover, she wants us to experience the reality of God in our lives, for she knows that once we do, we'll be transformed forever.

If you have difficulty relating to God, Mary can help. As St. Maximilian Kolbe put it, "God sends to us the one that personifies his love: Mary, the spouse of the spirit—a spirit of maternal love—immaculate, all beautiful, spotless, even though she is our sister, a true daughter of the human race, God confides to her the communication of his mercy to souls."

If you want to know God, get to know Mary.

Am I willing to accept a new vision of reality?
Am I willing to let go of old ideas?

I EXPERIENCE GOD'S REALITY IN MY LIFE TODAY.

Grief

In her groundbreaking research, Elisabeth Kübler-Ross introduced the world to the stages of grief. She pointed out that those who are dying go through distinctive and identifiable stages of denial, anger, bargaining, acceptance, and finally peace. Moreover, she asserted that everyone who's grieving a loss—whether that loss is big or small—goes through similar stages. Even though we all express the stages in our own way, we seem to follow an innate template for grief work.

Of all the losses we experience, the death of a loved one is by far the most devastating. As Dylan Thomas noted, "After the first death, there is no other." Once we have experienced death in all its horror, we're changed forever. It's at that moment that we can begin to recognize grief for what it is: God's analgesic for what would otherwise be literally unbearable.

Despite her elevated status as the Mother of God, Mary experienced the pain of the death of those she loved. The deaths of her parents and her husband, Joseph, most certainly, but there were probably others. In some way, perhaps those deaths helped prepare her for the death of her son. And yet, as anyone who has lost a loved one knows, no matter how prepared you are, grief still rips away your heart and makes you feel as if you too could die.

When we're grieving, Mary understands. She understands what it's like to lose a parent, a spouse, a child. She knows what it's like to feel as if your heart is hemorrhaging from the pain. If you're mourning the loss of someone you love, Mary is always there to comfort you by her example and with her love.

Have I experienced the "first death" Dylan Thomas talks about?

I'M GRATEFUL THAT GRIEF DOESN'T LAST FOREVER.

The Litany of Loreto

Loreto, Italy, is home to one of the oldest and most revered of Marian shrines. According to ancient tradition, Mary's house from Nazareth was miraculously transported (*translated* is the official term) to a hill in Loreto in 1291. Since its appearance there, Loreto has been the destination of pilgrims—including Pope John XXIII and Pope John Paul II—from around the world.

However, the most well known aspect of the shrine isn't the house; rather, it's the prayer associated with it: the Litany of Loreto. Consisting of a series of titles and the request for Mary's prayers, it's one of the oldest and most beloved devotions to Mary.

Holy Mary, *pray for us.*
Holy Mother of God,
Holy Virgin of Virgins,
Mother of Christ,
Mother of Divine grace,
Mother most pure,
Mother most chaste,
Mother inviolate,
Mother undefiled,
Mother most lovable,
Mother most admirable,
Mother of good counsel,
Mother of our Creator,
Mother of our Savior,
Virgin most prudent,
Virgin most venerable,
Virgin most renowned,
Virgin most merciful,
Virgin most faithful,
Mirror of justice,
Seat of wisdom,
Cause of our joy,
Spiritual vessel,

Vessel of honor,
Singular vessel of devotion,
Mystical rose,
Tower of David,
Tower of ivory,
House of gold,
Ark of the Covenant,
Gate of heaven,
Morning Star,
Health of the sick,
Refuge of sinners,
Comfort of the afflicted,
Help of Christians,
Queen of angels,
Queen of patriarchs,
Queen of prophets,
Queen of apostles,
Queen of martyrs,
Queen of confessors,
Queen of virgins,
Queen of all saints,
Queen conceived without original sin,
Queen assumed into heaven,
Queen of the most holy Rosary,
Queen of peace . . .
Pray for us, O holy Mother of God, *that we may be made worthy of the promises of Christ.*

What title of Mary appeals most to me?

I ASK MARY, THE MOTHER OF GOD, TO PRAY FOR ME.

Mountaintop Experiences

In his great freedom speech, Dr. Martin Luther King, Jr., talked about being on the top of a mountain and seeing the promised land. For him, the possibility of equal rights for men and women of all colors was a mountaintop experience.

Mary had mountaintop experiences as well (apparitions that are said to have occurred on mountaintops notwithstanding!). When she climbed into the hill country to tell Elizabeth about Gabriel's visit, when she stood atop the Mount of Olives, watching Jesus being taken into the heavens—these had to have been both literal and figurative mountaintop experiences.

Like Dr. King and the Blessed Virgin, we all have mountaintop experiences—events that so shape and change us that nothing remains the same afterward.

The temptation after such experiences is to want to remain with our head in the clouds. In fact, that's exactly what happened to Peter, James, and John when Jesus took them to the mountain and appeared before them in glory with Moses and Elijah. Peter wanted to put up three tents and camp out forever on that mountaintop.

However, we *can't* remain on the mountaintop. The view is outstanding, but mountaintops are dangerous places. Human beings weren't intended to live at the summit. We can only visit mountaintops, drink in their glory, and then take the memory and promise of that glory back with us to our valley homes.

Without mountaintop experiences life isn't worth living, but we must also remember that life can't be lived on the mountaintop.

When was the last time I was on the mountaintop?
What did I bring back to the valley from that experience?

I GIVE THANKS FOR THE MOUNTAINS AND THE VALLEYS IN MY LIFE.

Friends

When we picture Mary (except in thinking about the Annunciation), we tend to see her in the exclusive company of Jesus and Joseph. Even when we envision her at the wedding feast at Cana, we generally imagine her having that little chat with Jesus; we don't see her in the company of her friends, discussing the bride's dress. And rarely do we picture her in even more ordinary circumstances—laughing as she and the other women draw water from the well, for example, or haggling with a merchant as she visits the markets of Jerusalem at festival time.

Yet intuitively we know that Mary had to have had friends. Edward Young calls friendship "the wine of life"—and we all know what value Mary put on wine!

So who were Mary's friends? While we generally assume that Mary was close to Elizabeth (whom she visited right after the angel Gabriel dropped in with his news) and to her sister (who stood by her at the Crucifixion), we can't know whether Mary was close to these people simply because they were her relatives or because they had become friends as well.

Each of us has the option of becoming friends with Mary. As is true for all friendships, however, we must take time to learn about our new acquaintance and nourish the friendship by spending time with her. One of the best ways to spend time in the company of Mary is by praying the Rosary. The meditative quality of the Rosary, as well as its focus on the lives of Mary and Jesus, makes it ideal for beginning or continuing a close relationship with Mary.

Who are my closest friends?
Do I do what's necessary to both make and keep friendships?

1 NOT ONLY *HAVE* GOOD FRIENDS, 1 *AM* A GOOD FRIEND.

Mothers and Sons

Relationships between mothers and sons have some universal qualities. First, no matter how old the son is, he remains his mother's "little boy." Second, no matter what transpires in his life, a son always has a special place in his heart for his mother. Despite the strength of the mother-son bond, however, mothers and sons don't always have blissful, unruffled relationships. Indeed, at times disagreements can run quite deep.

Even Mary and Jesus weren't above the normal tensions of mother-son behavior. Take the wedding feast at Cana: Mary wanted Jesus to do something about the wine situation, but Jesus clearly wasn't excited about the prospect.

As M. Basil Pennington, OCSO, put it, "Things were not transpiring exactly as He might have planned. 'After all, Mother, do you want it to go down in history that the first sign the Son of God worked on his saving mission was to turn out more booze for the boys after they had drunk the house dry?'"

Although Fr. Pennington doesn't answer the question, it's clear what Mary's response would have been: "Why, yes, dear, that's *exactly* what I want." Then we can almost hear her add, "And we refer to it as *wine*, dear, not *booze.*"

Often it's much easier to be polite to strangers than it is to be polite to our family. Family members are so, well, *familiar.* Yet to be polite and respectful to those with whom we have the most frequent relations is a hallmark of true love. Although Jesus questioned his mother's interference, in the end he did what she asked (and we assume that he did so politely!).

Am I ever brusque or rude with my family members?
Do I put on a different face for strangers than for family?

¶ TREAT ALL PEOPLE WITH KINDNESS AND RESPECT.

Home

Home is the abode of the heart.

ELBERT HUBBARD

Where did Mary call home? Nazareth, where she lived as a young girl? Bethlehem, where her son was born and her husband had relatives? Egypt, where she lived as a young bride and mother? Ephesus, where she's believed to have lived out her last years?

It's hard to say. Home isn't so much a physical place as an emotional tie; it really is "where the heart is." While many of us have a deep attachment to the place where we grew up, the place that sings a siren call to our heart might be a location we've never even visited. Whenever we see pictures or TV footage of that area, our heart cries, "There, that's *home!*" Something in that place resounds deeply in our being and creates a powerful longing.

Wherever the place we recognize as home, it's merely a reflection of our heavenly home. It reminds us that we don't really live here on earth, that we're merely travelers on a cosmic journey awaiting, at the end of our voyage, our real home with its cozy hearth and welcoming fire. It's precisely because we can be reminded of home by a place we've never been that we can be sure that when we enter heaven, we'll be completely, totally, and finally at home.

If I could live anywhere on earth, where would I live?
What kind of places make my heart sing?

I KNOW THAT I'M MERELY VISITING ON EARTH;
MY REAL HOME IS IN HEAVEN.

Happiness

"There is no duty we so much underrate as the duty of being happy," wrote Robert Louis Stevenson.

Most of us don't consider being happy a duty. More likely, we think of it as an elusive goal, with emphasis on the word *elusive*. But the reason that we find happiness so elusive may be that we look for it in all the wrong places.

We tend to equate happiness with acquisition. The more we have and do, the happier we think we'll become. However, if we want to be happy, we must live out this paraphrase of President John F. Kennedy's famous quote: "Ask not what life can give for you, but what you can give to life." The truth is that happiness has very little to do with getting the most *out of* life. It has everything, however, to do with giving all we can *to* life.

Ironically, when we start to give freely and joyously, with no expectation of return, we discover that the more we give, the more we receive. When we engage life fully, life begins to engage us back. When we love without strings, we discover we're loved unconditionally.

Mary's life stands as an example of the fundamental rule of happiness: in order to be happy, we must first be willing to pour ourselves and our talents out for others, without expecting anything in return. Then, and only then, will we discover that happiness isn't something we find; instead, it's something that finds us.

Am I happy? What things that I've thought would make me happy didn't? When was the happiest time in my life?

I MAKE UP MY MIND TO BE HAPPY TODAY.

Opposing Roles

The two roles for which we most honor Mary seem at first glance to be diametrically opposed to one another. After all, motherhood and virginity aren't generally considered to be compatible! Moreover, if, as Catholic tradition teaches, Mary was not only a virgin at the time of Christ's birth but a *perpetual* (yet married) virgin, then the contradiction is even more profound.

It's tempting to dismiss Mary's situation as unique in the history of humanity—which of course it is!—but Mary's life holds a lesson for each of us as well.

Her life teaches us that while we're incapable of reconciling the contradictions in our lives, God not only *can* but *does* reconcile them. One of the great mysteries of God is that God is capable of allowing two entirely different realities to coexist simultaneously. We can barely fathom such a thing. In fact, Mary's question to Gabriel, "How can this be?" is our question as well. Because God's vision of what can be is so radically different from ours, we can no more begin to conceive of two simultaneous realities than Mary could conceive of being both a virgin and a mother (all puns intended!).

The realities God creates aren't those of science-fiction universes. They include the reality of a couple deeply wounded by infidelity who are able to forgive and forget. The reality of a dying child who radiates joy to all around. The reality of a man wrongly executed who calls out from his cross, "Father forgive them for they know not what they do."

Have I ever experienced two realities coexisting in my own life?
What contradictions would I like God to help me
reconcile right now?

I BELIEVE THAT NOTHING IS IMPOSSIBLE FOR GOD.

Crosses

Most of us who were raised in a Christian home are familiar with the phrase "Take up your cross." Applied to burdens and responsibilities, the phrase is intended to encourage us in difficult situations. So why do some people find it so much easier to bear crosses than others?

Perhaps it's because a cross is a cross only if you don't want to take it up.

The pieces of wood that made up Jesus' cross were no heavier than many of the beams he would have carried in the course of his work as a carpenter. Their emotional weight was heavier, however, because they were to be used in a crucifixion. When Mary saw Jesus carrying a beam on a construction site, she most assuredly didn't have the same reaction she had when she saw him carrying a beam as part of his cross. It wasn't the wood that had changed; it was Mary's perception of it.

In the same way, the daily crosses we must take up are crosses only if we see them that way. While Helen Keller never downplayed the handicap of being blind, she wrote that being deaf was more difficult for her. We could say that being deaf was more of a cross for her than being blind.

Once we're willing to embrace our crosses, their weight is automatically lightened; we're able to carry them with much greater ease. It's only when we resist taking them up that they become too crushing to bear.

What crosses am I resisting in my life? What do I think would happen if I were to accept those crosses without resistance?

I KNOW THAT I HAVE CROSSES I MUST BEAR,
AND I'M WILLING TO TAKE THEM UP.

John the Baptist

After being around for his birth, did Mary ever shake her head at the person John the Baptist—Elizabeth's son—turned out to be? If he and Jesus got together as youngsters, did Mary ever worry about John's influence on Jesus? Given the person he was as an adult—someone who went off and ate berries in the wilderness, lambasted the ruling classes, and generally made such a nuisance of himself that he got beheaded—it's not too far-fetched to guess that he was a bit of a handful as a youngster and teen as well.

It's entirely possible that Mary and Elizabeth got together at family gatherings with the other mothers to talk about their kids and what it was like to have them. It's not unlikely that they would have discussed the fact that motherhood hadn't turned out exactly as they'd expected.

Motherhood *never* does.

Having a child (or children) links all women in a common bond. A mother in Japan and a mother in Australia and a mother in the United States and a mother in Africa all know what it's like to give birth, to care for an infant, to deal with adolescence. Cultural differences create some variations, but since moms are moms and kids are kids the world over, we have more similarities than differences. And one of the great similarities is that what we project life as a mother to be isn't what life as a mother actually is. In some ways, of course, it's much more wonderful than we could have imagined. In other ways, it's much more difficult. Since Mary and Elizabeth were real moms, they must have felt the same way—at least once in a while!

How do I feel when the future doesn't turn out as I'd imagined
it would? Am I willing to live in the present and
let the future take care of itself?

I LIVE IN THE HERE AND NOW.

Goals

Goals are funny: once you achieve them, they shift. Even if you work for months or years to achieve something, as soon as it's a reality, you suddenly have a new goal. Part of the reason that we have such ambivalent feelings about goals and accomplishments in this country is that Western culture isn't set up to savor achievement; it's set up to savor the *quest* for achievement. We're told that we must never be satisfied. We must always achieve more and more and more. Well, if there's no limit to what we must achieve, a goal is merely a plateau, with the next level looming immediately before us. No wonder we feel so little satisfaction with life.

One antidote to this quest-oriented mind-set is to set spiritual rather than earthly goals.

There's no telling what Mary's goals in her earthly lifetime were. Getting Jesus raised to adulthood had to have been one, of course. All the promises of the Messiah notwithstanding, life in ancient times was difficult. Jesus could have died from anything from pneumonia to Herod's whim. Mary probably had many other, less substantial daily goals as well—perhaps such things as getting the wool carded and another tunic woven for Jesus or Joseph. Such goals were, by their nature, transitory.

Now, however, Mary's goal is completely spiritual—to spread her son's message throughout the world. Such a goal will last until time itself ends. If we want more than a fleeting feeling of accomplishment, we too must supplement goals that we can accomplish in the here and now with goals whose ending point is eternity.

*Are the goals I've set for myself a mixture of
the here and now and the eternal?*

¶ TAKE TIME TO SET GOALS FOR MY LIFE.

Options

How many times have you heard someone say, "I don't have a choice"? Such a statement simply isn't true. In every situation we have options, although we may not like the options we have. Take, for instance, people trapped in dead-end jobs. They may say that they have no alternative but to stay put, but that's not the case; they have the option of leaving (even if they find that option unacceptable). In such a case, saying, "I don't have a choice," really means, "I don't like the choices I have."

Mary had a choice when the angel Gabriel appeared to her. Despite his rather forceful statement ("Behold, you will conceive in your womb and bear a son, and you shall name him Jesus"), Mary could have said, "No, no. I don't think so." She had the option of refusing. The history of humanity would have been altered, God's plan of salvation would have been different—but Mary *could* have said no. It's our blessing that she said a resounding yes.

When you find yourself in a situation that seems to leave you no choice, follow Mary's example. Mary asked Gabriel a few rather pointed questions before agreeing to become pregnant. In the same way, we can take the time we need to evaluate the options we have. Having done so, we may decide that all but one of our choices are unacceptable. While a single viable option may seem to be the same as not having a choice, it's far different: by consciously and deliberately examining our options and then freely selecting the one that we know is best (even if we don't like it), we're better able to live out our choice without rancor or regret.

Do I believe I always have an option,
no matter what the situation?

I KNOW THAT I ALWAYS HAVE CHOICES,
EVEN WHEN IT DOESN'T FEEL THAT WAY.

Prayer

Have you ever prayed and prayed for something, only to receive a totally unexpected answer—an answer that, even if not disappointing, was completely unforeseen?

In such a case, perhaps what was answered was the "prayer under the prayer."

The prayer under the prayer is what we *really* want to have happen. Only if we're totally honest, and sometimes only in retrospect, can we recognize this underlying desire. Let's suppose, for instance, that one of your closest friends is offered a transfer across the country. You pray with all your heart that he or she won't have to move, and yet the moving van pulls up one day and your friend leaves. However, you stay in touch after the move, perhaps via regular e-mail. After a few months, you both end up in the same city for a convention, and you enjoy being together for an entire week. If you look carefully at what you really wanted to have happen when you prayed that your friend wouldn't move, you'll see that you hoped to maintain the friendship. *And that's what happened.* Despite the distance, you remained close friends. The prayer under the prayer was answered.

Learning to pray the prayer under the prayer is at the heart of Jesus' words "Ask and you shall receive." You get what you're *truly* asking for, not what you *think* you want.

The key to recognizing God's answers to prayer is being completely honest with ourselves and God. In her few recorded conversations with Jesus, Mary was totally honest. She didn't pull punches. When she was upset in the Temple, she said so. When she wanted more wine, she asked for it. Mary got what she asked for, and so will we—if we learn to pray beneath our prayers.

Do I try to trick God into giving me what I want
by pretending to want something else?
Do I ever give my conversations with God a "holy paint job"?

I'M HONEST WITH GOD IN MY PRAYERS, EVEN WHEN
WHAT I'M SAYING DOESN'T SEEM "HOLY."

Career Choices

Career planners tell us that in order to get ahead, we have to decide what we want to do, make a plan, and then execute it. We have to chart the course of our own lives, they say, or we'll be blown aground by the winds of fate.

Mary's life gives us a very different model. Mary says that rather than powering our way (no matter what) in a particular direction, we have to be willing to sail with the wind of the Spirit, allowing ourselves to be taken in new and unexpected directions.

From ancient tradition, we're told that Mary had planned on being a dedicated virgin. She and Joseph may have been idealistic young people planning on serving the Temple together, or (as some accounts suggest) Joseph may have been an older man who married Mary in order to allow her to preserve her virginity. In any case, tradition tells us that motherhood didn't figure in Mary's future. God obviously had other ideas, and today Mary is honored above all as the Mother of God.

All of us need to be open to new paths in life, especially as life expectancy continues to climb. We no longer have to decide what we want to do at age eighteen and stay with that choice until our death. It's *never* too late for a fresh start or a new career. Perhaps you're struggling with that issue now—sensing a pull in a new direction but feeling that it's too late for you to make a change, that you've invested too much now to try something new. If so, ask yourself if you'll be happier in ten years if you *don't* do what you want to do now. If the answer is no, then you've got nothing to lose by trying the new direction.

Do I ever look for reasons why I can't change right now?
Am I willing to settle for something less than
what I really want just because it's convenient?

I'M WILLING TO TRY NEW THINGS AND SEEK NEW DIRECTIONS.

Submissiveness

Spiritual writers over the centuries have touted many of Mary's virtues, including her submissiveness. She's held up as a model of acquiescence and pliability, with her words to Gabriel—"May it be done to me according to your word"—held up as proof positive.

The good news is that yes, Mary was submissive in all the right senses of the word. She allowed God to show her the way she was to travel. She allowed God to work through and with her to fulfill the promises of salvation. She bent her will to God's will.

The bad news is that all too often Mary's submissiveness has been used as an excuse for domination; and that's wrong.

Mary was submissive to God, but she wasn't *dominated* by God. God didn't force Mary to do anything. God didn't trample Mary into a doormat to be flung before the Pearly Gates. God asked Mary to freely and willingly let go of her own desires in order to put the divine plan into action. With her submission, God so elevated Mary that she became the Gate of Heaven itself.

True submission never means running up the white flag, rolling over, and giving up. True submission means changing your heart and mind so that you're willing to do what's necessary to serve a greater good.

If you feel that your rights are being denied and your very being is trammeled, you aren't being submissive; you're being dominated. And if Mary is proof positive of *anything*, it's that while God calls us to be submissive, God never asks us to be dominated.

Do I think I have to give up my very being in order to be
submissive to God? Do I ever let other people dominate me?

I SUBMIT TO GOD'S LOVING INTERVENTION IN MY LIFE.

Promises

All too often, a promise made is a promise broken. Life being what it is, we don't have a lot of experience with promises that are kept. As a result, we often expect that a promise will be, if not broken, at least bent a little. This is especially true for promises whose fulfillment is far in the future. We sometimes assume that the "Someday we'll . . ." kind of promise is mere wishful, wistful dreaming. It's hard to believe in way-off promises, because there isn't any confirmation that they'll happen until they actually occur.

Mary must have had similar experiences. She knew of the promise from ages past that a Messiah would come, for example, but that promise had been around for centuries. There was nothing to show the promise was going to come to fruition in her lifetime—and *certainly* there wasn't anything indicating that *she* would be the means by which the promise would be kept.

People have speculated for generations as to why Mary was the chosen one. Of course, we have no way of knowing why God chose her, but it might have been because, of all women, she believed most completely and totally in God's promise of salvation. Maybe more than anyone else she trusted that God's word would be fulfilled. Because she was so open to God, God was able to work the greatest of miracles through her. Maybe she was chosen not because she *hoped* that God would fulfill the promise but because she *knew* God would.

Do I believe—not just hope—that God's
promises will come true?

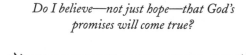

1 KEEP ALL THE PROMISES 1 MAKE.

Grace

"Hail, Mary, full of grace. The Lord is with you." These words—Gabriel's greeting to Mary—serve as the opening line of the Hail Mary, arguably the second-most-famous prayer of Christianity (the Lord's Prayer, of course, being the first). Even non-Catholics, most of whom wouldn't feel comfortable praying to Mary if their lives depended on it, have heard of it.

But what do the words really mean? More specifically, what does it mean when we say that Mary was "full of grace"?

Over the centuries, innumerable theological texts have been written on the topic of grace—in fact, some scholars have spent a whole lifetime trying to decipher its mysteries—so there's clearly no easy answer. However, distilled to its essence, the phrase "full of grace" means completely filled with God's presence. Unlike the rest of us, Mary didn't have any dark, dank, cobweb-cluttered corners of sin. Mary's soul was totally illuminated by God's love.

While we haven't been given Mary's special infusion of grace, we too can become filled with life and light and love. It's what God desires for each of us, what we were created for—to be filled with grace.

Such filling isn't quite like putting a glass under a faucet, however. It requires that we cooperate with God's plan by turning our hearts and minds toward what's good and positive and rejecting those things that are destructive and negative. It means that we must choose daily, sometimes even hourly, to do what we know is right in order to open the channels by which God's grace can enter our lives.

In what ways can I become more full of grace today?
What choices can I make to affirm life rather than destroy it?

I KNOW THAT GOD WANTS ME TO BE FILLED WITH GRACE.

Mirroring God

What does God look like? Artists over the centuries have tried, with varying degrees of success, to create visual representations of God. Some have opted for an old man with a long white beard; others, for more abstract images, such as a triangle with a central eye or even just a glowing light.

So what *does* God look like? The first book of the Hebrew Scriptures, Genesis, says that we were created in the image of God. This doesn't mean, however, that if we were to see God, we would see a human figure. Although some religions have tried to turn God into a flesh-and-blood person, the image of God that we were created to resemble isn't physical; rather, it's the very *essence* of God.

Because we were all created in God's essential image, we all mirror God to one another in some degree. However, God's *ultimate* mirror—that is, the person who most closely resembles God—is Mary. When we look at Mary, we see not only the best that human nature can produce but also what it means to be created in the image of God.

In Mary we see such divine attributes as unconditional love, forgiveness, mercy, and compassion. However, it's important to remember that although Mary mirrors God more perfectly than any other person, she isn't divine. The fact that she's just as human as each of us should give us great encouragement that we too can come to mirror God more perfectly.

When people look at me, what godly aspects do they see?
What godly aspects would I like them to see?
What can I change so that I more clearly mirror God to others?

I MIRROR GOD TO ALL I MEET.

Worship

One of the seven wonders of the ancient world was the immense statue of Zeus at Olympia. Not only did the locals worship there, but tourists from around the known world came to stand in awe before the marvel. Naturally, stories about amazing events that were alleged to have taken place there sprang up. Undoubtedly at least some of those who came to see the statue were hoping for a miraculous cure for illness, the healing of a failed relationship, or some other favor from Zeus.

Of course, the statue had no inherent power, and if any miracle occurred in response to requests from the heart, it was by the favor of the one true God, not the god Zeus.

The temptation to assign miraculous powers to something or someone other than God is still with us. Regrettably, Mary is one of the favorite targets. The line between Marian devotion and Marian adoration gets rather blurry at times. What should be proper honor becomes idolatry when Mary is worshiped not as the Mother of God but as a sort of goddess herself.

Mary is undoubtedly frustrated by having people worship her. Her entire earthly life was spent pointing the way to Jesus and his message. To have people focus on her rather than her son must aggravate her no end (assuming, of course, that people in heaven can be aggravated!).

Honoring Mary as the mother of Jesus (and by extension our mother), praising her for her example and her virtue, asking her for intercession and prayer—these are good and proper actions. But when Mary becomes more important to us than Jesus, warning signals should go up. Love for Mary should be part of the path to Jesus, not a destination in and of itself.

How important is Mary to my spiritual life?
Am I ever tempted to think that she can work miracles herself?

1 HONOR MARY AS THE MOTHER OF GOD, AND 1 LOVE
HER AS MY OWN MOTHER.

Freedom of Religion

One of the tenets of the U.S. Constitution is freedom of religion. Americans are guaranteed by law the right to practice their faith as they see fit. In fact, the United States was founded by immigrants escaping religious persecution in their native countries.

All too often, however, we interpret religious freedom to mean the freedom to try to make other people believe the way we believe. Not only do different religions quarrel, but people within any given faith squabble with each other.

In the Catholic tradition, Marian apparitions are a focus of disagreement. Some people can't imagine living a Catholic Christian life without believing that Mary has appeared and continues to appear throughout the world. Other Catholics live their whole lives without giving a single thought to Mary's travel itinerary. Disagreements between the two factions can become rather heated. Those who believe feel that disbelief is akin to insulting their mother; those who don't believe feel that belief strains credulity.

Neither side is likely to convince the other, nor should they try. That's what religious freedom is all about—the right to agree to disagree on matters that aren't central to salvation. Certain tenets, such as the virgin birth and the Resurrection of Jesus, are essential to being a Christian. When, where, and even if Mary is appearing today are not.

No matter what we personally believe about Mary's apparitions, freedom of religion demands that we allow other people to make up their own minds without our interference.

Do I feel personally affronted when someone doesn't believe
as I do about Mary's appearances in today's world?

1 KNOW WHAT 1 BELIEVE ABOUT MARY AND HER APPEARANCES,
BUT 1 RESPECT THOSE WHO DISAGREE WITH ME.

Wheat Fields

There's something ageless about fields of wheat gently waving in a warm afternoon breeze. The feathery heads and rich golden stalks hark back to the dawn of agriculture, when our remote ancestors first abandoned hunting and gathering to become farmers. The wheat fields we look on today, despite some genetic improvements, are basically the same crop that Mary would have seen growing in her lifetime.

If you have difficulty feeling close to Mary, one way to connect with her is to think of her when you experience some of the ordinary, everyday things she would have experienced.

The next time you look upon a wheat field, a vineyard, sheep dotting a hillside—think of Mary. The next time you smell freshly mown hay, sun-warmed grapes, showy narcissuses—think of Mary. The next time you hear the splash of waves at the side of a lake, the coo of a pigeon, the rustle of the wind—think of Mary. The next time you taste fresh-baked bread, a fine red wine, honey still in the comb—think of Mary. The next time you touch a piece of finely woven wool, a hand-thrown pottery bowl, a baby's cheek—think of Mary, and know that over the centuries, through the barriers of time and space, she is with you.

When do I feel the most connected with Mary?
When do I feel the most connected with other people?
Which of the five senses evokes the strongest memories for me?

I DELIGHT IN THE ORDINARY.

Ordinary Time

In Catholic tradition, the liturgical seasons are given particular names. The time before Christmas, for example, is called Advent. The forty days before Easter are designated as Lent. The days after Easter are called the Easter Season. Not every day of the year has a special event connected with it, however. Those times of the year that don't—summer, for example, when nothing extraordinary is going on—are called Ordinary Time.

At first glance, it seems somewhat ironic that many of Mary's great feasts occur in Ordinary Time: Our Lady of Lourdes, the Annunciation, the Visitation, the Immaculate Heart, the Assumption, the Queenship of Mary, and Our Lady of the Rosary, to name only a few. Mary, the most extraordinary woman of all times, is often stuck in the middle of Ordinary Time.

When we think about it, though, we see that Mary *belongs* in the ordinary. After all, it's in the ordinary times of our lives—those dreary, everyday, get-up-in-the-morning, go-to-work, come-home times—that we tend to lose sight of the eternal plan. It's easy to get so bogged down in the daily details that we forget that this life is only part of the cosmic journey to eternity. That's when Mary and her example become essential. During her lifetime, Mary didn't work a single miracle. She achieved her holiness by walking every ordinary day in the company of God. In doing so, she transformed not only herself but the course of the entire world.

Do I crave excitement? Do I get bored easily?
Do I ever take risks just to "stir things up"?

I ACKNOWLEDGE THE IMPORTANCE OF THE ORDINARY IN MY LIFE.

Maturity

One of the great heresies that has plagued Christianity almost from the beginning claims that Jesus couldn't have been fully human since he was divine. Even today that heresy has a certain appeal. We're inclined to see Jesus through his divine filter, forgetting that he was human in every sense of the word as well.

Take the story of Jesus staying behind in the Temple after the Passover Feast.

Mary obviously thought that Jesus was somewhere in the caravan—perhaps with Joseph and the other men. Joseph obviously thought that Jesus was either with Mary and the women or with the other kids.

And Jesus obviously thought . . . well, it isn't obvious what he thought. He might have thought that Mary and Joseph wouldn't mind if he stayed behind. He might have thought that one of the other kids would tell his parents where he was. Or it's just possible that he didn't think at all. After all, he was twelve at the time, and twelve-year-old boys aren't noted for clear and astute thinking where their parents are concerned, even if they're destined to be the Messiah.

The fact that Jesus might have acted before thinking when he was a boy doesn't detract from his divinity. There isn't, after all, any sin in simply being immature. And Jesus was once immature. In fact, Luke's Gospel says that after the Temple incident, "Jesus advanced [in] wisdom and age and favor before God and man."

When we act without thinking, we should take comfort in the realization that even Jesus made a few mistakes on the road to full maturity.

Do I blame myself excessively for my mistakes in judgment?
Do I tend to put mistakes in the same category as sins?

1 REALIZE THAT 1 MUST GROW IN MATURITY
ALL THE DAYS OF MY LIFE.

Touch

Michelangelo's *Pietà* is one of the great art masterpieces of all times. Portraying Mary and Jesus just after Jesus' body was taken down from the cross, it captures Mary's sorrow and Jesus' humanity in a way that leaves only the most hard-hearted viewer untouched.

Perhaps one reason that the *Pietà* is so moving is that it shows the tender touch with which Mary held her son. All human beings need to be touched. Babies who are deprived of physical contact can't survive even if their other needs are met. Furthermore, studies have shown that children who grow up in homes where affection is shown by hugs, backrubs, and other nonsexual touching are less likely to become involved in early sexual experimentation. Because their innate human need to be touched is satisfied, these children are better able to differentiate between love and sex.

Unfortunately, modern culture has become so sex-obsessed that even the most innocent touch can be misconstrued. Some overly conscientious parents refrain from touching their children too much for fear of molestation charges. Friends keep their distance for fear of being thought too forward. Co-workers forbear any physical contact for fear of being accused of harassment. The result is a society that's oversexed and undertouched.

While no one would suggest that you go around touching everyone you meet, practicing "safe touching" in the form of a hug, a pat on the shoulder, or a backrub is one way to "feed the hungry" in today's society.

How do I feel when someone I don't know well touches me?
How do I feel about touching other people in nonsexual ways?

I'M NOT AFRAID TO REACH OUT AND TOUCH SOMEONE.

Play

When was the last time you went out to play? Not to participate in an organized sporting event, but just to play—to run on the beach, to blow bubbles in the breeze, to let loose and do something totally and utterly frivolous.

If you're like most adults, it's been quite a while. One of the many reasons we stop playing is that it doesn't seem dignified or grown-up. Another reason, for some people, is that play doesn't seem "holy." After all, compare the number of times you've seen a picture of Jesus or Mary praying with the times you've seen a picture of one of them playing. The score is probably in the neighborhood of ten thousand to zero.

While it's true that we don't have a direct record of either Jesus or Mary actually playing, what do you suppose happened at wedding feasts in their day? Just for starters, there would have been singing, dancing, good food, and good wine (at least at one wedding!).

Play is one way we learn to awaken to the excitement of life, to see things in a new and refreshing way, to reconnect with the child within. While we put a great deal of emphasis on the importance of being grown-up, Jesus has a different idea. He tells his followers, "Amen, I say to you, whoever does not accept the kingdom of God like a child will not enter it."

While Jesus is certainly not condoning childishness, he's saying that we need to give ourselves permission to see life through the eyes of a child, to celebrate the wonder of creation—yes, to *play!*

When was the last time I went out to play?
If I could ask someone to play with me, who would I ask?

1 KNOW WHEN TO WORK, BUT 1 ALSO KNOW WHEN TO PLAY.

Guilt and Innocence

The American judicial system is based on the presumption of innocence: a person is innocent until proven guilty. The burden of proof falls not on the accused but on the prosecution. While the point of the system is to ensure that no one who's innocent is accidentally convicted, it has another, less desirable effect: when a person is found "not guilty," that verdict doesn't necessarily mean that he or she is innocent; it may mean merely that the prosecution didn't prove its case. Thus there can be an enormous difference between being not guilty and being innocent.

Pontius Pilate acknowledged the fact that Jesus' prosecutors hadn't proven their case when he said, "I find him guilty of no capital crime." However, Jesus was more than merely "not guilty"; he was totally and completely innocent.

How difficult it must have been for Mary to know that her son was innocent, to watch him declared "not guilty," and *still* to see him condemned to death. The utter unfairness and mockery of justice must have weighed heavily on her soul, yet we don't read that she uttered a single word of protest.

Why is that? Why wouldn't Mary have spoken out on behalf of her son?

The obvious answer is that since she was a woman, she wouldn't have been listened to by the men of the courts—but that's not the whole story. Mary didn't speak out because she knew that God's righteousness would prevail. Even though she didn't understand exactly why her son had to die, she had faith that God's will would be done and justice would ultimately be served. Would that we, when we find ourselves unjustly or unfairly confronted, could have half so much trust as Mary.

What do I do when I'm on the receiving end of an injustice?

I TRUST THAT JUSTICE WILL PREVAIL IN THE END.

Negative Emotions

Have you ever wondered what negative emotions Mary experienced? We're told that she was greatly troubled when the angel appeared. We know that she was anxious when Jesus was lost in Jerusalem, and we assume that she was brokenhearted when he was put to death. However, anger, frustration, annoyance, disappointment—these aren't emotions we typically associate with Mary, perhaps because of her Immaculate Conception. However, the fact that she was born free from the natural inclination toward sin doesn't mean that she never experienced any negative emotions other than sorrow.

Take disappointment, for instance. It's only natural to feel disappointed when things don't turn out the way we want or hope. Undoubtedly Mary was disappointed when her bread didn't rise the way she wanted or when it rained on a day that she'd planned to hang out the wash.

Or take frustration. If a ewe jumped the fence three times in one morning and Mary had to chase it back home, she probably felt just a wee bit frustrated with the beast. If she called Jesus and Joseph to dinner and they didn't come promptly, she probably felt frustrated as she watched the lentil soup cool.

Like all other feelings, negative feelings are neither right nor wrong. They just *are.* It's what we do with our negative feelings that makes them right or wrong. Beating the sheep or yelling at Jesus and Joseph would have been unthinkable for Mary. But feeling frustrated or annoyed—that's just part of human nature.

Do I tend to judge my feelings or the feelings of others?
Do I ever say, "You shouldn't feel that way"?

I'M ENTITLED TO MY FEELINGS.

Going for Quality and Quantity

At times quality and quantity are positioned as polar opposites—quality time versus quantity time, for instance. But in reality, quality and quantity needn't be at odds; there's a time and a place for each. A farmer needs a quantity of seeds in order to produce a crop for market, for example. One quality seed can't take the place of the needed quantity of seeds. However, sometimes quality is more important than quantity. One expensive, well-tailored jacket will take you through most social situations, while a closet full of cheap, trendy fashions will ensure that you're never properly dressed for *any* occasion.

In our prayer lives too, both quality and quantity have their place. Over and over in her appearances, Mary begs, "Pray always." Such an admonition clearly points to the need for *quantity* prayer. With constant, insistent prayer, even wars and natural disasters can be averted, she says, urging her followers to attend Mass regularly and pray the Rosary daily.

At the same time, Mary points out the need for *quality* prayer. In one of her apparitions, she's believed to have said, "I do not need two hundred Our Fathers. It is better to pray one, but with the desire to encounter God." On another occasion, she offered this advice: "When you pray, do not keep looking at your watch."

Mary understands that we need both quality and quantity prayer if we're to know, love, and serve God, just as we need both quality and quantity communication in any meaningful relationship.

Do I enjoy praying?
Do I find it easier to talk with God or to recite set prayers?
Do I have a special time of day when I pray?

I MAKE MY LIFE PRAYER AND PRAYER MY LIFE.

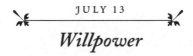

Willpower

Despite their fancy titles and deceptive marketing ploys, most diets rely on one thing: willpower. Whether a diet touts the fat-burning power of grapefruit or cabbage, the importance of twenty minutes of exercise a day, or the magic of a low-cal beverage, it boils down to one thing: having the willpower to eat less and exercise more. Since willpower comes naturally to very few of us, most diets are doomed to fail. Doing things by our own willpower generally means hanging on for dear life. If we let go for one instant, we're lost. This can be seen most readily with alcoholics. Those who depend entirely on their own willpower to stay sober generally fall off the wagon sooner or later. Those who don't fall sometimes become so bound by and rigid with the necessity of maintaining control that they're unable to live life fully.

The answer to the willpower dilemma is simple: stop trying to do it alone. Mary didn't depend on her own willpower to get through life. She let God handle those things God could handle best. As an example, take letting Joseph know about her pregnancy. Mary didn't even *try* to explain. She let God take care of the situation while she was visiting her cousin Elizabeth.

Letting God take over in place of our own willpower goes against human nature. It's difficult to trust that God really does love us enough to take care of our difficult situations. But until we learn to let go and let God, we're doomed to a never-ending struggle with our own lack of willpower.

Am I willing to trust God with my most difficult struggles?

1 DO ALL THAT 1 CAN AND LET GOD DO THE REST.

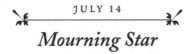

Mourning Star

Mary is traditionally called the Morning Star, because a new dawn of creation began with her acceptance of God's call. However, she could also be called the Mourning Star, because although she shines as a bright sign in the heavens, she remains in mourning until all of creation is united under her son.

We're just beginning to rediscover mourning as a *process*. It's not something that can be accomplished in a designated time-frame, and it *certainly* can't be crammed into the traditional three days we assign between a death and a funeral.

Unlike acute grief, which has certain definite steps, mourning ebbs and flows, sometimes over the course of a lifetime. We can continue to mourn long after our intense grief has subsided. While mourning is part of the way we cope with loss, it also alerts us to the fact that we still have some emotional or spiritual work to do in our lives. Once we've completed that work, we no longer have the inner need to mourn.

If you're currently in mourning, take some time to figure out what life-lessons your mourning is trying to teach you. If, for instance, you're mourning the loss of a parent, perhaps you're being gently pushed to learn how to become your own nurturer, supporter, and comforter. There's always a lesson underneath the mourning, just as underneath Mary's mourning is the desire for all God's children to be united in the common bond of love.

Am I currently mourning the loss of something
or someone important in my life?
What lessons am I supposed to be learning right now?

I ALLOW MYSELF TO TAKE AS MUCH TIME AS I NEED TO MOURN.

Trust

"Just trust me on this!" The minute you hear those words, your best bet is to run for the hills. When someone asks you to trust him or her, chances are you're going to end up wishing you hadn't. Because we've all had so many experiences with being let down, learning to trust God may not come easily. It's only logical: if we can't trust the people we know and can see, how can we begin to trust a God we *can't* see?

If Mary teaches us anything, it's to trust God. She trusted God at the Annunciation, she trusted her son at Cana, she trusted in the Resurrection. Throughout her life, she trusted even when logic demanded that she doubt.

How did Mary learn to trust God? The same way each of us does—simply by doing it. There's no secret. You can't mix two parts hope, one part knowledge, and three parts confidence to come up with a magic formula for trust. You can't ask other people how they did it and then copy their technique. The only way to trust God is to *trust God.*

Is it easy? Of course not.

Is it frightening? More so than *Jurassic Park* and *Nightmare on Elm Street* combined.

Is it possible? Absolutely.

If you find yourself wary of trusting God, ask Mary to pray that you'll have the courage to make the necessary leap of faith. Ask her to share her own unwavering confidence in God's power. Ask her to help you have the confidence to fall into God's loving arms of trust.

Do I trust God? Why or why not? Have I ever tried
to trust God without reservation?

I TRUST YOU, GOD. HELP MY DISTRUST.

Mt. Carmel

Known in Hebrew as Ha-Karmel, Mt. Carmel is a holy mountain in northwestern Israel. From the sixth century A.D., it's been associated with the veneration of Mary. Greek monks established a church and a monastery there about the year 500, and the Carmelite order was founded there around 1154. According to legend, Mary appeared to St. Simon Stock at Cambridge in 1251 and declared that wearers of the brown Carmelite scapular would be saved from hell and taken to heaven by her on the first Saturday after death. While the Catholic Church has never confirmed the legend as true, the scapular devotion is one of the most ancient devotions to Mary.

The brown Carmelite scapular is one of eighteen scapulars used in the Catholic Church. While Carmelite priests and sisters wear a long garment that drapes over the head and shoulders, extending almost to the feet over the chest and back, laypeople wear around the neck a much modified version consisting of two small pieces of cloth—one in front, one in back—connected by two long cords.

Although a scapular is in and of itself merely a piece of cloth, it symbolizes the desire of the one wearing it to be united in mind and purpose with Mary and all others who dedicate their lives to living out the call of the Gospel. Just as a wedding ring symbolizes the unity of a husband and wife, so a scapular indicates the spiritual unity of believers. Not a talisman or good luck charm, it's a private and personal symbol of faith and an intimate reminder to live out that faith in everyday life.

If someone were to look at my home, would he or she see any symbols indicating my religious beliefs or spiritual commitments?

I'M NOT AFRAID TO LET MY FAITH SHOW.

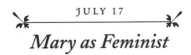

Mary as Feminist

The word *feminist* has gotten a bad reputation. A feminist is often seen as a male-basher, a rebel, a radical who rejects all tradition and takes equality between the sexes to illogical conclusions.

Given that interpretation, it's hardly surprising that Mary isn't touted as a feminist. And yet, in the truest sense of the word *feminist,* that's exactly what she is.

A true feminist isn't someone who seeks to destroy traditional roles or denies the God-given differences between men and women. Rather, a true feminist seeks to liberate the human spirit through the expression of what's best in both men and women. From that perspective, Mary was and remains an ardent feminist.

Mary's message over the centuries to all people—men and women alike—has been to become whole, creative, unique individuals. She doesn't ask us to fit into predefined roles. Instead, she encourages us to find our own special gifts and use them for the good of creation. Just look at a few saints who've had deep devotion to Our Lady. You couldn't find two more radically different individuals than St. Maximilian Kolbe, who gave his life in place of another prisoner at Auschwitz, and St. Gertrude the Great, an abbess and Latin scholar who lived in the thirteenth century. Or St. Dominic Savio, the boy mystic, and St. Philip Neri, the practical joker. Or even Pope John XXIII, the jolly peasant, and Pope Paul VI, the dignified scholar.

Mary doesn't want us to become photocopies of each other; rather, she wants us to discover who we are and what we do better than any other person who ever lived. In her desire to have each of us fulfill our God-given capabilities, Mary is an example of a true feminist.

Who am I? If I could be anything or anyone
when I grow up, who would I want to be?

I KNOW THAT I'M SPECIAL AND HAVE GIFTS TO SHARE WITH OTHERS.

Weeping

At the cross her station keeping,
stood the mournful mother weeping,
close to Jesus to the last.
(Stabat mater Dolovosa by Jacopone da Todi)

Not too many years ago, it was fairly common (and acceptable) for women to cry and very uncommon (and unacceptable) for men to. In recent years, however, as women have moved into positions traditionally held by men, feminine tears became increasingly less socially acceptable. Nowadays, with crying generally seen as a sign of weakness, it's uncommon for *either* men or women to cry publicly.

What a loss! The ability to weep is one of God's great gifts to us. When people say that they feel better after a good cry, they're telling the truth. Red eyes and stuffy nose notwithstanding, we do tend to feel better after we've cried.

And it isn't just our imagination. Scientists have discovered that the tears we cry out of sorrow have a different chemical composition than the tears we cry out of shame, embarrassment, anger, or laughter. The tears of sorrow actually have a cathartic effect: they help to cleanse our bodies of the chemicals we produce when we're under intense stress.

The next time you're moved to tears, don't maintain the proverbial stiff upper lip and blink back your feelings. Let the tears come, knowing that with them will also come comfort and healing.

When was the last time I had a good cry?
When someone cries around me, how does it make me feel?

I'M NOT ASHAMED OF MY EMOTIONS.

Health

Holiness and health don't go hand in hand. Many of the saints suffered from grave illnesses, and even those who enjoyed good health weren't spared the normal wear and tear of life. Thus it seems entirely possible that Mary could have suffered from arthritis, bursitis, or some of the other ailments that often accompany aging. Perhaps, being the Mother of God, she wasn't subject to the normal frailties of the human condition, but there's no evidence suggesting that she was miraculously immune from colds, viruses, and other pesky infections. To think that her body didn't obey the same laws of nature as all other bodies (to imagine, for instance, that she didn't get a welt when she was stung by a bee or didn't have to guard against infection if she was accidentally cut by a pottery shard) elevates her to a supernatural status.

While it's true that she was super*human*, embodying all that humanity can and should become, she wasn't super*natural.* The very fact that she's human makes her the ideal example for us. We can never hope to emulate supernatural creatures such as angels, because we weren't created with their gifts or capacities. But Mary is one of us. Perfected, protected, and elevated, most assuredly—but one of us nonetheless. She knows what it's like to be miserable and hurting; that's why she has intense compassion for the sick and injured. She knows what it's like to grieve; that's why she can be a comfort to the sorrowing. She knows what it's like to be fully human; that's why she can teach us how to develop our potential.

Do I allow myself to experience the full
range of human experience?

¶ REALIZE THAT GOOD HEALTH IS A GIFT FROM GOD.

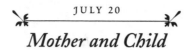

Mother and Child

When artists want to present a warm, loving image of Mary and Jesus, Jesus is usually drawn as a baby. Depending on the conventions of the artist's time, Jesus can be anything from a kid-size adult to a cuddly infant, but he's rarely portrayed as being much older than one or two.

What you almost never see is Jesus as a teen—and with good reason. Who gets soft and mushy at the sight of a kid with a skimpy beard and pimples on his chin? An adorable baby is a much more pleasant image than any adolescent could hope to be.

But Jesus had to go through adolescence, with all its physical and emotional changes. He didn't leapfrog from the stable to the Temple to his life's work. He went through all the normal stages everyone goes through—including adolescence.

All children grow up. That's what they're supposed to do. We can't keep them trapped in their baby mold forever. What's more, by letting Jesus grow up in our minds, we allow Mary to mature as well; we allow her to become a wise woman rather than a teenage virgin.

Why is it important that we let Mary grow? Because in order to accept Mary as our mother in all the stages of our lives, we're forced to grow ourselves. If we see Mary as the mother of a baby only, then we're unable to accept her as our mother once we ourselves begin to grow out of the babyhood of faith.

When I think of Mary as my mother, how old
do I imagine myself as being?

1 KNOW THAT 1 NEED TO GROW AND DEVELOP IN FAITH.

Stars

Did Mary ever wish upon a star as a little girl? We have no way of knowing, of course, but we do know that when we gaze into the night sky, we see very much the same thing Mary would have seen.

One of the most amazing aspects of stargazing is that what we see isn't the present but the past. Because it takes thousands and hundreds of thousands of light-years for the light from distant suns to reach us, what we see is the universe as it was in the past. For all we know, the stars we currently see may have been extinguished centuries ago. In fact, the universe may have already ended and we just don't know it yet!

In his essay "The World's Last Night," C. S. Lewis says something similar. He talks about life being akin to a play. He points out that even though we think we know the plot, we really don't. We don't know which act we're in, we don't know who's playing the lead, and we have absolutely no idea when the play is going to end. In fact, we aren't even sure we'll know the end when it comes. "When it is over, we may be told," Lewis says.

Because we can't know the future, it's imperative to live in the present. Wishing upon a star is one thing; living with our head in the clouds is quite another.

Do I worry about the end of the world?
If this were the world's last night, would I be ready?

I LIVE EACH DAY AS IF IT WERE MY LAST.

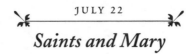

Saints and Mary

Although many Catholic churches are named St. Mary, the Blessed Virgin isn't usually referred to that way in ordinary Catholic conversation. In fact, if you were to say that St. Mary appeared at Fatima or Lourdes, it would sound rather odd to Catholic ears. People might even ask who you were talking about.

But by strict definition, Mary is indeed a saint. According to the *Catholic Dictionary,* saints are

1. Those persons in heaven, whether or not canonized, who lived lives of great charity and heroic virtue. They now live forever with God and share in His glory.
2. Those persons, according to St. Paul, who follow Christ (cf. Col. 1:2).

Since Mary not only lived a life of great charity and followed Christ, but is known to be in heaven (by virtue of her Assumption), she's clearly a saint.

Although few of us will become canonized Saints with a capital *s,* we're all called to become saints with a small *s.* We're all called to live lives characterized by charity and virtue, and we're all called to follow in the footsteps of Christ—even if we, like Mary, aren't officially referred to in the terminology of sainthood.

What do I think saints are like?
Have I ever thought of myself as a saint?

I SPEND TIME EVERY DAY DEVELOPING MY SPIRITUAL LIFE.

Heart Transplant

When Mary and Joseph presented the infant Jesus in the Temple, the prophet Simeon told Mary that her heart would be pierced. Mary would have known what heart-piercing entailed, because a lance-blow to the heart was the final action in a Roman crucifixion (and crucifixions were relatively common in first-century Israel). Indeed, it's entirely possible that Mary would have actually witnessed such an action. But the details aside, Simeon's prophecy wasn't just a warning of impending sorrow. He went on to explain *why* Mary's heart would be pierced: "so that the thoughts of many hearts may be revealed."

If Simeon were giving his prophecy to Mary today, instead of predicting that her heart would be pierced by a sword, perhaps he would predict that she'd be a heart-transplant donor "so that the lives of many others could be saved."

A heart transplant is an image that we can relate to more easily than the coup de grâce in a Roman execution. We've all read about or seen television documentaries on heart transplants. Despite the fact that most of us will be neither the donor nor the recipient in an actual heart transplant, when we risk forming intimate relationships with others we take part in a heart transplant of a different sort. Whenever we fall in love, connect with a soulmate, give birth to a child, or form a deep, intimate relationship, we give away our heart, or at least part of it. Sometimes the transplant takes and we get back as much as we give; other times the tissue isn't a close enough match, and we end up being hurt. Most of the time, however, the reward of love is worth all the pain and the risk.

Am I afraid to love? What do I think would happen
if I let myself love and be loved?

I'M WILLING TO RISK LOVE.

Self-Denial

We live in a self-indulgent culture. The only area we're willing—in fact, eager—to express self-denial in is the physical. We're determined to deny ourselves food, leisure, relaxation, and sometimes even relationships in order to have thin, toned bodies. We may think we're denying ourselves, but in fact we're indulging ourselves, because our primary motive is self—more specifically, our bodies. Our self-denial is merely thinly disguised self-indulgence.

Genuine self-denial has an "other" focus. We give up something we want in order to let someone else have something. Mary could be called the Queen of Self-Denial. She denied her dreams for her life in order to become the mother of Jesus. Although we don't know what her dreams were, we do know that she was willing to deny herself for the good of all humanity.

Often we're afraid that God will ask too much of us, that God will take a mile if we offer an inch. However, only rarely does God ask for the supreme sacrifice of martyrdom, and even in those cases God gives believers the strength and grace to endure. For most of us, the sacrifices are much less onerous—denying ourselves a Danish with our coffee in order to give a dollar to a begging street kid, refusing to buy an outfit we really like because it was made in a Third-World sweatshop, giving up our favorite television show in order to spend time with an elderly relative.

What's God asking me to give up today? Am I afraid that God will demand more of me than I'm willing to give?

I'M WILLING TO DENY MYSELF FOR THE GOOD OF OTHERS.

Detachment

Learning to differentiate between detachment and disinterest is one of the hardest lessons of adult life. We all know what it's like to feel disinterest, but detachment is another story. Letting go of emotional attachment for the outcome while still caring passionately about the process feels like a total contradiction in terms. How can you be completely engaged in something and yet be removed from the result? How can you want to be hired for a job you know you'd love, for example, and still be able to desire without reservation that the person best qualified for the job be hired (even if it's not you)?

It isn't easy, but it is possible—with God's help. God wants to teach us how to become detached from the final results while working as hard as possible to achieve them. It's the way God operated in Mary's life, and it's the way God operates today.

Mary cared deeply that the promises God made to the prophets of old would be fulfilled. She was willing to do all she could to help bring them about, and yet she was willing to let God bring about fulfillment in God's own time and way. She was passionately engaged in rearing her son, yet she was able to let him go to fulfill his destiny.

All too often, we think that being detached means not caring. That's not true. *Disinterest* means that we don't care; *detachment* means that we care so much we're willing to let God make the choices for us. It's a distinction that may take a lifetime to sort out.

Have I ever been able to experience the liberation that comes
with letting God make the right choice for me?

I'M DETACHED FROM ALL THINGS EXCEPT GOD'S WILL.

Heaven (on Earth)

Where is heaven? Most of us think it's somewhere "up there." A tabloid newspaper recently published pictures of a supposed city in outer space glimpsed by Russian cosmonauts. The article suggested that the city in the clouds might be heaven.

In several of her appearances, Mary has indicated that heaven isn't a place somewhere "out there" but a place within each of us. Jesus said much the same thing when he told his disciples that the kingdom of heaven was at hand.

Most of us get little glimpses of heaven on earth—in the eyes of a child, in the words of a lover, in the strains of a symphony. But such glimpses are brief and fleeting. All too soon we're back in our earthbound routine.

If we want to experience the heaven on earth that Mary and Jesus talked about, we can't expect other people to create heaven for us. We must seek heaven in our own souls, for heaven isn't so much a *place* as it is a *state of being*—a state marked by peace, tranquillity, and faith.

Over and over again, Mary tells us that if we're to experience heaven, we must first change our lives. We must turn from sin and self-desire and focus our attention on prayer and penance. Once we do so, we'll experience heaven on earth for ourselves.

How do I picture heaven? Do I realize that I have some
role in creating heaven—at least here on earth?

I LOOK FOR HEAVEN WITHIN, NOT SOMEWHERE "OUT THERE."

Unexpected Directions

Once in a while you meet a person who set a course early in life and followed it without deviation. For most of us, however, life is a series of switchbacks and curves, dead ends and U-turns, with only the occasional straight stretch. More often than not, we find ourselves in a place we never expected to go in the company of people we never expected to meet.

If you're feeling that way right now, Mary can undoubtedly empathize. Her life certainly took an unexpected direction when Gabriel appeared. With just a few words, God entered her life in a new and different way, and nothing was the same ever again.

What's true for Mary is true for us as well: when we let God fully into our lives, we have to be ready to go in unexpected directions. God will take us down paths we didn't even know existed. Along the way, we'll find challenges, sorrows, and struggles, but we'll also find unimaginable joys. What God has planned for us is much more wonderful than anything we could have planned for ourselves.

In order to experience the wonder of God, we not only have to be willing to go places we never expected, we also have to be willing to keep our eyes and ears open for signposts indicating the direction we should travel. The signs may be subtle, but when we're open to the prompting of the Spirit, we won't miss the turns!

When I've let God do the leading in my life,
what has been the result?
Am I afraid to let God set my direction?

I TRUST THAT MY LIFE IS UNFOLDING EXACTLY AS IT SHOULD.

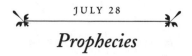

Prophecies

Tabloid newspapers are fond of prophecies, ranging from the improbable to the impossible. Often the prophecies are so ludicrous that it's hard to imagine anyone believing them—but someone must, or the papers wouldn't keep printing their outrageous headlines.

We tend to think of prophecies as predictions of impending events (usually unpleasant ones). But prophecies in the spiritual sense aren't crystal-ball foretellings of the future: they're messages from God that point the way to a new creation.

Gabriel's message to Mary is an ideal example of biblical prophecy. While it did contain some information about the future, it was more of a preview of coming attractions than a detailed synopsis. The bit of actual news ("You will bear a son") wasn't nearly as important as the rest of the message ("He will be great and will be called Son of the Most High, and the Lord God will give him the throne of David his father, and he will rule over the house of Jacob forever, and of his kingdom there will be no end").

God doesn't give prophecies just so that we can know what's around the next corner of life. God gives prophecies so that we can have new and abundant life.

In her appearances, Mary reminds us of some of the prophecies of God that we can cling to in times of trouble. For instance, prayer can change the world, God has a plan for each of us, and love is the answer to all questions.

If I could, would I choose to know my future?
Am I willing to leave my future in God's hands?

I LOOK FORWARD TO EACH NEW DAY.

Holiness

The life-duty of every person is to become holy. Such a deceptively simple statement!

One of the difficulties is that while each one of us is called to holiness, there's no such thing as holiness per se. Mary exemplifies holiness, but it's her own unique form of holiness. We can look at Mary's life for direction, we can call on Mary for assistance, but we must discover what kind of holiness God wants for *us*.

God doesn't call us to become clones of Mary. We're called to become our own holy selves, which means that each of us has a different path to travel. A mother has a different road to holiness than does a father, for instance, even when they share the raising of their children. A husband has a different road than a wife, a worker a different path than a retiree, a wealthy person a different path than a poor person. Each of us has our own unique route.

We must be holy, yes, but we must be holy in our own way, if we're to be authentic. And God wants authentic children, not clones of anyone—not even of Mary. We can admire Mary, we can honor Mary, we can emulate Mary, but we can't *become* Mary.

How does God want me to become holy?
Have I ever thought about the road to holiness
that I'm to follow?

I KNOW THAT GOD WILL SHOW ME THE PATH TO HOLINESS.

Night

Before the invention of fire, night was terrifying. Our ancestors, puny and vulnerable, without fangs or claws for protection, were at the mercy of beasts prowling in the darkness. After fire was harnessed, beyond the protective pool of firelight the night still held unspeakable terrors. Even in spiritual terms, night represents primordial fear and suffering. In his great masterpiece, *The Dark Night of the Soul,* St. John of the Cross talks about the "bitter and terrible" night of the senses and the "horrible and awful" night of the soul.

With the advent of electric light, we no longer have a great fear of the night. Yet countless generations have left their imprint on our collective soul. The night is still the time when we shut down and draw inward. Night is the time when confidences are most easily shared, when barriers are most easily broken, when words of love are most often uttered.

This evening, instead of trying to banish the night with the glare of television, take time to appreciate the blanketing quiet. Let your soul lie still, to be nourished by the stars, the nocturnal animals, the sounds of stillness that have been muffled by the hubbub of the day. As you do so, think of Mary, who surely spent time at night, gazing at the sky, looking for the star that heralded her son's birth, wondering exactly what destiny lay before them. Then finally, in the rich fullness of the summer night, bless the darkness as it blesses you with sleep and peace.

What do I do when I'm unexpectedly awakened in the middle of the night? Have I ever spent an entire night in prayer?

I KNOW THAT I'M SAFE NIGHT AND DAY.

Meals

There are more than twenty references in Scripture to a "land flowing with milk and honey." To the ancients, that land was a metaphor for safety, security, and prosperity. But if you think about it, a place with that much milk and honey would be sticky, messy, and potentially sour-smelling. In fact, it sounds a little like the kitchen floor after lunch with a toddler!

Fixing meals for toddlers is a relatively thankless job. If they like the food, they tend to make a huge mess. If they dislike the food, they tend to make a huge mess. Actually, fixing meals for a family tends to be a relatively thankless job, regardless of the ages of the people eating. Meals are so, well, *daily.* Three times a day the cook has to think of something to prepare with the ingredients available. Some days inspiration strikes; other days nothing sounds good.

When Jesus and Joseph came in the door of the house at Nazareth and asked, "What's for dinner?" Was Mary ever tempted to say, "I haven't a clue"? Since fast food hadn't been invented yet, she couldn't order takeout. Since there probably weren't any public eating establishments in Nazareth, she couldn't suggest that they go out to eat. Maybe, on those days when Mary just didn't feel like cooking, she served milk and honey, with a little bread on the side!

Do I look at the meals I must prepare as a way to serve those
who live with me or as a chore I would rather avoid?

I GIVE THANKS THAT I HAVE ENOUGH FOOD TO PREPARE A MEAL.

Dealing with Overwork

Summer is a time when many of us feel like chanting, "So much to do, so little time." Everything from the garden to the house to the family demands our attention. By August we've come to realize that we aren't going to get to half the things we'd planned to accomplish this summer, even if we work our tails off during the remaining weeks. What's more, most of us still have an innate fondness for the schedule of school and resent having to work during the summer.

When we feel overworked and undertimed, it's easy to become short-tempered and cranky. It's only natural. Then, when the pressures build up, we express our frustration to the people nearest us— well, we *hope* we express our frustration. What often happens is that we take our feelings out on the people around us.

If the Gospel account of the Finding in the Temple is any indication, Mary sometimes felt just as stressed, overtired, and cranky as we do. However, Mary understood the difference between expressing her feelings and taking her feelings out. Because she was able to tell Jesus exactly how she felt (worried and anxious), he got the message and was able to respond appropriately (getting up and going home).

This time of year, when we find ourselves getting irritable and cranky, let's ask Mary to help us remain calm, to express our true feelings, and to react appropriately.

Do I schedule more things than I can possibly accomplish?
How do I react when I feel pressured and trapped?

I DO ALL I CAN AND NO MORE.

Street Smarts

Some people seem to be born with street smarts, while others acquire such knowledge through practice. (Some people *never* seem to get it, but they don't count!) When it comes to matters of faith and religion, we all need a share of heavenly street smarts.

Everywhere we turn, charlatans try to convince us that they have the "real" message of God. Sometimes the frauds stoop so low as to use Mary as part of their schemes. They claim to have had a vision or heard a voice or seen a statue weep and then try to foist off their own ideas as having come from Mary.

While it's true that Mary has appeared in certain places and to certain people around the world, not everyone who claims to have seen Mary has had a mystical experience. That's why the Catholic Church takes such a long time to verify any alleged appearance.

In looking at Marian apparitions, it's important to use our heavenly street sense. If Mary's message is in opposition to the Hebrew or Christian Scriptures in any way, then the appearance can't be real. Likewise, if Mary's message contradicts any of her previous messages, then the appearance should be treated with skepticism. Finally, if Mary's message points to any way other than that designated by Christ, the appearance should be rejected out of hand.

While we often long to have a concrete taste of the mystical, we must be discerning as to what we accept as real. Just saying that something happened doesn't make it so. We must be willing to put all alleged appearances of Mary to the most rigorous of tests, confident that those that are real will survive any and all questioning.

Am I gullible when it comes to mystical experiences?
Do I ever feel that it isn't spiritual to put alleged
Marian appearances to subjective tests?

I USE MY HEAVENLY STREET SMARTS WHEN IT
COMES TO MARY'S APPEARANCES.

Work

We all have work to do, a job we've been called to at this particular moment in time. Perhaps your job is to be a stay-at-home mother. Perhaps it's to be a corporate president. The exact nature of the work doesn't matter, for all honest work is valuable. A physician's task is no more honorable than that of a writer. A CEO's function is no more valuable than a janitor's. As St. Paul told the residents of Corinth, "If the whole body were an eye, where would the hearing be? If the whole body were hearing, where would the sense of smell be? . . . If they were all one part, where would the body be? But as it is, there are many parts, yet one body." Likewise, in the overall scheme of life, we each have our particular work to do.

In this, Mary is one of us. She has her own particular work as well. One great temptation we face is to see Mary's work as being the same as her son's. When we make that assumption, we're in danger of misinterpreting Mary. For instance, Mary doesn't heal. At Medjugorje she's believed to have said, "I cannot cure. God alone cures. I am not God." She's made it clear that she doesn't work miracles in and of herself.

So what's Mary's work now? Her work today, as during her earthly life, is to point us toward her son. She says to each and every one of us, as she did at Cana, "Do whatever he tells you."

Do I honor the work I do as having been given to me by God?
Do I believe that my work is as valuable as everyone else's?

I DO THE BEST JOB I CAN AT ALL TIMES.

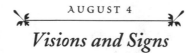

Visions and Signs

Outside most of the major Marian shrines, such as that at Lourdes, souvenir dealers fill the streets, hawking their (often tacky) wares. Glow-in-the-dark Rosary beads, cheap plastic bottles filled with holy water, gaudy pictures, and all kinds of other kitschy memorabilia are for sale. Like pilgrims in the Middle Ages buying a vial of the Virgin's milk or a snippet of Jesus' swaddling cloths, some modern-day pilgrims purchase trinkets in the hope that they may have been infused with miraculous power.

While it's easy to chuckle over other people's gullibility, some small part of us may secretly hope that our picture of Mary will weep real tears or that our silver Rosary beads will turn gold. There's nothing wrong with that hope, it's consistent with our natural human desire for visions and signs. Because it can be so difficult to believe, we'd like to have a concrete sign to help our unbelief. A weeping picture or a golden Rosary seems like a small thing to bolster faith.

But what if we *don't* get a sign or a vision? What if our Rosary stays solidly silver and the only moisture that appears on our picture comes from spilled coffee? Even more galling, what if we know people who *have* been given signs and wonders? Where does that leave us?

Remember the words of Jesus, "Blessed are those who have not seen and have believed." Since it's more important to be blessed than to see signs and wonders, we can take great comfort in continuing in our faith in the absence of visions and miracles.

If I could, would I want to have a vision of Mary?
Do I find it difficult to believe without seeing?

I DON'T NEED SIGNS TO BELIEVE.

Making Diamonds

When you come right down to it, a diamond is nothing more than a piece of coal transformed by enormous pressure. Out of ordinary fuel comes an extraordinary gemstone.

Mary is humanity's perfect diamond. She was made of the same "stuff" as the rest of us, yet out of that ordinary stuff, divine pressure created an extraordinary creation.

While Mary was extraordinary, God doesn't limit transforming pressure to her alone. The same spirit that transformed Mary can transform us as well. When we allow the Spirit of God to enter our hearts and souls, we too can become more than mere flesh and bones. We can become children of God.

There's a catch to all this, however. Just as a piece of coal must be subjected to enormous pressure before its molecular structure is altered into that of a diamond, so too our transformation process requires that we be subjected to what can feel like crushing pressure.

Jesus didn't promise us an easy life here on earth. Time and again, Mary repeats that same warning. We may have to experience great sorrow, loss, pain, hurt, and anguish as we're transformed from one nature to another. When the pressure feels overwhelming, consider which you would rather wear on your finger—a piece of coal or a diamond—and hang in there. The struggles will be worth it in the end.

*Am I ever tempted to give up when life's pressures
seem too great? Do I see my struggles as part of my
transformation into a new creation?*

I KNOW THAT I'M A DIAMOND IN THE MAKING.

Purity

One of Mary's traditional titles is "Virgin Most Pure." Not only was Mary a total and complete virgin, she was the most pure virgin who ever lived.

The fact that Mary was virginal at the birth of Christ has had some interesting practical repercussions for the rest of us. Because of Mary's virginity, some of the greatest teachers in the Church have assumed virginity is a purer state than marriage (at least a consummated marriage).

But purity doesn't hinge on sexual experience or lack thereof. A person can easily be impure without ever having had sex. For instance the French refer to a woman who has engaged in sexual activity up to, but not including, intercourse as "half-virgin." By not "going all the way," she gets to maintain a tenuous claim on virginity, but one would be stretching the truth to call her "pure."

Purity actually refers to living our lives honestly and in accord with our state in life. Someone who is married not only can, but should, express love with his or her spouse through sexual relations. Someone who is single should refrain from using sex as a means of expressing love. Purity is that simple: do what you have been called to do by God at this particular time in your life.

Am I living a pure life according to my particular state?
Do I encourage others to live pure lives,
by my word and example?

I DO MY BEST TO LIVE IN PURITY AND HONESTY.

All in the Name

The Sea of Galilee isn't really a sea. A sea, by the usual definition, is an expanse of salt water surrounding a continent. Since the Sea of Galilee is both landlocked and freshwater, it's actually a lake, although Galilee Lake doesn't sound nearly as poetical as the Sea of Galilee.

Not only is it a lake, it's a not very big lake—only about thirty-two miles in circumference. Yet because of its name, many people think of the Sea of Galilee as a large body of water.

It's all in the name.

Social scientists say that a person's name can have a dramatic effect on his or her future. A Gertrude will never be considered as attractive as a Jennifer, for example. And a Horace is unlikely to rise as far in the corporate world as a Robert.

Mary was named by her parents, but Jesus' name was foretold by the angel Gabriel: "Behold, you will conceive in your womb and bear a son, and you shall name him Jesus." The name *Jesus,* generally believed to mean "God is salvation," refers to the role Mary's son would play in the history of the world. Incidentally, the name *Christ* isn't his last name; it's a title meaning "the anointed one." Jesus' last name, if he had one, would have been something like *Ben Joseph,* meaning "son of Joseph."

Our names, too, can have special meaning. Not the least of which is the fact God calls each of us by our own name.

What does my name mean?
If I could have any name, what would I call myself?

I KNOW THAT GOD CALLS ME BY NAME.

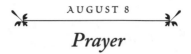

Prayer

Mary is said to have told the seers at Medjugorje, "Always pray before your work and end your work with prayer. If you do that, God will bless you and your work. These days you have been praying too little and working too much. Pray therefore. In prayer you will find rest."

It's one of the great paradoxes of faith that time spent in prayer isn't lost; rather, it's somehow mysteriously returned to us. We find that we can indeed accomplish more in a day hemmed by prayer than we would otherwise.

We have only scanty records regarding Mary's prayer life after the birth of Jesus. Other than allusions to her keeping things in her heart, the only Gospel reference to Mary praying puts her in the Upper Room with the disciples, waiting for the Holy Spirit: "All these devoted themselves with one accord to prayer, together with some women, and Mary the mother of Jesus. . . ." Nevertheless, we know that she had to have been a woman of prayer, because prayer goes hand in hand with holiness.

Sometimes we get the idea that we have to say set prayers, such as the Rosary or the Lord's Prayer, in order to be truly *praying*. But prayer is nothing more than a conversation with God. When we talk with our close friends, the only time we use pat formulas is when we're in a hurry: "How's it going?" "What's happening?" "How are you doing?" The rest of the time we let the conversation go where it will, knowing that what's important isn't the words but the communication itself. Likewise, we don't need to use set prayers with God; we can simply let the conversation flow out of our friendship.

What is my prayer life like?

WHEN I PRAY, I TALK TO GOD FROM MY HEART.

A Mother's Fears

Imagine the scene: Jesus is about two and a half, right at that "helping" age. He wants to go into the workshop and "help Daddy." Joseph looks at Mary for her verdict, and Mary thinks, *Saws! Nails! Splinters! Heavy boards! Dangerous things! My baby!* No matter how much she trusts Joseph to watch out for Jesus, she's a mother, and mothers worry about their children's safety. But she acknowledges her fears and lets Jesus explore and learn in the workshop.

Skip ahead a few years. Jesus is twelve. On the way to Jerusalem for the Passover Feast, he asks his mother if he can "hang out" with the men and other boys on the way, instead of walking with the women and little children. Mary looks at him and thinks, *Bad influences! Dangerous desert! Could get lost! Could get hurt! My baby!* Despite her trepidation, she undoubtedly acknowledges her fears and lets him go. (We won't talk about what she might have said after he lingers behind in the Temple, however.)

Now skip ahead a couple decades. Jesus is thirty-three. He tells his mother that things are getting a bit sticky with the Pharisees, but he has to go to Jerusalem for Passover. She looks at him and thinks, *Dangerous time! Could get hurt! Could get killed! My baby!* But knowing that his destiny awaits him, she acknowledges her fears and lets him go.

We can't protect those we love from the dangers of the world, no matter how much we try. There come times when all we can do is acknowledge our fear and let our loved ones go, just as Mary did.

What's my first reaction when someone I love is in danger?
Do I know when to step in and when to step back?

¶ GIVE THOSE ¶ LOVE THE FREEDOM TO
MAKE THEIR OWN DECISIONS.

Caesar Augustus

Because Mary belongs to all ages, we sometimes overlook the fact that she lived at a specific historical time. What was the world like in which Mary lived?

First and foremost, it was dominated by imperial Rome. Because of the Pax Romana, Roman influence blanketed the entire Mediterranean world. Even the backwater country of Judea had been entwined by Roman tentacles of power. Caesar Augustus, the grandnephew (and adopted son) of Julius Caesar, ruled the empire. Although his influence was great, Augustus ruled only a few provinces in his vast empire directly. One of these was Judea.

At the time of Mary and Jesus, Roman legions were stationed in Sebaste (in Samaria) and Caesarea (on the coast). Although the Jews had a great deal of freedom, Rome appointed the head of the Sanhedrin (the chief Jewish political assembly) and chose the Jewish high priest. In addition, Rome extracted high taxes from the Jewish people, including a land tax, a general tax, and a head tax or tribute. It was for this last tax that Mary and Joseph had to travel to Bethlehem to be counted. ("In those days a decree went out from Caesar Augustus that the whole world should be enrolled.") Caesar Augustus died when Jesus was in his late teens. It was under his son-in-law, Tiberius, that Jesus was sentenced and executed.

Placing Mary in her correct historical period not only helps us picture her more accurately, it also allows us to see how the time in which we live helps to shape our own lives.

What's the most significant historical event I can remember?

I GIVE THANKS FOR THE TIME AND PLACE I WAS BORN.

Role Models

Mary's life is a collage of role models for women in virtually every state of life: daughter, unwed mother, teenage mother, second wife, stepmother, widow, spiritual grandmother. From her own life experience, Mary can identify with the joys and sorrows of the many seasons of a woman's life. While some of the stages are readily apparent—that of a daughter, for instance—others may not be quite as obvious.

Mary was quite young when the angel visited her—perhaps as young as fourteen, by some accounts—which would make her a teenage mother. Since she wasn't married at the time, she would have experienced the stigma of being an unwed mother. People being people, a lot of the neighbors were probably counting the months between the wedding and the birth.

Mary's stature as a second wife is open to conjecture. Many ancient traditions say that Joseph had been married before and Mary was his second wife. If that's indeed the case, the brothers and sisters identified in Scripture could be Jesus' stepsiblings, making Mary their stepmother (with all the ins and outs that stepparenting entails).

Finally, since Joseph died before Mary, she knows what it's like to be a widow; and although she didn't have any grandchildren of her own, she was undoubtedly a spiritual grandmother to the children of Jesus' "brothers" and "sisters" as well as to some of the disciples.

What a comfort to know that no matter what life situation we find ourselves in, Mary not only understands, she's been there before us!

In what ways can I use Mary's example as a model
for the stages of my life?

I REJOICE IN EVERY STEP OF MY LIFE JOURNEY.

Passion

The word *Passion* has a specific theological meaning, referring to the events surrounding Jesus' trial, torture, and Crucifixion. While we usually think of the Passion in connection with Christ, it's also intimately linked with Mary.

On one level, that first Holy Week was the most glorious time of Mary's life, for it was at that point that her response to the angel Gabriel—*"Fiat!"* ("Let it be!")—was finally brought to full fruition. But on a human level, it was the worst time—bar none—she could have imagined.

It started with the Last Supper. Because she was a woman, she probably wasn't in the same room with Jesus during the meal; she would have been in another room with the other women. Even though she wasn't at his side, however, she had to have heard his ominous words: "Now I will no longer be in the world, but they are in the world, while I am coming to you." She must have been concerned when Jesus and the disciples set off for the Garden of Gethsemane. Undoubtedly she waited with the other women, peering into the darkness, looking for Jesus and the others to return. When the disciples came back without Jesus, saying that he'd been arrested and taken to trial, Mary must have been almost overwhelmed by a sick, sinking feeling.

Then came the road to Calvary, the Crucifixion, and Jesus' death. At that moment, it would have been of no consequence to Mary that she had the sure hope of salvation. Her child was dead! Her heart was broken! It's at this point that Mary is most like us— and it's in our greatest sorrow that Mary, our mother, comes the closest to us.

Have I ever thought about what Christ's Passion was like for Mary? Do I assume that because she knew things would turn out fine, it wasn't all that difficult for her?

WHEN I GRIEVE, I ASK MARY FOR HER
UNDERSTANDING AND COMFORT.

Birthdays

In our culture, birthdays are important personal feast days. We give presents, throw parties, and (depending on the particular birthday being commemorated) tease the birthday person unmercifully. It's one time when we allow ourselves to pull out all the stops and have a good time just because.

We don't know the date of Mary's birthday, even though it's traditionally celebrated on September 8. Moreover, it's unlikely that Mary celebrated her birthday in anything resembling modern fashion, since birthdays weren't as important in her time as they are today. In fact, we can't be sure that the average person commemorated birthdays at all. We know that the wealthy did, however: it was at a birthday celebration for Herod that Salome performed the dance which so delighted Herod that he gave her the head of John the Baptist on a platter.

We know that Mary enjoyed celebrations and parties in general because of what the New Testament tells us about the wedding feast at Cana. Clearly Mary knew what it took to have a good time. All too often, we think of religion as serious business. Mary's example at the wedding feast shows us that it's okay to have fun. God is close to us in our tears, but God is also present in our laughter.

Today take a holiday from the serious stuff of religion to celebrate the fun of faith. Rejoice in the creation and rejoice in the day that the Lord hath made!

Am I ever tempted to think that a dour and serious demeanor
is more pleasing to God than celebrations and fun?
If I could celebrate my birthday any way I wanted,
what would I do?

I TAKE EVERY LEGITIMATE OPPORTUNITY TO CELEBRATE.

Marian Devotion

The oldest known Marian prayer is the *Sub Tuum Praesidium,* composed about A.D. 250. In this early prayer, Christians asked Mary for her help and intercession. At a time when many theological nuances were still being hammered out, devotion to Mary was already firmly established. Mary was already seen as mother, virgin, protectress, and interceder for all Christians.

Devotion to Mary has a simplicity and a clarity that transcend theology. It centers on the love of a mother for her children and the confidence of children in the care and concern of a loving mother.

When we find ourselves overwhelmed by the barrage of theological differences and torn between conflicting ideologies, turning to Mary and asking for her help may be the wisest move we could make. At those times, let's pray these words with believers from the early days of the Church:

> We fly to your patronage,
> O holy Mother of God.
> Despise not our petitions in our necessities,
> but deliver us from all dangers,
> O ever-glorious and blessed Virgin.

> *Am I ever tempted to try to think my way to faith?*
> *If I have trouble believing in God's love for me,*
> *can I believe in Mary's?*

WHEN I FEEL PRESSED BY LIFE, I ASK MARY FOR HER HELP.

The Assumption

One of the standard jokes in Roman Catholicism is that the Feast of the Assumption is the day the Church "assumes" Mary was taken body and soul into heaven. While it's true that that's the *assumption* on the Assumption, this feast is more than a recognition of one of Mary's special privileges. It is, in fact, a celebration of the importance of our bodies.

Christian theology teaches us that we'll be reunited with our bodies in the afterlife. (Many of us undoubtedly are looking forward to a new and improved version.) The Assumption of Mary is verification that it isn't just our souls that are important; our bodies have value as well.

Sometimes we're inclined to go to extremes with our bodies. Either we pamper and indulge our physical selves, or we employ harsh discipline to keep our base natures in check, as St. Francis of Assisi did. (To St. Francis's credit, at the end of his life he asked forgiveness of his body, calling it Brother Ass and admitting that he had been overly harsh in his self-mortification.) Both extremes are harmful; rather, we should give our bodies the attention and care they deserve, remembering that moderate discipline is always the goal. After all, we'll be joining up again with those bodies in the next life.

Do I mistreat my body by not feeding it nutritious foods, not giving it proper exercise, or not allowing it enough rest?

I GIVE MY BODY WHAT IT NEEDS TODAY AND EVERY DAY.

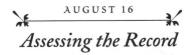

Assessing the Record

"Laughter is the closest thing to the grace of God," according to Karl Barth. If that's true, Mary must have laughed a great deal (although we have no record of her merriment), since she's closer to God's grace than any other person.

Making suppositions about Mary and trying to figure out what she was really like may seem irreverent to some people. Ironically, the stress over that issue arises because Christians believe that everything in the Bible is true. However, there's a big difference between *containing truth* and *containing ALL truth*. If something is in the Scriptures, it's true, yes; but the fact that something *isn't* in the Scriptures doesn't mean that it's necessarily false.

For instance, the Scriptures don't say anything about Mary sleeping, but common sense tells us she had to have slept. They don't mention her diapering the baby Jesus, preparing a meal, going for a walk, talking with Joseph, or going to the market either, but we know that she had to have done those things too, even though the Bible is silent on those topics.

The Bible is the major Christian source of God's direction for humanity. In it God gives us the concepts we need to make sound moral decisions, but God doesn't give us all the detailed information we need to make every single life decision. That's what our intelligence is for. We have to make up our own minds about a good many things, from the mundane (what to have for dinner) to the more complex (whom to marry). It's not that God doesn't care about these things; God cares about *all* our decisions. But God doesn't want us to consult a book when we need guidance. God wants to have an active, creative conversation with us when we formulate our life decisions.

> *Do I ever act as if the Bible were the be-all and end-all*
> *of knowledge? When I need to make a decision, do I*
> *use all the resources God has given me?*

I TREASURE THE BIBLE FOR WHAT IT IS, NOT FOR WHAT IT ISN'T.

Spiritual Shortcuts

Have you ever had a fellow traveler say, "Let's go this way; it looks like a shortcut"? If so, you know that shortcuts seldom work. They end up being longcuts at best, disasters at worst. Mary's message to the world is that there are no shortcuts on the road to heaven. The path is the same as it's been since the beginning of time: prayer, fasting, penance, and faith.

Consider just a few messages attributed to Mary from the seers at Medjugorje:

"Let prayer be your everyday food."

"If you pray and fast, you will obtain everything you ask for."

"Pray, fast, do penance, and help the weak."

"Men must be reconciled with God and with one another. For this to happen, it is necessary to believe, to pray, to fast, and to go to Confession."

While a shortcut may be tempting, it's seldom worth the time it takes to go back and start over (which is what almost inevitably happens!).

When it comes to our journey toward heaven, it's not only best, it's also safest, to take the way that Mary and the saints have pointed out for the past two thousand years. In the long run, it's much faster than any so-called shortcut could ever hope to be.

Am I ever tempted to try an "easier" way to spiritual growth than the way Mary has shown me?

1 SPEND TIME PRAYING, FASTING, AND DOING PENANCE.

A Metaphor for God

A metaphor is a poetic expression that compares or combines two dissimilar things without using the words *like* or *as*. For instance, "the heart is a lonely hunter" is a metaphor. No one thinks that a heart actually is a hunter, lonely or otherwise, but the metaphor helps create an image in our minds that can give us insight into the human heart. The notion of someone in love being solitary in his or her search for the beloved helps us comprehend a bit of the essential nature of love.

In somewhat similar fashion, Mary can be thought of as a metaphor for God. Certainly no one believes that Mary *is* God, but looking at her helps us understand the nature of God and the way God deals with creation.

Let's look at just a couple of examples:

God never forces us to do anything against our free will. God asks us to participate in the divine plan, just as God asked Mary to become the mother of the Messiah. We always have the choice of saying no, just as Mary had that choice.

God never gives us a trial without also giving us a way out. Mary was an unwed mother in a culture where such behavior was potentially punishable by death. God protected her by intervening with Joseph, assuring him that it was acceptable to marry Mary.

When we look at Mary's life, we see God. Can the same be said
about our own lives? In what way does my life reflect
God's goodness? How can I become more like
Mary (and thus more like God)?

I SEE THE FACE OF GOD IN EVERYONE I MEET.

Good Counsel

Mary is sometimes called the Mother of Good Counsel. To put that in more modern parlance, we could call her the Mother of Good Advice. Of all Mary's titles and roles, Giver of Good Advice is one of the most comforting, for who among us doesn't need good advice?

One of the difficulties in asking Mary for help is learning to listen for her answer. As with so many other matters in the spiritual realm, it's difficult to sort out the conflicting voices echoing in our heads. Depending on our childhood experiences, as well as other factors, several different pieces of advice might be playing on our mental radios. Is it Mary we hear, or is it our own mother? Is it the voice of the Mother of Good Counsel or the voice of the Church? Is it Mary or our own desires?

How can we know what advice comes from Mary and what comes from other, perhaps less reliable sources?

First, Mary's advice will always be loving. She'll never tell you to do anything that's destructive to yourself or to others. Second, Mary's counsel will always direct you to a place of greater wholeness and holiness. She'll guide you in ways that allow you to become more authentic, more real, more you. Finally, Mary's wisdom will be surrounded by a feeling of peace and centeredness. If you get a knot in the middle of your stomach trying to follow a bit of advice, you can be certain it didn't come from Mary.

*Is there something troubling me right now that I could use
advice from Mary to resolve? Have I asked Mary
for her help? If not, why not?*

I BELIEVE THAT MARY'S ADVICE IS ALWAYS IN MY BEST INTEREST.

Wisdom

When Mary finally found Jesus in the Temple with the priests, she was astounded by Jesus' wisdom. (What parents wouldn't be, finding their twelve-year-old chatting comfortably with the most learned men of the time!) Still, the most remarkable part of the story isn't Jesus' wisdom but Mary's.

Mary was wise enough not to abdicate her responsibility as a parent just because she had a son who was capable of learned discourse in the Temple. She didn't let Jesus' wisdom cause her own wisdom to falter.

Sometimes we back off from our responsibilities because we lack the confidence to do what God has given us to do. We let our fears get the best of us, and in the process we let wisdom fly out the window.

Mary knew that she was supposed to rear Jesus to manhood. Even though he had more spiritual knowledge than all the Temple priests combined, he couldn't simply rear himself. Mary understood that, so she did what she was supposed to do: see that her son was properly cared for. She had the wisdom to know what her responsibility was—and to do it.

Jesus may have exhibited his spiritual erudition and divine wisdom when he spoke with the priests in the Temple at Jerusalem, but Mary exhibited her maternal wisdom when she made him go home.

Do I believe that God has given me the wisdom I need
to make the right decisions for my life?

I USE MY GOD-GIVEN WISDOM TO MEET MY RESPONSIBILITIES.

Vision Quest

Mary has a vision for the world—a vision she repeats over and over in her appearances. That vision is simple to express but complex to achieve: peace, love, harmony, and belief in her son and his message. Many of the great saints have had a similar vision for humanity. Indeed, anyone who wants to accomplish any lasting good in this world has to have a vision not unlike Mary's.

One of the hallmarks of Native American spirituality is the vision quest. Although the exact activity varies from tribe to tribe, generally a vision quest entails a young person going off alone to spend time in the wilderness awaiting divine revelation and insight. The young man (less often a young woman) endures cold, hunger, exposure, and other hardships until finally the physical loses its hold on the spiritual and the soul is freed to experience new insight. The result is a clarity of understanding and a sense of unity and integrity with all of creation.

Non–Native Americans don't usually go on formal vision quests, but we all need to find our unique vision for life in some way. Like the Native American who goes on a vision quest, we must expect a bit of effort and sacrifice as we attempt to discern our vision. We have to be willing to put our lives on the line—though perhaps not quite as literally as do those who spend days in the wilderness—in order to gain the insight we need. It doesn't just happen; it requires conscious, active work on our part. It's only after we've realized our vision for our own lives that we can begin to share that vision with others.

Have I ever spent time figuring out what my vision is?
Could I go on a vision quest of some sort?

I KNOW WHAT I WANT FOR MYSELF AND THOSE AROUND ME.

The Queenship of Mary

Many people have a good deal of trouble thinking of Mary as Queen of Heaven. Having a queen implies the presence of a king, and a king and a queen seem like a matched set, more or less equal in power and rank. Thus if Jesus is King of Heaven and Mary is Queen of Heaven, it sounds as if Mary is equal to Jesus.

That, of course, is heresy. Mary isn't now—nor can she ever be—equal to Jesus, who is both God and man. While theologians have offered many explanations as to why Mary is Queen of Heaven (including the obvious reason: that the mother of a king is a queen by default), many people still have difficulty with the title, in part because of their misunderstanding of what constitutes a monarch, particularly a "just monarch" in the biblical sense.

In the ancient Middle East, ideal justice wasn't so much laying down the law impartially as it was seeing that help and protection were given to the weakest members of society. Therefore, a just monarch was one who led by example in assisting the poor. Because Mary leads us in understanding our responsibilities to the less fortunate, she acts like a just sovereign in the biblical sense. Ergo, Mary is a queen; and since she's in heaven, she's Queen of Heaven.

In the end, though, it doesn't matter whether or not you think of Mary as Queen of Heaven. What does matter is that you follow her example in caring for those who need your love and attention.

How do I react when I encounter a beggar on the street?
Do I take personal responsibility for helping the needy?

1 REALIZE, WHEN 1 SEE THE POOR AND SUFFERING, THAT "THERE BUT FOR THE GRACE OF GOD GO 1."

Procrastination

Reading between the lines in the Gospel account of the wedding feast at Cana, we can sense that Mary was getting a little impatient with Jesus' reluctance to get on with his mission. It's almost as if she gave him a motherly little push to get a move on.

"Mom, I'm just not ready yet!" Jesus protested.

"Trust me: you are. Now go do something about the wine situation."

There's a time for patience and a time for pushing. Mary seems to have understood the difference and given her son a little push when he was procrastinating.

Sometimes we *all* need a nudge, even if we're Jesus.

Occasionally, though we know what we ought to be doing, we (for whatever reason) fail to get off our duffs and get on with it. Sometimes we procrastinate because we're afraid of failure; other times we procrastinate because we're afraid of success. Still other times we procrastinate just because we procrastinate!

Analyzing the reasons for procrastination can help us figure out how to avoid similar situations in the future, but it does little to eliminate present procrastination. If you're avoiding doing something that you know you should be doing, there's only one cure: get on with it. Come to think of it, Mary said almost the same thing to Jesus!

Is there something I've been putting off doing that I know I
should do*? What's keeping me from "doing it"?*

1 DON'T LET PROCRASTINATION RULE MY LIFE.

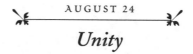

Unity

We know very little about Mary's life in Palestine, and we know even less—in fact, absolutely nothing—about her life in Egypt after she and Joseph escaped Herod's wrath. We don't know where they went, what they did when they got there, or how long they stayed. All we know is that they went to Egypt and stayed there at least until Herod died. (Incidentally, since Herod died in 4 B.C.E., some scholars think that Jesus must have been born sometime around 6 B.C.E.)

During this most hidden time of Mary's life, she was a stranger living in a strange land. How did that experience shape Mary? What insights did it give her?

It's hard to say, but that sojourn as a foreigner had to have had an effect. It's interesting to note that non-Christian Egyptians today have a special devotion to Mary. At Zeitoun, where ancient tradition suggests that the Holy Family stayed during the flight into Egypt, thousands of people are said to have witnessed numerous apparitions of Mary above St. Mary's Coptic Cathedral between 1968 and 1971. In 1986 thousands of others claimed to see the Blessed Virgin inside and above the Church in Damiana.

Mary is claimed to have told the seers at Medjugorje, "Love your Muslim brothers and sisters. Love your Serbian Orthodox brothers and sisters. Love those who govern you."

Mary the Jew, who lived in the land that had enslaved her ancestors, tells us by word and example what St. Paul expressed in his letter to the Galatians: "There is neither Jew nor Greek, there is neither slave nor free person, there is not male and female; for you are all one in Christ Jesus."

Do I harbor secret prejudices?

I BELIEVE THAT ALL PEOPLE ARE EQUAL IN THE SIGHT OF GOD.

Money

In our culture, money makes the world go round. Trying to live without any money at all is well-nigh impossible. Our entire economic system is based on monetary exchange. Yet God says that money is the root of all evil, right?

Well, no. Actually, it's the *love* of money that's the root of all evil. Money itself is neither good nor bad. It's what we do to obtain money and what we do with it after we have it that's good or bad.

Take Mary, for instance. She had money. At the very least, she had a fair amount of gold from the Wise Men, not to mention the frankincense and myrrh. For a time at least, Mary would have had more than enough money, but obviously it had no detrimental effect on her.

Why some people have more money than they could possibly spend and others must struggle in poverty is a mystery. It's tempting to assume that those with the most money are the most blessed by God, but no correlation exists between corporal cash and celestial credit. Some of the most despicable villains the world has ever known haven't wanted for a single thing, while many of the most holy individuals have been poor to the point of destitution (sometimes voluntarily).

Jesus makes it clear that financial prosperity isn't a guarantee of spiritual reward. "Blessed are the poor, for the kingdom of God is theirs." It's not wrong to want the blessing of money, but having money isn't a guarantee of God's blessing.

How important is money in my life?
Do I use money, or do I let money use me?

1 KNOW THAT 1 HAVE ENOUGH TO MEET MY NEEDS.

Fear

Many of the messages attributed to Mary in her appearances have a distinctly apocalyptic flavor. They refer to the end-times and the final judgment, with vivid visions of hell and purgatory. They talk about the devil's torments and catastrophic events that will befall the earth. They contain secret messages that only the seers can know.

Little wonder that along with inspiring devotion, Mary's appearances often produce a sense of fear. Hints of awful things that could be just around the corner naturally make people afraid. For some people, the fear translates into life-transforming action; they begin to reform their lives by praying more, fasting, doing good works, and turning to God. For others, however, fear gets the upper hand; they're terrified into inertia.

If you're the kind of person who's inspired by Mary's messages, then by all means read and reflect on them. If, however, you're the sort who becomes overwhelmed by terror when you read about upcoming chastisements, don't spend your time dwelling on them. Read them if you must, but then put them aside and get on with your life.

Mary wants us to reform our lives and turn our hearts to her son. She doesn't want us to sit around, scared to death of future events. Her messages are meant to encourage us to virtue. If they have the opposite effect on someone, then maybe they aren't meant for him or her.

When I read what some of the seers claim Mary has said, how
does it make me feel? Am I encouraged or scared to death?

I ALLOW GOD TO SPEAK TO ME IN THE WAYS GOD
KNOWS ARE BEST FOR ME.

Wrinkles

It's interesting that facial wrinkles appear to be hard and harsh, but when you touch them, they're very soft. A natural reaction to age and exposure, they add depth and character to a face. A young, unblemished face has a kind of ethereal beauty, but an older face has character written in every line. Consider Mother Teresa of Calcutta, for example. Her life of love and sacrifice is clearly shown in the lines on her brow and cheeks.

Although most paintings and statues of the Blessed Virgin show her as wrinkle-free, they can't be accurate depictions of the older Mary. Living in the Middle East, being exposed to the weather, going through the sorrows and tribulations she had to face, Mary would have had her share of wrinkles. Her life would have been recorded on her face, just as Mother Teresa's is on hers.

Although we can't decide what kind of wrinkles we're going to get, the choices we make affect the lines on our faces. If we scowl and frown, we get different lines than if we laugh and smile. Not all of Mary's wrinkles would have been caused by pain and sadness. Surely she would have had laugh lines at the corners of her eyes and mouth as well. Since most of us will get at least some wrinkles during our lives, let's make sure a portion of them are created by joy!

What kind of wrinkles am I developing?
What life-events show on my face?

† LET JOY AS WELL AS SORROW REGISTER ON MY FACE.

Patience

One virtue we all must learn to cultivate is patience. Mary is no exception. She had to have patience while waiting for Joseph to find out about her pregnancy, she had to have patience while they lived in Egypt, she had to have patience as she and Joseph searched for three days for their son, she had to have lots of patience waiting for him to do something about being the Messiah, she had to be patient until the Resurrection, and now she has to be patient for the end of time.

There's no reason to suppose Mary is naturally any more patient than the rest of us since patience involves waiting and waiting is no fun, especially when we don't know what we are waiting for or we suspect we won't like what happens at the end of the wait.

We often want to hurry things along, to skip ahead to the last chapter of the book of life. But we can't. We have to allow time to unfold at its own pace. We have to trust God is with us as we wait and one day all the waiting will make sense.

Along with Mary, we have to learn to have patience.

Am I a patient or impatient person?
How do I feel when my patience is sorely tried?

I PRACTICE PATIENCE THROUGHOUT MY DAILY LIFE.

The Right Questions

One of the truisms of a successful business is that to get the right answers, you have to ask the right questions. Once you've asked the right questions, the right answers are often obvious. (Warning: the right answers aren't necessarily the answers you want. There can be a big difference between what you *want* to hear and what you *need* to hear!)

Figuring out what questions we need to ask can be difficult. We get muddled by trying to anticipate answers, by trying to manipulate responses, and by allowing preconceived notions to influence our thinking.

Despite the paucity of dialogue given in the Gospels, it's clear that Mary's questions were always right to the point. She asked the questions that got her the answers she needed. For instance, she asked Gabriel, "How am I going to have a baby if I haven't had sex?" When she found Jesus in the Temple, she asked, "What are you doing here? Didn't you know we'd be worried?" She didn't meander around the point. She asked directly and got direct answers: "You'll have a baby because God is going to make it happen"; "I'm doing my Father's business."

Although she might not have liked the answers she received, and she might not have understood all their implications, Mary at least *got* answers—and it was because she asked the right questions. Like her, we need to learn to ask the questions that will give us the answers we need.

How good am I at asking direct questions? Do I ever try
to phrase questions in such a way that I'll get
the answers I think I want to hear?

I'M NOT AFRAID TO HEAR THE ANSWER TO ANY HONEST QUESTION.

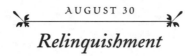

Relinquishment

The verb *relinquish* sounds as if it means to give up, to let go, to stop caring. In reality, however, relinquishment is empowering. Once we relinquish the need to be in control, to be right, to be in charge, we open the gates for God's grace to take over.

Mary relinquished control over her life when she said, "May it be done to me according to your word." Despite that relinquishment, she didn't roll over, give up, hide in the back room, or meekly await the consequences. She continued to take charge of her life, although she realized that God was now in ultimate control. She went to Elizabeth's. (There's no indication that she asked anyone's permission to go; she just packed her bags and went.) She married Joseph. She had her baby. She lived her life fully, completely, and authentically—despite the fact that she'd relinquished control to God.

We can do the same thing. We can let God have ultimate control while still living an empowered life. While it's possible, no one's saying it's easy. We have to be willing to go places we never expected to go; we have to be willing to change our direction at a moment's notice; we have to be willing to give up cherished ideals in order to make room for new goals.

If you're feeling as if God isn't answering your prayers, perhaps it's because you're still trying to tell God the way things should be, instead of letting God lead you on the paths God knows are right for you. Perhaps it's because you're *retaining* control instead of *relinquishing* it to God.

> *Do I feel as if God is answering my prayers right now?*
> *Am I giving God room to work in my life?*

I HAND OVER MY LIFE TO GOD, TRUSTING THAT GOD
WILL GIVE ME ONLY GOOD.

The Future

When the prophet Simeon told Mary, on the occasion of Jesus' Presentation in the Temple, what the future would hold, it's little wonder that she and Joseph were amazed. Most of us would be amazed if someone told us our future with such conviction and authority.

Most of us think we'd like to have a glimpse into the future. That's one reason psychic readers, Tarot cards, crystal balls, and fortune tellers have been in demand for thousands of years. We figure that if we could just get a little peek into the future, we'd be better prepared to deal with it.

Not true. To know the future is a burden. To know what will happen tomorrow robs today of its joys. In fact, it's a good thing most of us *don't* know the future or we wouldn't be willing to go through with it. Looking ahead, we'd think we didn't have the strength to go through with the difficulties and pain. Yet most trouble is a bit like a distant storm. On the horizon the clouds look impenetrably black, but when the storm is directly overhead, generally there are glimmers of silver and patches of lighter gray. Likewise, to see future trouble is to see only the darkest aspects. Once the trouble actually arrives, we almost always have the strength and ability to cope.

Mary was given a glimpse of what lay ahead in life by Simeon. Likewise, we occasionally get brief insights into our future. When that happens, we should ponder those insights in our heart, as Mary did, but not let them preoccupy our present.

Have I ever had an insight into the future?
How did it make me feel? If I could choose to see
the future, would I make that choice?

I'M WILLING TO LIVE ONE DAY AT A TIME.

Nothing Too Small

Jesus' actions at the wedding feast at Cana prove that nothing in our lives is too small for God's attention and concern. Jesus objected to Mary's request that he deal with the shortage of wine not because he thought running out of wine—a major faux pas—was unimportant, but because it wasn't yet time for him to reveal his power and his mission. He wasn't being asked to do something he was *unwilling* to do; he was being asked to do something before he was ready to do it.

Nothing in our lives is too small or insignificant to bring to God. Even those things that we think aren't significant enough to bother the Creator of the universe with are important to God. God isn't just the Mighty One; God is also our loving parent, who wants us to share all the intimate moments of our lives. God wants us to ask about everyday things (such as keeping face at a social event) as well as extraordinary things (such as medical healings).

Often it's hard to believe that God cares about us as individuals. It's easy enough to think that God cares about the *big* things—war, injustice, hunger, poverty, and so on. But wine at a wedding? Our common sense says, "Oh, come on. God doesn't have time to be bothered with piddly little things like that."

But God *does* have time—all of eternity, to be exact. And God cares deeply about each one of us. As our parent, God wants us to live an abundant and blessed life, but God can't give us all the joys awaiting us unless we approach saying, "We have no wine."

Do I tell God all the details of my life, or do I save
my prayers for special occasions?

I BELIEVE THAT GOD CARES ABOUT ME AND THE DETAILS OF MY LIFE.

Old Age

What we know about Mary could fit in a thimble. What we *don't* know about Mary could fill a reservoir. One of the many things we don't know is how old Mary was when she died. Some accounts say she died a few years after Jesus; others say she died as many as twenty-five years later, but we don't know for sure. We do know, however, that she achieved old age, at least by standards of the time.

In other times and cultures, old age has been revered for its wisdom, endurance, and strength. In our culture, on the other hand, old age is the enemy. We do all we can to escape it—if not actually, at least outwardly, through cosmetic surgery and exercise. But no matter how much we try to ignore our own aging, we can't prevent the passage of years. A trim, tucked, tanned seventy-five-year-old body is still a seventy-five-year-old body.

Rather than trying to deny and defy age, perhaps the wiser course is to learn to celebrate it. Despite its obvious drawbacks, growing older has a few advantages over youth—among them, the wisdom that comes from experience, a decreasing concern with what people think (and an increasing concern with what God thinks), and the ability to *be* instead of always having to *do*.

Since none of us has any alternative to growing older, let's look to those who have aged well—such as Mary—as an example for the journey.

Do I fear being old? How old do I think "old" is?

I'M AT THE PERFECT AGE FOR ME.

Tangible Love

Just before Jesus began his public work, he headed out into the desert for forty days of prayer and fasting. When he told his mother his plans, did she try to pack him a little something to tide him over? Maybe a loaf or two of bread or a skin of goat's milk?

Even though Mary and Jesus are now seen as co-workers for a common good, Jesus was still Mary's kid—and she must have behaved toward him as moms usually do toward their sons. She must have occasionally pampered him, fixed his favorite foods, packed him a lunch for the desert. Like any good mother, she must have let him know how much she loved him by doing things for him.

We put a great deal of emphasis on the words "I love you," but it isn't enough to *tell* the people we love that we love them; we have to *show* them as well. We have to make our love tangible.

When it comes to love, the old axiom "Actions speak louder than words" is all too true. A person who belittles or abuses another, then tries to smooth things over by saying, "But you know I love you," is a liar. Love is more than words. It is also action.

What do I do for those I love? Is there something tangible
I could do today for someone I love?

1 SHOW MY LOVE IN CONCRETE WAYS.

The Rosary

Of all the devotions associated with Mary, the most famous is the Rosary. Legend has it that Mary gave the Rosary to St. Dominic. Although St. Dominic and his followers are certainly responsible for the promulgation of the prayer, its origins extend beyond that group.

In part, the Rosary developed out of the monastic practice of praying the Psalms each day. The educated brothers would read Scripture, and the illiterate brothers would say 150 Our Fathers (which explains why Rosary beads are sometimes called *Pater Noster*—or Our Father—beads). Somewhere along the line, the Our Fathers were replaced by Hail Marys. The "mysteries" or meditations associated with the Rosary seem to have developed out of a number of medieval devotions to Our Lady, although (with the exception of the Assumption and the Coronation of Mary in the final set of "glorious" mysteries) they have their origins in the events of Scripture.

Regardless of its beginnings, the Rosary is one of the favorite prayers of the Roman Catholic Church. Clergy and laity alike have found sublime comfort in it. Its repetitive nature offers an entrée into meditative prayer, and its dual emphasis on the life of Christ and devotion to Mary provides an introduction to scriptural events.

Moreover, it's one prayer you can say virtually any time and any place, with no more specialized equipment than your own fingers. Even if you think you don't like praying the Rosary, try giving it another chance. Along with Pope John Paul II, you may discover that it "introduces us into the very heart of faith."

What's my favorite form of prayer? Am I willing to try other types of prayer, even if they feel a bit odd at times?

¶ TRY DIFFERENT FORMS OF PRAYER.

Hyperdulia

According to Catholic theology, there are three different kinds of respect: *dulia*, *hyperdulia*, and *latria*. The first is the respect given to angels and saints, the second is the respect given to Mary, and the third is the respect reserved for God alone.

The terms themselves aren't all that important, but the concepts are. The honor we accord to Mary is unique, because she's unique in the history of humanity. As the *Theotokos*, or "God-bearer," she gave human life to Jesus. For that reason, if for none other, she's honored above all the other saints and holy men and women.

However, we must be careful not to allow *hyperdulia* to slip into *latria*. In other words, we have to make sure that the honor we rightfully accord to Mary doesn't infringe on the worship belonging to God alone.

Worshiping Mary is tempting. For one thing, Mary seems much more approachable than God. We sometimes think that she understands us and our needs more easily than God, who can seem remote and distant. Additionally, since she's a mother, we may feel more confident coming to her with our problems: a mother will, after all, love us no matter what.

However, when we fall into the trap of worshiping Mary, we do both her and God a disservice. Mary deserves our highest respect (*hyperdulia*), but she doesn't want, nor can she accept, our worship. She will, however, always join us in worshiping God—which is even more rewarding than worshiping her.

How do I envision God?
Am I ever tempted to pray to Mary instead of to God?

I HONOR THE SAINTS, I HIGHLY HONOR MARY,
AND I WORSHIP GOD ALONE.

Practicality

So many of the verbal and physical portraits of Mary depict her as a wimp. From the wide-eyed teen serenely smiling at Gabriel to the insipidly docile woman standing at the foot of the cross (a single tear gleaming on her cheek), Mary rarely comes across as being strong, forceful, or practical.

Yet Mary was all of those things. Just look at what she said to Gabriel: "How is this pregnancy going to happen, since I haven't had sex?" Now that's the question of a woman who isn't intimidated by anyone or anything—even an angel. And take the wedding feast at Cana. Many women, if told off by a son as Mary was would crumple into a self-pitying heap. Not Mary. She figured Jesus would come around to her way of thinking, so she went ahead and laid the groundwork for changing the water to wine.

Being holy doesn't exempt a person from the need for practicality. Look at Mother Teresa of Calcutta. The entire world recognizes her as a saint, yet she's eminently practical. Her life's work includes praying for the sick and dying, but it also encompasses tending to their physical needs of bathing, clothing, housing, and healing. If Mother Teresa is capable of combining great holiness and great practicality, surely Mary was as well.

Do I see religion as practical or merely spiritual?
How can I put my faith to practical use right now?

'I VALUE MY PRACTICAL SIDE.

Weddings

At first glance, it seems a bit odd that Jesus' first miracle was performed at a wedding feast. Wouldn't a cure have been more appropriate, since he spent much of his public ministry healing the sick? But no, his first miracle was a sign of sheer joy at that most joyous of occasions—a wedding. He turned ordinary water into wine so that the celebration could continue.

Of course, we can't overlook the fact that he performed the miracle at his mother's request. And that brings to mind one of the lingering questions about the miracle: Why was Mary involved? There are a few possibilities. Maybe she was a bit of a busybody who just happened to notice the situation (though that seems totally out of character). Maybe she was related to the bride or groom, who informed her of the situation (a scenario that's certainly possible). Maybe Mary had a special interest in weddings because she didn't get much of one herself (having been at least three months pregnant at the time she married Joseph, which made a big event inappropriate). Or maybe she herself was putting on the wedding for one of the "brothers" or "sisters" of Jesus who are mentioned in the Gospels.

Whatever the reason, Mary took a special interest in the celebration and insisted that Jesus do the same. In "encouraging" him to perform his first miracle at a wedding celebration, Mary made sure we had concrete proof that every detail of our lives has merit in the sight of God. In addition, she showed us that she's willing—and able—to ask her son for favors on our behalf. We have only to ask.

Do I let Mary know when the wine in my life is running out?

I BELIEVE THAT MARY WILL INTERCEDE
ON MY BEHALF IF I ASK HER TO.

The Birth of Mary

Although no one knows for certain when Mary was born, her birthday is traditionally celebrated on September 8. This date was chosen simply because it's nine months after the feast of the Immaculate Conception—the celebration of Mary's own conception. Similarly, the date of the Annunciation is placed nine months before Christmas. (Incidentally, we're fairly certain that Jesus' actual birthday wasn't December 25, because Christian Scriptures say that the shepherds were in the fields. Through other historical records, we know that shepherds spent the night in the fields only during the spring and fall, certainly not in midwinter.)

According to legend, Mary's parents were Anna and Joachim; her father was an official at the Temple at Jerusalem. It's believed that they'd been married about twenty years when an angel appeared to them, telling them that they'd have a daughter whose entire life would be dedicated to God.

The legend goes on to say that Mary lived and studied at the Temple from the time she was three until she was fourteen. At that point, she moved back to Nazareth with her parents, who arranged for her to marry Joseph, the carpenter.

The legend is lovely, but it's *only* legend. Despite a multitude of private revelations about Mary's birth and childhood, we know for certain only what Scripture tells us—and that's almost nothing.

If the legend and private revelations help you appreciate Mary more fully, feel free to enjoy them. If, however, they seem too difficult to believe, stick to the Mary we know from Scripture and let the legend be.

What do I recall most vividly from my childhood?
What do I appreciate most about my growing-up years?

I LEAVE THE PAST IN THE PAST AND GO ON FROM TODAY.

Romancing Mary

Mary's life-story has been romanced almost beyond imagination. In fact, almost all the life has been romanced out of it.

Yes, she had her baby in a stable, but it was the cleanest, tidiest stable you could ever hope to set foot in, with the nicest, sweetest animals you could possibly envision. And yes, a bunch of shepherds visited her right after the birth, but they all took showers and used deodorant before they came in. And yes, she had to flee to Egypt to escape Herod's death threats, but since she and her family came back safely, it must not have been that big a deal. And yes, she lost Jesus in the Temple, but since she found him, all's well that ends well. And yes, Jesus did die on the cross, but he rose from the dead—so what's the fuss all about?

With a few cleansing swipes, we eliminate all of the grit of Mary's life, making it into a romance. But it *wasn't* romantic, as the Dominican priest Edward Schillebeeckx points out:

> Her life does not follow the pattern of a fairy tale, like that of Snow White. No little forest birds hold her clothes in their beaks and carry her away out of the reach of danger to the accompaniment of sweet, heavenly music. If this were so, she would not be an example of strength for us in our day-to-day struggles with the harsh realities of a life which is anything but a fairy tale. . . . [Sh]e showed us, by her example, how faith in the mystery of the living God is stronger than human life; stronger, too, than death—even the death of her own Messiah.

Do I ever wish that my life were more like a fairy tale?
Am I envious of those whose lives seem easier than my own?

I'M GRATEFUL FOR THE CHALLENGES IN MY LIFE.

A Feminine Face

In recent years, devotion to the Blessed Virgin has taken an upturn. It's really not surprising: the more stern, the more wrathful, the more distant God seems; the more fearful, the more frightening, the more unpredictable the world seems; the more people—even Protestants—turn to Mary. Forrest Church, a Unitarian pastor, says this of Mary: "She lends the idea of God a feminine face and makes the idea more available, less exclusionary."

Despite debate (even dispute) over the Catholic Church's Marian dogma, Mary herself has a universal appeal. Every age has emphasized and taken comfort from some aspect of Mary. Sometimes she's been seen as a submissive maid who allowed God to do whatever God wanted with her. Other times she's been seen as a bold prefeminist who made her own decisions. Even today there's no unanimity: for some of us, Mary is a frail wisp of a girl; for others, she's a robust peasant woman. No matter how Mary is envisioned, one fact remains—she allows us to put a feminine face on faith.

In Christianity, with its strongly masculine images of God the Father and Jesus the Son dominating the theological landscape, Mary provides a softening touch. Whereas God the Father is seen as Creator/Judge and Jesus as Redeemer/King, Mary is the humble mother who comforts her children and wipes away their tears.

Moreover, in her sublime humanity, Mary shows all of us what it's like to live an authentic, holy, and whole life. In Mary, doctrine, dogma, and division are erased by a mother's embrace.

How would I describe Mary? Can I apply any of the
characteristics I ascribe to her to my own life?
Do I want to apply them to myself?

I SEE GOD WHEN I LOOK AT MARY.

Opportunity

If we humans had been given the job of setting up the world, we'd probably have done a number of things differently. One thing we might have changed is the way so many opportunities come disguised as problems. We'd make opportunities more, well, *opportune*.

Like it or not, in the world as God designed it, opportunities are often cloaked under the mantle of problems. One of the lessons Mary teaches us, both in her life and in her appearances, is that every problem provides an opportunity to trust in God's solution.

Because we have limited insight, we tend to be limited in our ability to see potential solutions to any given problem. Say, for instance, that you're in debt. The solution seems clear: getting a raise. Losing your job definitely seems *counter*productive. But let's say you *do* lose your job. What does that mean in terms of your problem? How can the problem be turned into an opportunity?

Well, maybe God has another job waiting for you. Maybe you're meant to use your new free time to create a dept-payback program. Or maybe the solution is something else entirely—something that God reveals to you once you're unemployed but that wouldn't have occurred to you had you stayed in the security of your old job.

If you're feeling bogged down or trapped, don't restrict yourself to your own solutions; turn the "opportunity" over to God and see what creative action emerges!

What am I worried about today?
Have I asked God to help me find a solution?

1 LOOK BEYOND MY PROBLEMS TO SEE THE SOLUTIONS.

Devotion

We can't live without a little salt in our diet; however, too much salt can kill. Salt is also an excellent preservative, if not used in excess.

Religious devotion is a lot like salt. Without some devotional practices, we can't live spiritually, but if we spend too much time on devotions and not enough on our responsibilities, we can poison our whole life. For instance, a mother who prays the Rosary all day and neglects her children isn't racking up heavenly points; a father who races from one shrine to the next while allowing his business to suffer and his family to go into debt isn't meriting graces.

The key is to choose one or two devotional practices and let them become a sprinkling of salt in our spiritual life, rather than the basis of our entire diet. As St. Frances of Rome, who lived in the fifteenth century, said, "It is most laudable in a married woman to be devout, but she must never forget that she's a housewife. And sometimes she must leave God at the altar to find Him in her house-keeping." St. Frances apparently practiced what she preached. Her biographers report that on one occasion, when she was reading the office of the Blessed Virgin, she was interrupted four times by household duties. When she finally returned to her prayers, the words were written in gold!

What devotional practices are important to me?
How much time do I spend on them?
Is it enough or more than enough?

I HAVE BALANCE IN ALL ASPECTS OF MY LIFE.

Unconditional Love

We all long to be loved completely, totally, and unconditionally, but if we look for such love from other human beings, we're bound to be disappointed. No human is capable of loving unconditionally—not even Mary. Unconditional love is the prerogative of God; only the God who is complete love can love completely.

Mary comes as close to loving unconditionally as any of us can hope to come, however. Because she's so completely filled with God, she mirrors God's love as completely as any human being ever could. In other words, her love is as close to God's love as is humanly possible. In fact, that's what Mary encourages from each of us: striving to love as God loves, to love without conditions.

What does loving unconditionally mean? That's a tough question. It's almost easier to say what it *doesn't* mean. It doesn't mean tolerating all behaviors. It doesn't mean allowing others to walk roughshod over us. It doesn't mean giving up our selves in order to give to others.

Loving unconditionally means not saying, "I'll love you *if*. . ." It means giving our love without expecting any payment in return. When we love for the sake of loving (not for what we might get out of it), when we love because we can do no other—then we approximate God's unconditional love.

What do I expect from the people I love?
What do the people I love expect from me?

I KNOW THAT I'M LOVED UNCONDITIONALLY BY GOD.

Smother Love

The difference between mother love and smother love is the difference between buying children new shoes as their feet grow and binding their feet so tightly that they can't grow.

What does mothering really entail? Basically, it's determining the line between letting go and hanging on. While babies are in the womb, mothers have no choice but to allow their children to grow at their own speed. After all, a mother doesn't *grow* a baby. Nothing a mother does can speed up cell division or fetal development. A mother can provide a safe environment for the baby—one unpolluted by drugs, alcohol, and other dangers—but she must leave the actual growing up to her child (though many a mother, near the end of the nine months, would be willing to do almost anything to hurry up a baby's growth!).

The same is true once the baby leaves the womb. It's a mother's job to provide a safe environment for growth, but it's up to a child to do the growing him- or herself—and not just physically, but mentally and emotionally as well. When a mother tries to take over the growth process, mother love becomes smother love—and a child suffocates or dies instead of developing.

Mary obviously understood her role, or else we wouldn't have been told that "Jesus advanced [in] wisdom and age and favor before God and man." Mary understood that her role was to mother Jesus, not to smother him.

Was I mothered or smothered when I was growing up?
How can I be a good mother to those who are
literally or spiritually my children?

I KNOW THE DIFFERENCE BETWEEN MOTHERING AND SMOTHERING.

Our Lady of Sorrows

We know that Mary had many sorrows in her life, but why was she sorrowful if she knew that everything would turn out fine in the end? Why didn't she just adopt *Hakuna matata* as her mantra and sail through her struggles, Pollyanna-confident that all would be okay?

Well, she probably *didn't* know that it would be okay. Today, in heaven, she knows what the future holds; but when she was living on earth, she didn't have that gift. Like us, she had to walk in faith rather than certainty.

It's always easy to look back and see God's protective hand guiding our lives, but at the time we're going through struggles, it's not so easy. In fact, sometimes it's well-nigh impossible. God has promised always to answer our prayers, but when we've asked and asked and gotten the opposite of what we were begging for, it's mighty difficult to trust that promise.

What's true for us is also true for Mary. She had been promised that her son would be the Messiah, but at Calvary, the promise paled before the cross. On that hill, she saw only her child—beaten, bruised, defiled. Gabriel and his promise might as well have been a dream, for all she cared at the moment.

Knowing that Mary had to summon courage when doubt loomed large should encourage us to do the same. It isn't easy for us, but then it wasn't easy for Mary either.

Do I assume that everyone else has an easier time
believing than I do?

I HAVE THE COURAGE I NEED TO BANISH DOUBT.

Secrets

To keep your secret is wisdom; but to expect
others to keep it is folly.
SAMUEL JOHNSON

Can you keep a secret? Most of the time, despite our best intentions, a secret burns its way to our lips. Then, of course, it's no secret, for a secret revealed (even once) is a secret no longer.

Secrets have a special fascination for us, and the secrets surrounding Mary are among the most fascinating of all. In most, if not all, of her appearances, she's said to have given the seer (or seers) certain secrets. The seers at Medjugorje, for instance, have said that each was given ten secrets. Some of these secrets were personal and private; others were designed for public revelation at a specific time.

The most famous Marian secret is the Third Secret of Fatima, which is widely believed to contain specific predictions about the end of the world, although only the seer and the pope, who was given a written version by the seer, know for sure.

Trying to figure out the secrets Mary has disclosed to seers is, to put it bluntly, a waste of time. Any speculation is just that—*speculation.* Until and unless the seers reveal the contents, the secrets aren't our business. We've been given all the information we need to live worthy lives, and any facts contained in the secrets would only confirm the knowledge we've already received. If they purport to give a *new* direction, then they're not only secret but also false, for God reveals truth to all who seek with an open heart and mind.

Do the secrets Mary has given the seers
intrigue me or frighten me?

I KEEP THE SECRETS THAT I'VE BEEN TOLD.

Keeping Your Mouth Shut

If wisdom is the better part of valor, then sometimes silence is the better part of wisdom. Mary must have known that, because she let God and an angel reveal her pregnancy to Joseph. She didn't try to explain her situation; she kept her mouth shut and let God handle things.

How often do we get into trouble because we don't have enough sense to keep quiet when we should? When we say something we regret, we often frantically scramble to pull our words back the second they're out of our mouths. But a word once spoken can never be retracted. It can be mitigated or spoken over but never taken back.

Rather than placing ourselves in situations where we have to eat our words, it's far better not to serve them up in the first place. Before you say anything to anybody today, take a few seconds to engage your brain before your tongue. Consider the consequences of your words: Will they hurt the person who hears them? Will they be damaging in any way? Are they truthful? Are they loving?

If the pit of your stomach tells you that you should keep still, then keep still. However, silence isn't *always* the best policy. To remain mute in the face of injustice is just as wrong as it is to speak out unthinkingly. If you feel strongly that you *should* speak out, then speak. But if you feel strongly that you *shouldn't* speak out, then keep your mouth shut.

Am I willing to take a stand for things I believe in?
Do I choose my words with care?

I TRUST MY INSTINCTS REGARDING WHEN TO SPEAK
AND WHEN TO KEEP SILENT.

Rejection

We've all experienced the pain of rejection. Not making the team. Not getting the job. Being dumped in a relationship. There's no point pretending rejection is fun. It isn't. It hurts—sometimes unbelievably so.

To think that Mary never experienced rejection is unrealistic. In fact, a superficial reading of the Gospel of Matthew would lead us to believe that Jesus rejected her on one occasion:

> While he was still speaking to the crowds, his mother and his brothers appeared outside, wishing to speak with him. [Someone told him, "Your mother and your brothers are standing outside, asking to speak with you."] But he said in reply to the one who told him, "Who is my mother? Who are my brothers?" And stretching out his hand toward his disciples, he said, "Here are my mother and my brothers. For whoever does the will of my heavenly Father is my brother, and sister, and mother."

No matter that Jesus was trying to make a point; his words still must have stung Mary. We aren't told what Mary did after Jesus made his comment, but she apparently didn't stomp off in a huff. She kept on trying to comprehend what Jesus was doing and why he was doing it.

The way Mary handled this apparent rejection says as much about her as it does about the kinship rules of heaven. Jesus teaches us a lesson in his words to the crowd, but Mary instructs us in her behavior.

Have I forgiven those who've rejected me in the past?

I DON'T LET REJECTION DESTROY ME OR MY SELF-ESTEEM.

Honesty

Being honest can be hard. Not the kind of honesty that returns an overpayment at the store or files accurate income-tax returns. *That* brand of honesty is relatively easy. In fact, it's often easier to be honest in such situations than it would be to cheat.

The most difficult honesty is self-honesty.

Mary was bluntly honest with herself. While we might think that her self-description to Elizabeth—"All ages will call me blessed"—sounds boastful, we must remember that honesty acknowledges good as well as bad, success as well as failure. False humility has no more place in real honesty than does misplaced arrogance.

Being honest with ourselves is difficult, because it demands that we see the truth. It forces us to see ourselves without the masks of self-deception and self-delusion. It insists that we strip away the old varnish of life to see the naked wood beneath.

When we look at ourselves honestly, we sometimes learn things we'd rather not know. Maybe we discover that we're made of knotty pine instead of oak. Maybe we realize that the blows life has dealt us aren't just marks on the surface but gouges marring our very being.

Moreover, being honest usually means that we have to make changes in our lives. We have to put on a new finish, so to speak.

That's the downside of personal honesty. But there's also an upside: through self-honesty we can become more authentic, holier people. Like an old piece of lovingly refinished and refurbished furniture, we're able to become a treasure in one of the mansions of heaven.

Have I ever made an objective inventory of both my good
qualities and my faults? Am I willing to take a look
at myself and see who I really am?

I'M WILLING TO BE HONEST WITH MYSELF, BECAUSE I KNOW
THAT SELF-KNOWLEDGE IS NECESSARY FOR GROWTH.

The Whole Story

We seldom know the whole story behind events, but that doesn't stop most of us from thinking that we know exactly what's going on. Consequently, we feel perfectly comfortable judging other people.

Consider Mary for a moment. When she returned from Elizabeth's house, her neighbors must have noticed that she'd put on a bit of weight around the middle. They probably assumed that she'd had a little affair on the side while she was visiting her cousin. Tongues must have danced as people speculated about what Joseph was going to do, who the father was, and what punishment Mary would have to suffer. Although they thought they had the whole story figured out, they couldn't have been more wrong if they'd tried.

If you see someone in an unexplained situation, do you automatically think the worst? If, for instance, you see a friend in a close tête-à-tête with a man who isn't her husband, what pops into your mind? They're having an affair, perhaps? They might be, of course, but they could equally well be planning her husband's surprise birthday party. Alternatively, they could be relatives or just good friends. The point is this: until you know the whole story, don't judge.

In fact, even if you *do* know the whole story, be careful about judging. After all, Jesus said, "Stop judging, that you may not be judged. For as you judge, so will you be judged, and the measure with which you measure will be measured out to you."

Have I ever been judged unfairly? What was my reaction?
Have I ever judged someone else and later found
out I was gravely mistaken?

I DON'T JUDGE OTHERS. PERIOD.

Speaking Truth in Love

Honesty may be the best policy, but when you speak the truth, speak it in love. That's what Mary always does in her appearances. Despite the firmness of her messages, they are always bound round with love. She urges us to repent because the time is drawing short and punishment awaits those who don't reform, but she also emphasizes how much God loves us and reminds us that God desires each of us to live abundantly and joyfully.

Mary comes to us as God's messenger of truth. She tells us what we need to hear, but realizing that the truth can sometimes be hard to take, she envelops it in love. She seeks not to force us into obedience but to exhort us to become the best we can be. She knows that we aren't perfect, but she keeps encouraging us to try and try again. Even as she points out our faults, she also reminds us of our potential. We hear her words of warning, but because they come packaged with love, we obey out of a desire to please rather than a fear of punishment.

When we have to correct or advise another, let's strive to emulate Mary. May we always speak the truth, but may we also be careful to present the truth in a way that builds trust, confidence, and the desire to change.

How do I react when someone tells me an unpleasant truth?

I TELL THE TRUTH, BUT I DO SO WITH CARE.

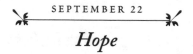

Hope

We don't use the word *hope* correctly, for the most part. We tend to employ it as a synonym for *wish*. If someone says, for instance, that he hopes he'll win the lottery, what he's really saying is that he *wishes* he'd win the lottery.

Hope has a quality of expectancy that wishing doesn't. Hope sees with the eyes of faith, while wishing sees mainly with the eyes of desire. Hope is confident that all *shall* be well, while wishing is desperate that all *will* be well.

Mary didn't wish; she hoped. In her great prayer, she said, "The Mighty One has done great things for me, and holy is his name." At the time she said this, the "great things" hadn't yet happened. All that had occurred was that Mary was pregnant without the knowledge of her husband-to-be—hardly what we'd call a "great thing." Moreover, the initial fulfillment of Gabriel's prophecies for her unborn son was three decades in the future, with the final fulfillment thousands of years in the future. Yet Mary was able to give thanks, even for what hadn't yet happened, because she had hope in God. In giving thanks prior to seeing results, Mary cooperated in the fulfillment of the things she hoped for.

It's odd, but true: when we have confident hope in God's ability to give us what we desire, we make it possible for God to give us that very thing.

> *What am I hoping for right now that I can begin
> to thank God for in advance of its fulfillment?*

WISHING IS SOMETHING DONE ON A STAR. I HOPE IN GOD.

Walking

Although most of us envision Mary riding on a donkey as she and Joseph made their way from Nazareth to Bethlehem, it's more than likely that they walked (though it's nice to think that Joseph might have provided a donkey for Mary). Walking was the ordinary means of travel in those days; in fact, Mary would have walked most of the places she went. As Alban Butler's *Lives of the Saints* puts it, "[H]er bare feet [were] dusty, not with the perfumed powder of romance, but with the hard stinging grit of Nazareth, of the tracks which led to the well, to the olive gardens, to the synagogue."

Nowadays we walk mostly for exercise, not for transportation. Walking is indeed good exercise, but it's also an unparalleled way to come into intimate contact with the world. You have to slow down when you walk. You have to encounter nature, up close and personal. You have to feel the sun on your face, the breeze at your back, the ground under your feet.

In short, walking allows you to reconnect with the world that passes by unnoticed through a car window. What's more, early fall is one of the best times of year to walk. The weather is still pleasant, and the landscape changes daily as it begins its inexorable transformation to winter. This fall, experience the world in a new way: slow down and take a walk!

Do I ever feel as if I'm racing through life?
Can I take a half-hour in the next day or so
just to walk through life?

I'M THANKFUL FOR FEET THAT WALK, HANDS THAT GRASP,
EYES THAT SEE, EARS THAT HEAR.

Relatives

If Mary, Jesus, and Joseph lived all alone, isolated from their relatives, they were an anomaly; if the three of them huddled together, excluding all others, the neighbors certainly talked about them behind their backs and avoided them at the city well. In first-century Israel, families didn't live miles and miles from their relatives as we do today. People were born, lived, and died in the same town—sometimes in the same house—as their relatives. In fact, the extended family was highly valued in Jewish society—hence the importance of the genealogies of Jesus.

Although we don't have much information about Mary's family, we believe that she had at least one sister since the New Testament mentions her being with Mary at the foot of the cross. Add a handful of cousins, aunts, uncles, and other folks, and Mary had more than enough family members to contend with.

As we all know, relatives can be our greatest champions or our worst detractors. How did Mary's relatives react to her and her son? Did they stand in solidarity with her, or did they throw verbal stones? Were there relatives on both sides of the proverbial fence?

In the end, though, how our relatives treat us isn't as important as how we treat them. We must try, insofar as is possible, to live in harmony with our relatives, respecting their right to their own opinions, decisions, and way of life and according them the same politeness we would a stranger. While nobody says our relatives have to be our best friends, they shouldn't be our worst enemies either.

Whom do I consider part of my extended family?
Is there an estranged member of my family with whom
I'd like to reestablish contact?

I APPRECIATE THE UNIQUENESS OF MY FAMILY.

Harvest

In an agrarian culture, harvest time is often the best time of the year. The difficult work of planting and tending crops is over, and the bleak days of winter are still to some. For the moment, there's plenty to eat and there are plenty of hands to help with the work. It's no wonder that virtually every culture has a harvest celebration.

The harvest festival for the Jews—the Festival of Sukkoth, also known as the Festival of Tabernacles (or Booths)—comes soon after Rosh Hashanah, the Jewish New Year. This Sukkoth celebration commemorates the forty years the Jews spent wandering in the wilderness before settling in the Holy Land, but it also celebrates the fall harvest that will feed the people, the autumn rains that will fall, and the faith of the ancestors who knew that they'd eventually enter the promised land.

Mary and Jesus would undoubtedly have celebrated this festival, since it was one of the major feasts of the Jewish calendar (not to mention the fact that it was one of the most fun). One of the highlights of the celebration was the building of a *sukkah*, or small booth, in memory of the huts the Jews had had in the wilderness. Families then lived in the booths during the festival. Imagine the sense of fun and excitement such an activity would create! Since Mary and Jesus were known to enjoy a good time, it seems a sure thing that the Festival of Sukkoth must have been one of their favorite times of year.

Do I celebrate each season as it comes along?
What's my favorite time of year?

1 GIVE THANKS FOR THE YEAR AND ALL ITS CELEBRATIONS.

Trials

No one gets through life free of difficulties. Some people have easier lives than others, but everyone has his or her share of suffering.

When looking at your life and its struggles, consider the story told of a man who was suffering from many difficulties. He asked God to take away his trials, so God showed him a large, bulging bag. The man was told to exchange his problems for any of the other problems in the bag. The man carefully took all the trials out of the bag and examined them one by one. In the end, however, he put them all back and kept his own, saying that while he could bear his own difficulties, the others seemed impossible to accept. God then reached out and helped the man carry his trials.

Mary often tells us, in her appearances, that we'll have to suffer trials. But she also says that God will provide a means through the suffering. For instance, she's said to have told the seers at Medjugorje, "I wish to inform you that God wishes to send you trials; you will be able to overcome them with prayer. God tries you in your daily occupations. Pray, therefore, so as to be able to overcome every trial in peace."

God is always willing to help us overcome our trials, but it's up to us to ask for help. If we don't ask, it's no wonder we don't receive.

What do I consider my greatest trial at the moment?
Am I trying to bear it alone?

I KNOW THAT I CAN BEAR MY PROBLEMS IF I ASK GOD
TO HELP ME CARRY THEM.

Assistance

Over the centuries, many of the great saints have requested Mary's assistance. If you find it difficult to ask Mary for help, consider making their words yours:

> Virgin Mary, hear my prayer: through the Holy Spirit you became the Mother of Jesus; from the Holy Spirit may I too have Jesus. ST. ILDEPHONSUS

> O my Mother, you who always burned with love for God, deign to give me at least a spark of it.
> ST. ALPHONSUS DE LIGUORI

> Ah, tender Mother! Tell your all-powerful Son that we have no more wine. ST. BERNARD

> Earnestly pray for us to Jesus, your Son and Our Lord, that through your intercession we may have mercy on the day of judgment. ST. JOHN CHRYSOSTOM

> Holy Mary, help the miserable, strengthen the discouraged, comfort the sorrowful, pray for your people, plead for your clergy, intercede for all women consecrated to God.
> ST. AUGUSTINE

> Remember me, dearest Mother, and do not abandon me at the hour of death. ST. FRANCIS DE SALES

> My beloved Mother, grant . . . that I may love God with burning love like yours. ST. LOUIS DE MONTFORT

What request do I have for Mary?
Do I believe that she loves me enough to intercede on my behalf?

HAIL, MARY, FULL OF GRACE. PRAY FOR ME NOW
AND AT THE HOUR OF MY DEATH.

Vision

Albert Schweitzer once commented on the mystery of human relationships:

> We wander through this life together in a semi-darkness in which none of us can distinguish exactly the features of his neighbor. Only from time to time, through some experience that we have of our companion, or through some remark that he passes, he stands for a moment close to us, as though illuminated by a flash of lightning. Then we see him as he really is.

In one sense, Mary is like that flash of lightning. When she appears, we see the world as God sees it, with all its beauty and its horror, its glory and its sin. Moreover, Mary, the woman cloaked in the sun and stars, illuminates our lives so that we can begin to part the darkness and distinguish the features of our neighbors.

Once that happens, even though the world may not change, we do. Our focus shifts from objects to people. Realizing that the only thing we'll take with us from this life is our relationships, we no longer go through life seeking only success and possessions. We begin to understand that love is all that really matters, that without love the semidarkness of life may become total, impenetrable blackness. Once our vision clears, we're able to see from the bounds of earth to the gates of heaven.

What's the most important thing in the world to me?

I VALUE MY RELATIONSHIPS, NOT MY POSSESSIONS.

Unpredictability

Have you ever noticed how unpredictable God is? God does things in ways we couldn't—and wouldn't—predict in a million years. Take the way most species propagate. If we were devising a method, it's a sure bet we wouldn't have chosen the means God selected. Or take the way God decided to redeem the world. The crucifixion of God's only son would never have entered our minds. Or take Mary's appearances. If we were choosing people for Mary to appear to, we wouldn't put poor, uneducated children high on the list. (Let's be honest: we wouldn't put them on the list at all!)

One aspect of God's unpredictability that we've all experienced lies in divine responses to petitionary prayer. Prayers are seldom answered the way we think they should be. We may pray that our child makes the varsity basketball team, for example, yet she plays more poorly than ever at tryouts and fails to make even the junior varsity team. Does that mean God didn't answer our prayer? Does it mean God *did* answer, but with a resounding no? Or is there another possibility?

When prayers aren't answered the way we think they should be, we need to remember three things. First, God is unpredictable. Second, God doesn't say no without reason. Third, God may have (indeed, probably has!) answered in a way we never expected. As Helen Keller said, "[W]e look so long at the closed door that we do not see the one that has opened for us."

Am I prepared for the unpredictable when I pray?
Am I willing to accept God's answer, no matter what it is?

I EXPECT AN ANSWER FROM GOD, BUT I DON'T
DEMAND A *SPECIFIC* ANSWER.

Victims

In the waning days of the twentieth century, victim status is the excuse du jour. *I can't be blamed for my cocaine habit because my father was an alcoholic. I can't be blamed for my failed marriage because I grew up in a dysfunctional family. I can't be blamed for my poor work habits because the schools didn't teach me how to study.* We don't take responsibility for anything because nothing is our responsibility. It's always someone else's fault; we're merely innocent victims.

That's not to say we *can't* be victims. The target of a pedophile and the person who has the bad luck to cross paths with a violent criminal, for instance, are truly victims. But when people actively seek a way to be *seen* as victims, they're more than likely looking to excuse themselves for their own failings.

While victimhood is very tempting—after all, being a victim excuses us—it cripples us severely. Jesus was truly a victim, but he didn't claim victim status. In fact, he said, "Father, forgive them, for they know not what they do." He chose the cross; he didn't let it choose him.

Nonetheless, discarding victim status takes courage. It means being willing to forgive those who've hurt us in the past and to leave that past in the past. It means accepting accountability for our own actions, without looking for mitigating or extenuating circumstances. It means acknowledging that bad things happen to good people.

If you find yourself making excuses for your life, ask Mary and Jesus to help you determine whether you're guilty of claiming victim status. Then, if you have to admit that you are, ask them to help you shed that role. Finally, trust that they'll help you and then get on with your life.

*Am I willing to admit that most of what happens to me
is the result of my own choices?*

I'M A SURVIVOR, NOT A VICTIM.

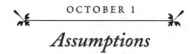

Assumptions

To assume is to presume something is true. When it comes to Mary, we assume a great deal. Catholics assume, for instance, Mary was conceived without sin, she was taken body and soul into heaven, she was ever-virgin, she has appeared and still is appearing throughout the world.

While assumptions about Mary are generally fairly safe, assuming things about other people isn't always as prudent. As one wag points out, to assume makes an ass out of "u" and "me."

In fact, making assumptions is one way many of us get in deep trouble. For instance, assuming the gas tank is full before starting on a long trip is one way to ensure you'll be walking to the nearest gas station. Making assumptions in relationships can be equally dangerous. You may assume a relationship is much more serious than the other person does. Guess who is going to get hurt when the truth comes out?

Although we can safely make certain assumptions—that the sun will rise tomorrow or that the law of gravity will remain in effect, most of the time we should approach assumptions with the same wary caution with which we approach a snake in the grass. It might turn out to be harmless, but it could very well be a rattler, just waiting to strike when our guard is down.

Do I ever assume something to be true
without first checking the fact?

I AM CAREFUL ABOUT MY ASSUMPTIONS, ESPECIALLY WHEN IT COMES TO PEOPLE AND RELATIONSHIPS.

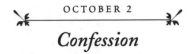

Confession

Confession is good for the soul. It allows us to acknowledge our faults, admit our failings, and take inventory of our lives. While confession is necessary for spiritual growth, we don't need to confess everything to everyone. That's exhibitionism, not confession. After all, some things don't need to be revealed to the world.

That's one reason that the Catholic Church has differentiated between the act of confession with a small *c* and the sacrament of Confession with a big *C*. Small-*c* confession is disclosing something to someone primarily to get it off our chests. Big-*C* Confession is telling something to God through the mediation of a priest in order to receive forgiveness. That difference is important. There are times when big-*C* Confession could restore harmony, while small-*c* confession might destroy it. For example, although a person might Confess harboring ill will and bearing a grudge toward his or her employer and feel cleansed of hostility, confessing such feelings openly (especially to the employer!) could have disastrous consequences.

Mary urges us to use both confessions wisely in order to grow in grace and wisdom. The seers at Medjugorje report that she said, "Do not Confess through sheer habit, in order to remain the same after it. No, it isn't good. Confession ought to give life to your faith. It ought to stimulate you and bring you back to Jesus. If Confession means nothing to you, really, you will convert with difficulty."

Do I use both Confession and confession appropriately?
Do I ever confess my failings just to make myself feel better,
not intending to change my behavior?

I KNOW WHEN TO CONFESS AND WHEN NOT TO CONFESS.

Heart-Knowledge

We don't know much about Mary's formal education. (Okay, we don't know *anything* about Mary's formal education.) Pious tradition says that she was instructed in the Temple, but we don't know for sure. We do know that at the time Mary was growing up, it would have been unusual for a girl to receive formal education outside the home. She would have been expected to focus on the skills she would need as a wife and mother, learning those from her own mother.

In Mary's case, her long prayer recorded in Luke indicates a familiarity with the Hebrew Scriptures, but that doesn't necessarily mean that she could read and write. After all, she was part of a culture with a strong oral tradition, and she would have heard Scripture read aloud every Sabbath in the synagogue.

While we don't know if Mary had much book learning, we do know she had an advanced degree in heart-knowledge. She knew and understood both the workings of human nature and the ways God deals with creation.

Heart-knowledge doesn't come from reading or studying. It comes from engaging life fully and enthusiastically. It comes from living each and every day as if it might be your last. Although formal education is good and often necessary, if you're forced to choose between getting more intellectual knowledge and gaining heart-knowledge, go for the heart. It's the only education that lasts for eternity.

*Do I rely more on my formal education
or on my heart-knowledge?
When I need to make a decision, do I use both my book learning
and my heart-knowledge to come to the right conclusion?*

1 ALLOW LIFE TO TEACH ME THE LESSONS 1 NEED TO KNOW,
NOW AND FOREVER.

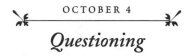

Questioning

There's an old saying, "To err is human; to forgive, divine." Actually, "To question is human; to answer, divine" might be more telling.

Anthropologists used to call us the tool-making animal (which isn't exactly true, since other primates make and use tools, but that's another issue). More accurately, we might be defined as the *questioning* animal. Human beings are the only creatures on earth who ask "who, what, when, where, and why?" And we're the only creatures who care about the answers.

In her appearances in the Christian Scriptures, Mary is often portrayed as asking questions. She asks Gabriel how she could have a baby when she hasn't been sexually active, she asks the preteen Jesus why he stayed behind in the Temple, she asks the adult Jesus to come out and talk with her and his "brothers." And if *she's* not asking questions, someone close to her is. For instance, as soon as she arrives at her cousin's house, Elizabeth asks why the mother of the Savior should come to visit.

Mary's example demonstrates that it's perfectly acceptable to ask questions—even of angels!

The key is to wait for the answer.

All too often, we ask questions but don't really want answers. Or we ask questions and ignore the answer if it's not what we'd hoped for. The point of asking isn't to have our own preconceived notions verified; rather, it's to gain insight and wisdom. If we aren't willing to hear the answer, then we shouldn't bother asking the question.

When I ask a question, am I prepared to accept the answer I get,
even if it's not what I wanted to hear?

1 THINK ABOUT THE QUESTIONS 1 ASK, AND 1 ACCEPT
THE ANSWERS 1 RECEIVE.

Promises

Mary knows what it's like to live in the shadow of a promise. For thirty years she watched her son grow up and work as a contractor, all the while carrying in her heart the promise that he was the long-awaited one, the Messiah, the Savior. At times she must have felt a bit downhearted. Thirty years is a long time to wait for something—anything!—to happen. Yet even though she saw very little proof to indicate that he was the Messiah, she never gave up hope. She clung to the promise despite scant evidence of fulfillment.

Clinging to God's promises in our lives is never easy. For one thing, we don't have any idea how long it will take for them to come true. After all, a day is as a thousand years and a thousand years is as a day to God. When we're waiting, we're tempted to point out that while God might have a thousand years, we don't!

As we attempt to practice patience, one thing that can help is to remember that God's timing is better than ours. God knows not just this moment but *all* the moments of our life. If God delays in fulfilling a promise, it's not because God hasn't gotten around to it yet but because the timing isn't yet right. And, as we all know, timing is everything. The flower bulbs we plant in the fall don't bloom immediately, not because they aren't growing but because it's not the right time. When the time is right, promises and flowers will both burst forth.

Do I ever get impatient with God's timing for my life?

I BELIEVE THAT GOD'S PROMISES TO ME WILL BE
FULFILLED AT THE PROPER TIME.

Projection

One reason we have difficulty trusting God is that all too often we misappropriate other people's life-stories, presuming that we know what those people prayed for and projecting our reactions onto their relationship with God.

Let's say we have a friend who's dying of cancer. This friend tells us that she prays every day for healing. When death comes instead of health, we may feel quite angry at God, since God clearly didn't answer our friend's prayers. The problem is that we don't really know another person's prayers. One woman told her children that she was praying for healing, but she confessed to her sister that she really was praying for death. When she did die, her children were disheartened initially, but their aunt was able to tell them that God had indeed heard and answered their mother's prayers.

If we use other people's lives as a way of judging the trustworthiness of God, we're bound to be disappointed. The only way we can come to know and trust God is to enter into an intimate personal relationship.

Mary knows God in a deeply personal way. We too can know God personally. In fact, that's the only way we can know God. Either we know God personally, or we don't know God at all.

Has God ever not answered one of my prayers?
If I think a prayer hasn't been answered, could it be that
the answer is "not yet" rather than "no"?

I DON'T BASE MY RELATIONSHIP WITH GOD
ON OTHER PEOPLE'S EXPERIENCES.

Motherhood and Pregnancy

Most of the time when we use the word *pregnant,* we're describing someone who's expecting a child. But one can be pregnant in other ways as well—pregnant with anticipation, pregnant with hope, pregnant with desire. Likewise, we can give birth to something other than a baby—an idea, a dream, a concept. Pregnancy always results in *some* form of motherhood, however.

In his encyclical *Mulieris Dignitatem,* Pope John Paul II wrote,

Motherhood has been introduced into the order of the Covenant that God made with humanity in Jesus Christ. Each and every time that *motherhood* is repeated in human history, it is always *related to the Covenant* which God established with the human race through the motherhood of the Mother of God.

Mary was pregnant with a child, certainly, but she was pregnant with more than that. She was pregnant with the hope of salvation for all people. In her womb, she carried the future of humanity and the new covenant God would make with each of us.

Each of us, male and female, has the potential to carry to term and give birth to new life—not in the literal sense, of course, but in other ways. We can give birth to creativity, to love, to wholeness, to empathy. What are *you* carrying that's crying out for birth?

Am I mindful of the creative life within me? Am I willing to go through the pangs of birth in order to bring life to life?

I CELEBRATE MY ABILITY TO BRING FORTH A NEW WAY OF LIFE.

Gold

Gold is one of the most precious of all metals. In Mary's time, it was probably *the* most precious, given that only six metals (gold, silver, iron, lead, tin, and copper) are mentioned in Scripture.

Besides being valuable, gold is also malleable. It can be beaten into filaments as fine as a hair or made into a throne fit for a king. In fact, gold is often considered a sign of royalty. That's one reason the Magi brought it as part of their gift offering. Seeking a king, they brought the baby Jesus royal gifts.

Over the centuries, men (and a few women) have sacrificed virtually everything, including their souls, to acquire gold. Today we don't generally collect actual gold (gold coins notwithstanding), but that doesn't mean we've evolved beyond the trap of acquisition. Even if our gold is only a VISA gold card with an unlimited credit line, we act at times as though we're willing to sacrifice anything for it.

The myth of King Midas, who wanted everything he touched to turn to gold, has a lesson for us in the twentieth century. Midas learned the hard way—by touching his daughter and turning her into a golden statue—that life and love are much more valuable than cold metal. When the gods saw Midas's anguish over his daughter's fate, they took pity on him and restored the girl to life.

If we're sacrificing our lives for something akin to gold, we may end up learning the same difficult lesson. We can only hope that we get a chance to correct our mistake, as did Midas.

Do I ever place possessions above people?
What's the most important thing in my life?

¶ INVEST IN PEOPLE AND RELATIONSHIPS, NOT POSSESSIONS.

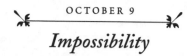

Impossibility

Over and over in both the Hebrew and the Christian Scriptures, we're told that nothing is impossible with God. An old woman past menopause bearing a son? No problem. A virgin giving birth? Not to worry. Resurrection from the dead? Under control. The message is clear: God can do anything.

But do we really believe that? Maybe we believe that God *can* do anything; but when push comes to shove, we have difficulty believing that God will do the impossible *for us.*

The issue comes down to trust. Do we trust—*really* trust—God?

Mary trusted God completely. If we learn nothing else from her life-story, we learn of her trust. She trusted that God would give her a son; she trusted that God would make her unwed pregnancy right in the eyes of the world; she trusted that her son would be the Savior. In short, she trusted that God would do the impossible in her life.

"Yeah, but she was Mary!" we may be tempted to argue. "It wasn't as hard for her to trust as it is for us." Not true. Mary wasn't given miraculous powers that enabled her to trust God to do the impossible for her. She had to achieve trust the same way we have to— by letting go and letting God.

When she did, God was there, working the impossible in her life. God didn't let her down; and God won't let us down either, but we have to be willing to trust. *Impossible,* you say? Remember, *nothing* is impossible with God—even learning to trust.

Do I really believe that God will do the impossible for me?
Do I trust God completely with my life?

EACH DAY I LEARN TO TRUST A LITTLE MORE.

Teaching

Our mothers are our first teachers. As his mother, Mary was Jesus' first teacher. She was the one who taught him both spiritual things (such as how to say his prayers) and everyday things (such as how to drink from a cup, wash his face, and put on his sandals).

As Edward Schillebeeckx writes,

> Mary's function in the Incarnation was not completed when Jesus was born. It was a continuous task, involving the human formation of the young man, as he grew up from infancy to childhood and from childhood to adulthood. . . . God, in his humanity, formed his first word, and there can be little doubt that it was "Mama."

Even after we become adults, we can still learn from our parents. Jesus was no exception to this generalization. At the marriage feast at Cana, Mary taught (or retaught) him a couple of important lessons. First, she reminded him of the necessity of paying attention to things around him. She lived out the adage "If a friend is in trouble, don't annoy him by asking if there's anything you can do. Think up something appropriate and do it." Second, she taught (or retaught) him that the Fourth Commandment ("Honor your father and mother") doesn't evaporate when a child becomes an adult. No matter how old we are, our parents are still our parents and deserve our honor and respect. Third, Mary taught Jesus that little things such as providing wine at weddings can be just as crucial to life as curing the sick or raising the dead. Finally, she reminded him that Mother (almost always) Knows Best!

If my parents are alive, how can I show them
my honor and respect?

I'M GRATEFUL FOR THOSE WHO'VE TAUGHT ME,
ESPECIALLY MY MOTHER AND FATHER.

Reconciliation

Is there someone in your life from whom you're estranged? One of Mary's recurrent messages in her appearances is the need to be reconciled with all around us. In some of her appearances, she's talked about loving those whose religious differences have sparked hatred, anger, and wars. She's also spoken of reconciliation within families, within nations, and within the world.

Without reconciliation, all is lost, she says. "My Son suffers very much because men do not want to be reconciled," Mary is believed to have said at Medjugorje. "They have not listened to me. Be converted, be reconciled."

Over and over Mary begs for reconciliation:

"Be reconciled, because I desire reconciliation among you and more love for each other as brothers."

"Peace. Only peace! You must seek peace. There must be peace on earth. You must be reconciled with God and with each other."

"I desire to be with you in order that the entire world may be converted and reconciled."

"Hurry and be reconciled!"

Peace and reconciliation don't begin on a nationwide level. They begin today—in our homes, our schools, our neighborhoods, our churches. Today is the day the Lord has made. Today is the day of reconciliation.

Is there someone in my life from whom I'm estranged?
Is there something I can do right now—such as calling or
writing to him or her—that might initiate a reconciliation?

I CHOOSE PEACE AND RECONCILIATION.

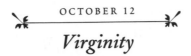

Virginity

Mary was a virgin when she gave birth to Jesus. But why? Why was it so important that Mary be virginal?

The easy answer is because the prophets had foretold that the Savior would be born of a virgin from the house of David. In order for that prophecy to come true, Mary (who was a descendant of the Davidic line) had to be a virgin.

But Mary had to be a virgin, not just for the sake of prophecy, but for the sake of Jesus. The Messiah couldn't be conceived by a natural father, for then he would be nothing more than an ordinary man. In order to ensure that conception couldn't be thought the result of ordinary sexual activity, the mother of the Savior had to be a known, consecrated virgin.

Mary's virginity is an important theological issue, but it's also an important personal issue. In being both virgin and mother, Mary shows us that no one state in life is superior to another. A virgin isn't better than a mother, and a mother isn't better than a virgin. Both states of life have merit, but for different reasons. If God is calling you to remain single, then to do so will bring you peace and fulfillment. If God is calling you to become a parent, then your satisfaction will be found in that role. Moreover, no matter which state God is asking you to live in, you can be certain that God will give you the help you need—just as God gave Mary the help she needed to be both virgin and mother.

Do I ever regret the choices I've made in life?
Have I asked God to bless me in whatever state
of life I find myself at this moment?

I KNOW THAT I'M IN THE STATE OF LIFE
RIGHT FOR ME AT THIS TIME.

Fatima

On this date in 1917, Mary appeared for the seventh and final time to three children in Fatima, Portugal. She identified herself as Our Lady of the Rosary and asked for prayer and penance as a way to end World War I. "I have come to exhort the faithful to change their life, to avoid grieving Our Lord by sin, to pray the Rosary. I desire in this place a chapel in my honor. If people mend their ways, the war will soon be over." As she delivered her message, the sun appeared to toss and tumble in the sky and crash toward earth. It's estimated that as many as thirty thousand people saw the phenomenon.

As part of her message, Mary asked that Russia and the world be consecrated to her Immaculate Heart. In 1942, Pope Pius XII obeyed her instructions. Both Pope Paul VI and Pope John Paul II have renewed the consecration.

While Fatima is one of the greatest sites of Marian pilgrimage in the world, its significance isn't in the 1917 visions or in the fabled secrets she revealed to the three seers; rather, it's in the great promise Mary left: "In the end, my Immaculate Heart will triumph, the Holy Father will consecrate Russia to me, and a period of peace will be granted to the world." In a world sorely lacking in peace, Mary's promise is good news indeed.

How can I bring peace to my little corner of the world?

I VALUE PEACE AND DO WHAT I CAN TO LIVE IN PEACE
WITH ALL PEOPLE.

Calvary

Bethlehem and Calvary are the locations most often associated with Mary and Jesus.

Bethlehem is a natural—cute baby, doting mother, darling animals, twinkling star, quaint shepherds. What's there *not* to like at Bethlehem?

Calvary is another matter. The place of execution for criminals of the Roman state, it was a hill just outside the walls of ancient Jerusalem. It had to have been a bleak, barren place; the Romans would hardly have allowed vegetation to grow on a site intended for maximum exposure to the elements. They wouldn't have wanted to provide either shade for the condemned or potential hiding places from which accomplices could stage a rescue attempt.

The condemned criminal carried only the crossbeam to his cross; the uprights were permanently anchored in place on Calvary. Since two criminals were executed with Jesus, there must have been at least three weather-worn crosses on the hill, but there could have been several more. The ground, hardened by the constant pounding of soldiers' and bystanders' feet, was probably spattered with bloodstains from previous executions. The surrounding area was probably littered with trash, since an execution was a public spectacle (and people tend to drop all sorts of things as they stand and watch community events). All in all, Calvary was a dirty, dreadful place to die. And yet it was the place where salvation would be won.

Few of us get to choose the place where we'll die, but we *can* choose the way we'll live. Let us always choose to live fully, remembering the price that was paid at Calvary.

Am I willing to live a life worthy of the price
that was paid for it?

1 LIVE FULLY AND IN THE NOW.

Water

Clean, potable water is literally life-giving. The infant death rate dramatically declines when a town or village obtains a reliable source of clean water. Conversely, sickness runs rampant when the water source is polluted.

Because most of us live in homes where fresh water is available with the twist of a knob, we forget what a valuable commodity water is, especially in desert climates. Without water, life literally ceases. Mary would have obtained her family's daily water needs from a well—probably much like Jacob's well, where Jesus met the woman who'd had five husbands. Mary would have gone to the well at least once a day, bringing home a jug filled with water for cooking, bathing, and other household necessities.

While water is absolutely necessary for physical life, Jesus tells us that the living water of truth is equally necessary for eternal life. When the Samaritan woman asked him about the living water, Jesus replied, "Everyone who drinks this water will be thirsty again; but whoever drinks the water I shall give will never thirst; the water I shall give will become in him a spring of water welling up to eternal life."

Today let's give thanks for the gift and wonder of water. Let's take a few minutes to count the many blessings water gives us, including cleanliness, health, and eternal life through baptism.

Do I ever take clean water for granted? Do I ever stop
to think about the miracle that occurs each time
I turn on the water faucet?

I'M GRATEFUL FOR ALL THE MIRACLES IN MY LIFE,
INCLUDING RUNNING WATER.

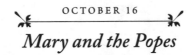

Mary and the Popes

Pope John Paul II has a particular devotion to Mary. He placed his entire papacy under her protection and gives her credit for saving his life when an assassin shot him at point-blank range. His motto, *"Totus tuus,"* means "All is yours, O Mary," and his coat of arms is a cross flanked by the letter *M.*

But Pope John Paul II is hardly the only pope to have had a special love and dedication to Our Lady. As early as the year 392, Pope Siricius spoke on the perpetual virginity of Mary. In more current times, Popes Leo XIII, John XXIII, and Paul VI have all expressed their commitment to the Virgin:

> Mary, show that you are our Mother; may our prayer be heard by that Jesus who willed to be your Son.
> POPE LEO XIII

> O Mary! Like you in Bethlehem and on Golgotha, I too wish to stay always close to Jesus. He is the eternal King of all ages and all peoples.   POPE JOHN XXIII

> Look down with maternal clemency, most Blessed Virgin, upon all your children. . . . Heed the anguish of so many people, fathers and mothers of families who are uncertain about their future and beset by hardships and cares.
> POPE PAUL VI

> O Most Blessed Virgin Mary, Mother of Christ and Mother of the Church, with joy and wonder we seek to make our own your Magnificat, joining you in your hymn of thankfulness and love.   POPE JOHN PAUL II

If the popes have turned to Mary throughout the ages, then we too can have the confidence to approach Mary as our guide and example.

When do I find the most comfort from Mary?
When have I turned to her in need?

I REJOICE THAT MARY IS MY MOTHER AND MY EXAMPLE FOR LIFE.

Archetypes

In classical literature, *woman* in the broadest sense fits into several different archetypes. Among them are the scarlet lady (the seductress, the temptress), the earth mother (the nurturer, the bearer of life), and the crone (the wise, strong willed matriarch).

Theological considerations aside, Marian imagery draws heavily on the roles of the earth mother and the crone, who have their roots in the old pagan religions.

While goddess and neopagan religions aren't compatible with Christian beliefs, that doesn't mean the old ways didn't have some grasp of the truth. They recognized, for instance, that there's a feminine element in life and in God, and that element remains strong despite attempts to suppress it. We refer to Mother Nature, for example, not Father Nature.

Over the centuries, Mary has often been used to archetypically represent the feminine side of God. Such representation is both good and bad. Although it allows us access to the divine in a way that strictly masculine images don't, it diminishes God by assigning God's feminine traits (such as compassion) to Mary and leaving the deity male. Moreover, limiting God to the masculine gender is a theologically inaccurate stance because God is neither male nor female.

If you have difficulty relating to God in the masculine, then by all means use Mary as a way to access the feminine nature of God. Or better yet, ask Mary to help you discover the feminine that is God.

Do I think of God as male? How does it change my image
of God to think of God as female?

I KNOW THAT GOD IS NEITHER MALE NOR FEMALE. GOD *IS*.

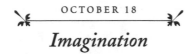

Imagination

The imagination is one of the greatest gifts God has given humanity. To imagine is the first step in making something come true. Thomas Edison imagined a way to illuminate the darkness, for instance, and the electric light was developed. Wilbur and Orville Wright imagined flying like a bird, and space travel became possible. Mary imagined being the mother of the Messiah, and salvation entered the world.

We've all been given the ability to imagine, but sometimes we allow that gift to atrophy. Perhaps we were put down as children when we imagined a pretend playmate, or maybe we were encouraged to direct our mental abilities toward more "practical" things.

What are you currently imagining? If you could let your imagination have free rein, what would you imagine? If you knew that you couldn't fail, what would you imagine doing? Do you think that God can help your imagined dreams come true?

Sometimes our prayers aren't answered simply because we haven't really prayed; we haven't imagined a better circumstance and asked God's help in achieving it. And sometimes our *big* prayers aren't answered because we haven't prayed *big* prayers. If we don't ask big, how can we get big? Yet what would it hurt to ask for our dreams—big and bold—to come true? If they don't, we haven't lost a thing. But if they do, think of what we've gained!

Do I pray small, "safe" prayers because I think
they'll be easier for God to answer?
What do I have to lose by praying a big, "dangerous" prayer?

1 BELIEVE THAT 1'LL GET WHAT 1 ASK FOR FROM GOD.

Reflections

Time and again, the Scriptures say that Mary pondered the events of her life in her heart. Clearly she was a woman of introspection.

We all need to become introspective people. We all need to take time to reflect on the events of our lives and examine their impact and meaning. The unexamined life is no life at all. However, our busy and demanding schedules often don't provide us the time we need to reflect thoughtfully. If that's the case, we must make or take the time (whichever is more accurate) for this all-important soul-work.

Don't let anyone kid you. It isn't easy. The moment you decide to devote time and energy to the work of the spirit, a thousand and one other incredibly urgent things will rush in, demanding your full attention. Suddenly everything will fall apart both at home and at work. You'll find yourself too busy to turn around, much less ponder things in your heart.

That's when it's vital to stop the mad rush. Very little is so essential that it can't wait a few hours. Give yourself permission to find a quiet place where you can let your soul refresh itself. If you can, go away, perhaps to a park or a church—anywhere you can sit and just *be*. If you can't get away physically, then create an oasis in the chaos. Select the quietest corner you can find, dim the lights, light a candle, and let silence soothe your soul. At first it may seem as if you're wasting time, but you'll soon discover that time wasted in this fashion is the best-spent time of all.

Do I take the time I need to lead an examined life?
Do I spend as much time on my inner life as I do on my outer life?

1 TAKE THE TIME 1 NEED TO DO MY SOUL-WORK.

The Upper Room

*When they entered the city they went to the upper room where
they were staying, Peter and John and James and Andrew,
Philip and Thomas, Bartholomew and Matthew, James son of
Alphaeus, Simon the Zealot, and Judas son of James. All these
devoted themselves with one accord to prayer, together with some
women, and Mary the mother of Jesus, and his brothers.*

ACTS 1:13

The author of Acts writes as if the reader is completely familiar with the Upper Room. Unfortunately, two thousand years later, we aren't so sure what the passage is all about.

What was it like in the Upper Room? What was Mary doing and feeling? Was she comforting everyone, or was she keeping things in her heart? We don't know. But we do know that at least two things were happening in the Upper Room: waiting and praying.

So often we find ourselves in the same place as the apostles and Mary: waiting for *what*, we aren't quite certain; praying for *what* we don't quite know.

Prayer does effect change in our life and the lives of those around us. But it isn't enough to just think about praying; we actually have to pray. We have to open our minds, our hearts, and our mouths. We have to ask God for guidance, knowledge, strength—whatever it is we need at the moment—for if we don't ask, we can't complain when we don't receive.

*Do I use prayer as my first recourse or as my last resort?
Do I spend more time praying or thinking about praying?*

I DEVOTE MYSELF TO PRAYER.

Religious Narcotics

In a much-quoted statement, Karl Marx once described religion as "the opium of the people." While his statement has been frequently disparaged, in some ways it's true. If we let religion take us away from real life, then it does act as an opiate. We can get so caught up in attending church that we forget that the real purpose of religion isn't to replace real life but to make our lives real.

And we can't be naive. Religion *does* sometimes take us away from real life. Doing work around the church, teaching Bible or catechism classes, working on retreats, helping out at parish functions—it's easy for a person's entire life to become filled with "religious" activity at the expense of other things—family, friends, and work.

In fact, unless we view Mary realistically, she can become an opiate as well. If we see her as escaping the sometimes-difficult work of faith or as offering us a way out of that same work, then she can become an opiate, impeding real spiritual growth.

If Mary hadn't lived a real, nitty-gritty life, she would indeed be a narcotic, and in following her we would be left with the dull ache of a hangover rather than the vibrant infusion of new life true faith brings.

Do I want to find an easy way to faith? Am I ever tempted to use Mary as a way not to have to examine my own life closely?

1 DON'T LET ANYTHING DULL ME TO THE WONDERS OF LIFE.

Poetry

Over the centuries, many of the world's greatest poets, some of them not particularly religious, have written about Mary and her virtues. Henry Wadsworth Longfellow extolled Mary's virtues:

> And, if our faith had given us nothing more
> Than this Example of all Womanhood,
> So patient, peaceful, loyal, loving, pure—
> This were enough to prove it higher and truer
> Than all the creed the world had known before.

Oscar Wilde found himself in awe of Mary's mystery:

> And now with wondering eyes and heart I stand
> Before this supreme mystery of Love:
> Some kneeling girl with passionless pale face,
> An angel with a lily in his hand
> And over both the white wings of a Dove.

Percy Bysshe Shelley was equally rhapsodic:

> Seraph of heaven! too gentle to be human,
> Veiling beneath that radiant form of Woman
> All that is insupportable in thee
> Of light, and love, and immortality.

Even Edgar Allan Poe, whom we usually associate with horror, addressed a prayer to the Blessed Virgin:

> At morn, at noon, at twilight dim,
> Maria, thou hast heard my hymn:
> In joy and woe, in good and ill,
> Mother of God, be with me still.

If I were writing a poem in praise of Mary, what aspects
of her life and personality might I single out?

I'M WRITING MY OWN LIFE-POEM.

Respect for Life

The words *respect for life* get bandied about a lot, especially in the political arena. In fact, they've taken on specific political connotations with reference to abortion. But *respect for life* means much more than the political slogans and the pro-life movement intend. *Respect for life* means recognizing that all life is connected in and through God. It means accepting God as the Creator of all life—plant, animal, and human.

Once we become aware of the intricate interconnectedness of all life, we begin to glimpse our essential bonds with everyone and everything. We begin to see that God doesn't limit interaction to our species but is acutely, passionately involved with all of creation.

Mary's message, from the Incarnation through her appearances in modern times, is one of respecting life, of celebrating life, of letting God's new life flow through each of us. Mary calls us to deepen our awareness of our own lives, and in doing so to deepen our awareness of *all* life.

Spend a few minutes today observing the abundance of life that surrounds you. Whether you live in the city or the country, life surges and flows all around you. From a weed struggling to come up through a sidewalk crack to a flock of late-flying geese, the mystery of life envelops you completely. Respect life—and in doing so, respect God.

When was the last time I gave thanks for the gift of life?
What am I doing to show my respect for life?

I APPRECIATE LIFE IN ALL ITS GLORIOUS ABUNDANCE.

Unreal Holiness

Does Mary seem too holy to be real? Do you find yourself agreeing with Mary Lee Bensman, who wrote, "Mary, you know I've had a hard time identifying with you, seeing you as a real person. I've tried lots of different things, lots of times—prayers, devotions, rosaries—but nothing has worked. I feel like there is a barrier between us that can't be broken. You're too holy for me to relate to."

If those words resound in your soul, you aren't alone. A lot of people find Mary too holy to be real. She's a delicate figurine in a nativity set, a statue on a side altar, a beatific face painted by an old master. Removed from the harshness of life, always sweet, always prayerful, always dutiful, always kind, always cheerful, always all things good and wonderful—this Mary is someone we can't relate to. If we're completely honest, we're not even sure we'd like this perfect woman if she were our neighbor. She'd be the person with the perfect home, the perfect marriage, the perfect kid, the perfect life.

Or *would* she?

Mary's life appears perfect only because we know how things are going to turn out. But she didn't live in a sacred bubble, protected from the world. She lived a real life—a life in which the house got dirty, she and Joseph disagreed, and her son was arrested and tried as a traitor. Mary too holy to be real? No, real enough to be holy!

Do I find Mary too holy to relate to?

I KNOW THAT THE MORE REAL I AM, THE MORE HOLY I CAN BECOME.

Return from the Dead

Scripture says that after Jesus' death and resurrection, other dead people also rose and were seen by many: "[T]he earth quaked, rocks were split, tombs were opened, and the bodies of many saints who had fallen asleep were raised. And coming forth from their tombs after his resurrection, they entered the holy city and appeared to many."

Somehow those lines conjure up images of Boris Karloff as the mummy in an old black-and-white movie. The vision of many people staggering around Jerusalem with their burial shrouds hanging in shreds isn't one we usually associate with The Easter Story. (It just doesn't seem to fit well with bunnies and colored eggs!)

Having the dead come back to life (or a sort of life) is standard fare for many horror films. In fact, it's a surefire way to scare the living daylights out of movie viewers. But Mary has returned from the dead many times, in all of her appearances, and she evokes no visceral fear. Perhaps the reason we're not afraid of Mary is that she returns from *life* rather than from *death*.

Mary's appearances show us that death isn't the end of life; it's the transformation of life. To an unborn baby, perhaps *birth* appears to be death. After all, life as the unborn baby knows it ends completely at the end of the birth canal. The baby has to go somewhere totally foreign, a place no baby has ever returned from. But who, once born, would return to the captivity of the womb? Perhaps it's the same with the life after this life. Once we've experienced that fuller, heaven-based life, perhaps we'll wonder why anyone would choose to return to this earthly womb.

Do I fear death? Have I ever thought about what will happen to me after I die? Do I believe in life everlasting?

1 SEE LIFE AND DEATH AND FURTHER LIFE AS PART OF
A CONTINUUM OF EXISTENCE.

Taking Risks

Are you a risk-taker? Not the kind of person who's willing to skydive, mountain-climb, or go white-water rafting at a moment's notice, but the kind of person who's willing to take the biggest risk of all—intimacy.

Physical risk-taking is one thing; emotional risk-taking is quite another. The latter means putting not just your life but your very being at risk; it means being willing to die not from exposure to the forces of nature but from exposure of the self.

In our culture, we tend to assume that the only real intimacy is that which occurs between lovers, spouses, and parents and children. While it's true that those relationships are often intimate, they're not necessarily so; in fact, they can be the very antithesis of intimacy.

Intimacy isn't contingent on physical connection. Sometimes the most intimate of all relationships are purely intellectual. What makes a relationship intimate is the depth of emotional involvement and the willingness to expose the true self, with its vices and virtues, to another person. Close friendships can have that kind of intimacy; and since intimate friendships aren't limited to people we can see and hug, a close friendship with Mary can be intimate.

Mary is willing to enter into an intimate bond with us—a bond in which she shows us the way to her son and in which we trust her with our secrets. Take a risk with Mary. What do you have to lose?

What are the most intimate relationships in my life?
To whom do I feel the most connected at this moment?

I'M WILLING TO TAKE AN EMOTIONAL RISK FOR INTIMACY.

Open-Heart Surgery

For a person with severe coronary problems, open-heart surgery is often the only alternative to death. When you think about it, though, open-heart surgery is rather grim. The patient allows a team of surgeons to cut through the chest wall, expose the heart, and literally cut and sew that organ. If we didn't know better, we'd think that such goings-on would be a sure way to end a person's life, not save it.

One of the traditional (and somewhat grim) images of Mary shows her Immaculate Heart cut away from her breast and on fire with love. While the picture might not appeal to everyone, it reveals an important truth: love is the ultimate open-heart surgery.

Love requires that we let our chest be opened and a piece of our heart be cut away. Like physical open-heart surgery, it's a dangerous operation. If the missing piece of our heart isn't repaired or replaced, we run the risk of being permanently scarred or of hemorrhaging to death. But there's also the chance that the missing piece will be exchanged; the person we love will take a piece of our heart, yes, but will hand us back a piece of his or her heart in return. Instead of being left with a gaping hole, we'll get a heart transplant.

Whom do I love? Who loves me?

I'M WILLING TO LOVE.

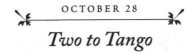

Two to Tango

In the apocryphal stories about Mary's childhood, she's said to have danced for joy. In fact, dancing is mentioned more than one hundred times in Scripture.

God apparently likes to dance. It's no wonder. Love itself is (or should be) a dance, for a dance is the joyous coming together of two people, each sustaining part of the pattern but together doing that which they could never do separately.

People who love each other must come to realize that love, like dance, isn't merely knowing which steps to take. It's also creating what's called a "framework." Both partners must shape their arms so as to hold the other person firmly but not restrictively, opening their arms to let their partner enter into the frame. Only then are the dancers able to move as one or spin free as the music dictates.

People who love each other must also learn that love, like dance, requires partnership. If one person is waltzing and the other doing the tango, neither one is dancing, no matter how perfectly each one does the individual steps. Compromising on the rumba might work, but when two people dance—or love—they must be willing to learn one another's steps.

Finding the perfect dance partner is never easy, unless you step into the framework of God's love. Then dance—and love—becomes possible, for God is, after all, the Lord of the Dance.

Do I find it hard to love? Have I ever danced with God?

I LET THE LORD OF THE DANCE LEAD ME
INTO THE BALLROOM OF LIFE.

Apparitions

We talk about Mary's appearances and apparitions, but exactly what is an apparition?

The *Catholic Encyclopedia* defines an apparition as "the sense-perceptible vision or appearance of Christ, the Blessed Virgin, angels or saints." It goes on to say that "the authenticity of apparitions is a matter for investigation and evaluation by the Church or an experienced spiritual director. Church approval is always required when a popular cultus arises in response to alleged apparitions."

While most apparitions are of Jesus, Mary, angels, and saints, diabolical spirits can also be apparitions. The saintly Curé of Ars was known to have seen the devil on several occasions.

The signs of authentic encounters, at least of the saintly kind, are defined primarily by results. Increased prayer, greater devotion, a sense of peace, and an upsurge of charity are indications that an apparition was authentic. However, the Catholic Church doesn't insist that anyone believe in any private apparition. After careful investigation, the Church sometimes says that an appearance is "plausible" or "credible," but it never gives a solemn or infallible declaration of authenticity.

Since the Catholic Church treats apparitions with healthy skepticism, we should do the same. In fact, if you think you're seeing an apparition, think again. St. Teresa of Avila claimed that most visions are the result of too little sleep and too much self-mortification. She should know: she had the real thing most of her life. If the apparition is authentic, you'll eventually know it. If it's not, a good night's rest and a decent meal should put things back in perspective.

Do I want a supernatural experience?
What would I do if Mary appeared to me right now?

1 USE COMMON SENSE WHEN IT COMES TO UNCOMMON EVENTS.

Prayer

Do you have trouble praying? Many people do—even the disciples, as this passage from Luke reveals:

> Jesus was praying in a certain place, and when he had finished, one of his disciples said to him, "Lord, teach us to pray just as John taught his disciples."
>
> He said to them, "When you pray, say: Father, hallowed be your name, your kingdom come. Give us each day our daily bread and forgive us our sins for we ourselves forgive everyone in debt to us, and do not subject us to the final test."

Even though we have Jesus' own advice on how to pray, we often aren't quite sure whether we're praying correctly or praying for the right thing. We rely on prayer formulas because we know that they work, but our hearts tell us that other kinds of prayer are possible.

If you have difficulty praying, ask Mary for help. She had the most intimate relationship possible with God, because Jesus was her child. She watched him grow up, and thus she knows him better than anyone else ever could. Because of her special relationship with Jesus, Mary doesn't have to rely on set prayers. She knows what it's like to talk with God one on one, face to face.

The words to an old hymn express it well: "Lovely lady dressed in blue, teach me how to pray. God was once your little boy, tell me what to say."

Today ask Mary to help you pray with confidence.

Do I have difficulty praying?
What kinds of prayer do I feel the most comfortable doing?

I KNOW THAT MARY WILL HELP ME LEARN
TO PRAY WITH CONFIDENCE.

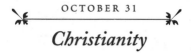

Christianity

Mary was a first-century Jewish woman. As a woman of her time and culture, she would have participated in the rituals, rites, and practices of Judaism. Such a statement seems self-evident, but sometimes we tend to think of Mary and Jesus as *Christians* rather than *Jews*. We forget that Christianity was first considered a sect of Judaism, not a separate faith. We overlook the fact that Jesus didn't come to set up a new religion; rather, he came to establish a new way of relating to God. Jesus himself said that he came not to abolish the law but to fulfill it.

So how does that relate to Mary? In her relationship with Jesus, Mary shows us that God desires not our fear but our friendship. God wants us to enter into a love relationship that will extend into eternity.

Because it can be difficult for us to imagine God relating personally with each of us, Mary shows us that our God is an approachable God. A mother doesn't fear to come close to her own child, so Mary gives us an example of the way we can approach her son Jesus.

Do I think of God as a distant deity or a close personal friend?
Have I ever asked Mary to help me know and love
God more personally?

1 ENTER INTO A LOVE RELATIONSHIP WITH GOD.

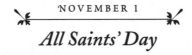

All Saints' Day

Today the Catholic Church commemorates all those men and women who have been declared Saints with a capital *S*. They include such famous individuals as St. Francis of Assisi and St. Catherine of Siena, and such obscure individuals as St. Honoratus and St. Mamertus.

Of all the saints, however, the Blessed Virgin Mary is considered the first and foremost. In his Encyclical *Redemptoris Mater* Pope John Paul II writes, "Mary was and is the one who is 'blessed because she believed'; she was the first to believe. From the moment of his birth in the stable at Bethlehem, Mary followed Jesus step by step in her maternal pilgrimage of faith."

Mary did what we're all called to do—follow Jesus step by step on a pilgrimage of faith. It's never easy. Just look at Mary. Her pilgrimage led her to become a stranger in a strange land when she and her family fled their comfortable homeland to seek refuge in Egypt, it led her to become a misunderstood mother whose son was deemed crazy by the neighbors, and finally it led her to become the mother of a convicted and executed criminal.

If we think our pilgrimage of faith will be any easier, then we haven't been reading the Scriptures. The Bible warns us time and again that the road to sainthood—whether with a capital or a lowercase *s*—is narrow and difficult. While such information can be disheartening, we can look at Mary and her life and take comfort from the fact that we need never walk the path alone. Mary's God—and our God—will always be with us, encouraging us on the way to sanctity.

Do I want to become a saint?
Do I think that sanctity is for other people but not for me?

I TRY TO LIVE A SAINTLY LIFE.

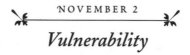

Vulnerability

Often the people we find the most appealing are those who are willing to show their weaknesses. In seeing their vulnerability, we can identify with them and in turn feel free to expose our own weaknesses.

Maybe we can. Then again, maybe not. The truth is that to become vulnerable is to open oneself to the possibility of pain. While most of us would rather avoid pain than embrace it, one of the facts of the spiritual life is that to grow we must become vulnerable. That means accepting the likelihood of pain.

No real growth occurs without some pain, because growth involves change and change creates discomfort. The pain doesn't have to be overwhelming—indeed, it can be relatively minor—but it's inevitable.

That was certainly true for Mary. Once she became vulnerable, opened herself to the will of God, she experienced more pain than she could ever have imagined. And yet along with the pain came incredible joy. That's another of the facts of the spiritual life: while growth requires vulnerability (and hence pain), it also creates joy.

Pain and joy may seem to be contradictory, but they aren't. In the play *Shadowlands*, C. S. Lewis talks about the incredible joy he experienced in his short and pain-filled marriage. In the end, he comes to accept the fact that it wouldn't have been possible to have the joy without the pain. In fact, the pain made the joy all that much sweeter. What was true in Mary's life and in C. S. Lewis's life is true in our own lives as well.

Do I try to avoid pain, or do I accept it as a necessary
part of becoming fully human?

I'M GRATEFUL FOR THE PAIN AS WELL AS THE JOY IN MY LIFE.

Bridges

There's something awe-inspiring about the way a bridge flings itself across an expanse, linking one riverbank with another. While we stand in awe of human-crafted bridges, the most magnificent bridge of all is one not built with human hands: it's Mary herself.

Mary not only managed to bridge the gap between God and humanity by cooperating in the Incarnation, she also managed to connect Christians and Muslims in their traditions and holy books.

The Christian and Muslim traditions are strikingly similar on the subject of Mary: Luke's Gospel tells us that Gabriel greeted Mary with the words "Hail, favored one! The Lord is with you," while the Koran reads, "God has chosen you and made you pure and he has chosen you above the women of the universe."

Pope Pius IX noted that "the Blessed Virgin Mary was, from the first moment of her conception, by a singular grace and privilege of almighty God preserved free from all stain of original sin." Likewise, according to the Koran, Mary, "a saintly woman, was destined, together with Jesus, her son, to be a sign to the universe."

In fact, one of the only differences between the two views of Mary is that there are more verses about Mary in the Koran than in the New Testament!

While wars and border skirmishes break out all over the Middle East, Mary quietly stands as the bridge between two religions and two cultures. It's no wonder that she's so often called the Queen of Peace.

How has Mary acted as a bridge in my life? In what ways
could I ask her to help bridge a gap between me
and someone from whom I'm estranged?

I STRIVE TO BUILD BRIDGES, NOT DIG MOATS.

Well-Chosen Words

The actual words of Mary, as recorded in the Gospels, are few:

"How can this be, since I have no relations with a man?"

"Behold, I am the handmaid of the Lord. May it be done to me according to your word."

"Son, why have you done this to us? Your father and I have been looking for you with great anxiety."

"They have no wine."

"Do whatever he tells you."

Although Mary doesn't say much, her words are well chosen and to the point. She doesn't waste time or energy with flowery phrases.

Her utterances were short and succinct. Since she saw no need to confuse things with a plethora of unnecessary words, neither should we—especially not in prayer. When we pray, we often think that we need to gussy up our speech or use someone else's well-chosen words. But do we really think that we could hide our true thoughts and feelings from God by covering them with fancy phrases? When we pray, let's take Mary as our example, saying what we mean and meaning what we say.

Do I pray with honesty and confidence, or do I try
to fake my way through my prayers?

I TELL GOD THE TRUTH, SINCE GOD ALREADY KNOWS IT.

Miracles

Have you ever experienced a miracle? Do you suspect you might have, but you aren't quite certain? Many of us feel that way. Miracles, like beauty, are in the eye of the beholder. Furthermore, they require an element of faith. In fact, if they didn't require faith, they wouldn't be miracles; they would be scientific facts. And if belief could be reduced to science, there would be no need for faith.

However, we can't reduce the spiritual world to scientific facts. More happens beyond the veil of our sight than we can possibly imagine. Folk tales from around the globe testify to that other world. And we respond strongly to those stories because they resound with the reality in our hearts. We know intuitively that there's another world where miracles themselves are science.

Mary is part of that world, and she allows us glimpses into it through her appearances. Those appearances are proof that the world we can touch and taste and smell isn't the *real* world. No, what's real is unseen most of the time.

Part of the great puzzle of spiritual growth is its paradox: to have, we must relinquish; to receive, we must give; to be loved, we must love. Once we understand the essentially paradoxical nature of spirituality, we begin to realize that we're surrounded by miracles every second of every day.

Have I ever experienced a miracle? Do I really want
to experience one, or would I rather just read
about other people's miracles?

I KNOW THAT I'LL EXPERIENCE A MIRACLE IF I ALLOW
MYSELF TO BE OPEN TO THE POSSIBILITY.

Tears

One of the more common phenomena in recent Marian apparitions is a statue of Mary that cries either blood or tears. People have flocked around these statues, trying to capture some of the mysterious fluid. On the occasions when scientists have been called in to analyze the fluid, they've noted that while it exhibits some of the characteristics of human blood or human tears, it can't be officially confirmed as either. Nonetheless, the tears have attracted enormous attention from both the pious and the impious alike.

If you're interested in that sort of thing, statues that weep are all well and good for inspiring piety and devotion, but it's the real tears of real people that we're called to wipe away. All the crying statues in the world shouldn't move us as much as the tears of one real person. If we're moved to pity by a statue, then how much more so should we be moved by the tears of a starving child, a homeless mother, or a victim of war?

While no one can say for sure that Mary's statues are crying, we can be certain that if they are, it's because we're ignoring the real tears of the world.

What sights move me the most? Am I influenced more by mysterious events or by actual people? What concrete actions have I taken recently to help wipe away the tears of the world?

1'M MORE MOVED BY INJUSTICE THAN MYSTERY.

Hagion

In her great prayer of gratitude to God, Mary says, "The Mighty One has done great things for me, and holy is his name." In the Greek translation of this text, the word for *holy* is *hagion,* the root of which lies in a phrase that means "without land." It's the same root that forms the base of a synonym for saints—*hagio*—and it's used in naming the biographies of the saints—*hagiographies.*

In one sense, those who are holy are "without land," for they've come to recognize that we're but travelers on this earth. We aren't meant to live here for eternity; rather, we journey through this life without putting our roots into the land.

Striving for holiness doesn't mean that we can't enjoy the good things of the earth, however. St. Francis of Assisi, the quintessential ascetic, asked for almond cookies on his deathbed. St. Francis Borgia (the white sheep of the notorious Borgia clan) was a gourmet par excellence. St. Francis Liguori was a connoisseur of music and the theater.

But holiness requires the recognition that all the good things of the earth are ours only to enjoy, not to possess. Mary most certainly understood this principle. She enjoyed life in all its fullness (including wine at weddings!), but she didn't seek earthly riches. Rather, she recognized and praised a God who "has thrown down the rulers from their thrones but lifted up the lowly. The hungry he has filled with good things; the rich he has sent away empty."

Do I want to be holy? What if holiness means giving
up some of the things I treasure most?

WITH MARY, I SAY, "THE MIGHTY ONE HAS DONE
GREAT THINGS FOR ME."

Flowers

By this time of year, most gardens are brown and barren. Seed catalogs, however, are already burgeoning with the promise of spring. For gardeners—in fact, for many people generally—flipping through the pages of these catalogs is a way of glimpsing the future—especially the glory of summer flowers.

In Greco-Roman times, it was common to place an offering of flowers on the altars of the gods and goddesses—Zeus, Aphrodite, Athena, Pan, and Daphne, among them. As Christianity spread throughout the world, flowers—along with the rest of nature—lost their association with pagan deities and became a sign of God's love for us. Even today our churches are often adorned with fragrant flowers, sometimes in the midst of winter.

Hundreds of flowers have become associated specifically with Mary's life and attributes over the years. In days past, many homes and castles had a so-called Mary garden, where plants that reflected Mary's joy or goodness or sorrow or intercession were planted. A few cathedrals and churches still have Mary gardens, and now and then you still see a yard where an image of Mary reigns over a mound or border of many different kinds of flowers.

Rather than planting a butterfly garden or a hummingbird garden next spring, you might want to consider planting a Mary garden. Then, when your marigolds, foxgloves, delphiniums, Canterbury bells, ferns, and violets begin to grow, you can offer praise to Mary—and through her, to her son Jesus.

Do I use nature as a way of praising God?

I RECOGNIZE GOD'S GOODNESS IN ALL OF CREATION.

R and R

In workaholic Japan, some companies have to order their executives to take vacations. With grim determination, those executives head off to "have fun," approaching their R and R with the same determination they show on the job.

While we may chuckle a bit at the thought of working at having fun, many of us have forgotten what it's like to play. Either we ignore play altogether, as some Japanese do, or we play so competitively that we turn every game into a contest to be won. We've forgotten how to do something for R and R that has no practical, extrinsic value.

In the painting "The Childhood of Mary Virgin," the pre-Raphaelite artist Dante Gabriel Rossetti depicted a young, pensive Mary sitting under a grape arbor with her mother, embroidering a glorious red hanging. What Mary is doing is "impractical," in the sense that her embroidery project isn't serviceable or functional. The hanging is pure decoration, made for fun.

Apparently Mary still has a sense of play. She's seen in a humble town in a war-torn nation on one occasion; the next time she's seen shimmering as an image on a skyscraper window, dancing over the roof of an ancient church in Egypt, or hovering above a quaint Irish village. She comes dressed as a Mexican peasant, a French woman, a glorious queen, a humble maiden.

No matter where she appears or what she says, Mary always brings a sense of joy and peace—not to mention at least a hint of playfulness.

What do I do for play? Do I think of play as a waste of time or
as something necessary to my spiritual health?

I FIND TIME FOR REST AND RELAXATION.

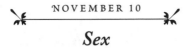

Sex

What did Mary know and think about sex? Does it seem irreverent to consider that she might have been a sexual being?

It's certainly a great deal easier to think of Mary as a beautiful waxen doll, created from all eternity to carry the infant Jesus in her womb. To think of her as a real woman, with all that that entails, seems, well, sort of disrespectful, doesn't it?

The fact is that Mary *was* a real woman. She had the hormones and anatomical features of every other woman. What set Mary apart, however, was the fact that she was the first in a long line of female saints and religious who were normal, healthy women but who offered their sexuality back to God. Being a normal sexual person doesn't mean that you have to *act* upon your sexuality. Mary obviously opted not to be sexually active in her relationship with Joseph. That doesn't mean, however, that she *couldn't* have been. She freely chose her stance.

What differentiates Mary and all others who dedicate their sexuality to God from the rest of humanity isn't that they know how to say no; rather, it's that they know how to say yes to God with every fiber of their all-too-normal bodies.

Do I treat my sexuality as a gift or as a burden?

1 GIVE THANKS FOR THE GIFT OF MY BODY.

Lover and Beloved

Some psychologists believe that there's a lover and a beloved in every relationship. Although the terms don't indicate degree of commitment or depth of love, they do serve to explain how some relationships operate.

The lover is the person who shows his or her love the most obviously. He or she is the one who tends to say words of love, give tokens of affection, and "pursue" the relationship.

The beloved, on the other hand, is the one who tends to receive the love. While he or she may be just as passionate about the relationship, his or her style is to be more restrained, to hang back a bit on the overt displays of affection. He or she is the one pursued.

While such a balance may work well, if one of the partners becomes stuck in either lover or beloved mode, the relationship may begin to show strain. If the person who's generally the beloved never assumes the lover role, for example, the lover may begin to feel neglected and taken advantage of. Conversely, if the lover never gets a change to feel beloved, he or she may find affection beginning to wane.

Sometimes when we think of Mary, we think of her as the lover and God as the beloved. But God is both lover and beloved to each of us. God both accepts our love and actively gives us love in return. The relationship that we—and Mary—have with God may be the only one where we're both lover and beloved simultaneously.

If I'm in a relationship at the moment,
am I the lover or the beloved?

I ALLOW MYSELF TO LOVE GOD AND BE LOVED BY GOD.

Self-Love

Jesus said that the first great commandment is to love God with your whole heart. The second great commandment is to love your neighbor as yourself. Though we work hard to get the *love God* and *love your neighbor* parts down pat, we sometimes overlook the *love yourself* part.

What does it mean to love yourself?

Clearly Jesus wasn't talking about the "me, me, me; I, I, I" self-aggrandizement of the evil queen in *Snow White,* who spent most of her time asking her magic mirror if she was still the fairest woman in the land.

There's a significant difference between the self-love that's merely self-indulgent and the self-love that's endorsed by God. *Genuine* self-love—the sort Jesus calls us to—is always directed toward God. The more a person is directed to God, the more he or she is directed toward wholeness. In fact, self-love is essentially recognizing and appreciating wholeness. Moreover, self-love stands up for itself and its values. When you love yourself authentically, you recognize both your faults (without self-deprecation) and your virtues.

No one in Scripture demonstrates authentic self-love better than Mary. On receiving Gabriel's message, she asserted confidently, and in a way that gave all the honor to God, that all generations would call her blessed. She's equally self-confident in her apparitions. For instance, she says, "I am the Immaculate Conception!" She doesn't fumble around muttering, "God told me to tell you that God says I could be considered the Immaculate Conception." She knows who she is—and in knowing herself, she's able to express real self-love.

If you're losing or destroying yourself for the sake of "love," then what you're experiencing isn't real love. Perhaps you need to ask Mary to help you learn what *self-*love means.

Do I find it hard to be nice to myself?
Do I ever feel guilty when I "treat" myself?

I LOVE MY NEIGHBOR, BUT I ALSO LOVE MYSELF.

Touchstone

In ancient times, although goldsmiths had no way of removing impurities from gold, they rubbed gold across a black stone called a *touchstone* to see what kind of impurities (such as copper) were present.

The prophet Zechariah says that God will test his people in the same way:

> I will bring the one third through fire,
> and I will refine them as silver is refined,
> and I will test them as gold is tested.
> They shall call upon my name, and I will hear them.
> I will say, "They are my people,"
> and they shall say, "The Lord is my God."

In one sense, Mary is our touchstone. By comparing our lives with hers, we can reveal our impurities. Her life, freed from sin through the Immaculate Conception and the salvific power of her son, allows us to see where we fall short of the ideal. But the notion of a touchstone isn't merely to point out the impurities; a touchstone also highlights the gold. Likewise, even when we see areas of our lives that need work, we can also see areas where the gold of grace is shining through.

What areas of my life do I know need some work?
Am I willing to use Mary as my touchstone?

❧ ALLOW MY LIFE TO BE TESTED, AS GOLD IS TESTED.

Justice

When we talk about justice, we tend to limit our thinking to legal action in a court of law. We believe that justice is done when criminals are convicted, murderers executed, and crimes punished.

When we talk about charity, on the other hand, we generally refer to acts of kindness to the less fortunate. We think of charity as giving a donation to a worthy cause or a handout to a street person.

The Hebrew Scriptures take a radically different view of these two words. What we call *charity*, it calls *justice*.

Mary stands as a living example of this scriptural interpretation of justice. The woman who announced to her son, "They have no wine," isn't afraid to go boldly before the throne of God to say, "They have no food, no home, no job." Completely absorbed by our human condition and human struggle, she prays now and always for our broken and confused world. But more than that, she devotes herself to praying for the forgiveness of sin. As an Orthodox Church prayer says, "O Mary the Virgin *Theotokos,* the holy and trusted intercessor of the human race, intercede for our sake before Christ, whom you bore, that He may grant us the forgiveness of our sins."

As you go about your daily life, do you see people in need of food, clothing, shelter, and forgiveness? If so, don't give them a token in the name of charity; give them all you can in the name of justice.

In what ways do I promote justice in the world?
Could I do more than I'm doing?

1 EXECUTE JUSTICE—AND 1 DO SO CHARITABLY!

Language

Apparently Mary is a skilled linguist, for in all of her appearances, she speaks the language of the person who sees her.

In 1531 a peasant who lived near Tenochtitlán (which is now Mexico City) saw a vision of a beautiful woman who identified herself as the Virgin of Guadalupe. At least that's what we're generally told. However, given that the peasant, Juan Diego, was a Nahuatl Indian, it's unlikely that Mary used the Spanish word *Guadalupe* when talking to him. More likely she described herself with the Nahuatl word *Coatlaxopeuh*, which is pronounced "quat-la-su-pay."

Dissection of the native word reveals something fascinating about Mary herself. *Coa* means "serpent," *tla* is a noun-ending interpreted as "the," while *xopeuh* means "to crush or stamp out." If this *is* the word Juan Diego heard from Mary, she identified herself as "the one who crushes the serpent."

This title is reminiscent of both the promise God made in Genesis—"I will put enmity between you and the woman, and between your offspring and hers; He will strike at your head, while you strike at his heel"— and these words of Revelation:

> A great sign appeared in the sky, a woman clothed with the sun, with the moon under her feet, and on her head a crown of twelve stars. . . . She was with child and wailed aloud in pain as she labored to give birth. Then another sign appeared in the sky; it was a huge red dragon, with seven heads and ten horns, and on its heads were seven diadems. Its tail swept away a third of the stars in the sky and hurled them down to the earth. Then the dragon stood before the woman about to give birth, to devour her child when she gave birth. She gave birth to a son, a male child, destined to rule all the nations with an iron rod.

What titles of Mary mean the most to me?

I KNOW THAT BOTH MARY AND GOD ALWAYS SPEAK
IN A LANGUAGE I UNDERSTAND.

Envy

Along with such favorites as pride and lust, envy is one of the so-called seven deadly sins. While Mary wasn't guilty of envy (or pride or lust or any of the other sins), it's quite possible that some of her neighbors might have been envious of her—at least until her son was arrested as a criminal and executed.

After all, for many years she lived a very nice life. She had a terrific kid who was clearly brilliant and a talented husband (God wouldn't have chosen an incompetent to be Jesus' foster father), and she was undoubtedly loved and respected by most people. Somewhere along the line, someone must have shown a few sparks of envy toward her.

How did Mary handle those who envied her? Of course, we don't know for sure, but we can speculate that she would have made every attempt to diffuse the envy, for envy unchecked can be fatal. (It isn't called a *deadly* sin for nothing!)

Since we aren't Mary, it's far more likely that we're on the envying (rather than envied) side of things. What can we do to combat this natural tendency?

One way is to recognize that God measures love not by what we have but by what we are. Once we stop concentrating on what we have (or don't have) and start focusing on what we can become—recognizing that we really do have all we need to become the people God wants us to be—envy will fade away.

Do I envy anyone?
If so, what do I envy the most about that person?

I'M GRATEFUL FOR WHAT I HAVE, NOT ENVIOUS
OF WHAT I DON'T HAVE.

Confidence

Sometimes groups do what are called "trust exercises." As an example, a person might stand in the center of a circle and fall backward, trusting that someone will be there to catch him or her before the ground hits.

The purpose of such an exercise is to graphically demonstrate confidence in others. While some of us might be willing to trust that we'd be caught if we fell backward in a circle, we're far less likely to have much confidence in others in the real world. Experience has taught us well: lean too far back, and you'll topple over.

One of Mary's greatest gifts to humanity is that she shows us the one Person worthy of our trust: God. Although she was "greatly troubled" when Gabriel came to announce that she would bear the Messiah, she was willing to place her confidence in God's plan and say—though she knew only the sketchiest of details—"Okay, I'll do it."

One way we can emulate Mary is by having confidence in God even when we don't have all the details spelled out. Perhaps the "God-shaped vacuum" that seventeenth-century philosopher Blaise Pascal said was in every human is really just the desire to trust the only One worthy of our complete trust.

Do I have trouble trusting people?
Do I have trust trusting God?

I KNOW THAT GOD WILL NEVER ABANDON ME.

Natural Human Emotions

All too often, we erroneously assume that holiness precludes natural human emotions—especially the darker emotions. It's hard to envision Mary so frustrated that she's ready to cry, for example, or so upset that she has to take a slow, deep breath before she speaks.

But emotions are one of God's great gifts to humanity, and Mary was fully, gloriously human. She had to have experienced all the emotions we do—the positive and the negative.

In point of fact, the closer we are to God, the more deeply we feel both pain and joy. But even animals, as we move up the evolutionary scale, experience emotion. Jane Goodall's studies of chimpanzees indicate that they experience such "human" feelings as grief, joy, anger, and contentment.

Certainly we often attribute emotional responses to our pets, especially our cats and dogs. And what we see as evidence of emotion is part of what we find so appealing about mammals. It's in part the lack of visible emotion in reptiles and fish that makes most of us feel so estranged from them.

Today take note of every emotion you experience. Don't evaluate or judge your feelings. Just *feel* them. And then give thanks to God that you're able to experience such a wide range of feelings.

What am I feeling right now? Do I tend to judge my feelings?

I KNOW THAT FEELINGS ARE NEITHER RIGHT NOR WRONG.

Depression

Depression still bears a stigma in much of our society. Even though many famous people, including Winston Churchill and Abraham Lincoln, have suffered tremendously from depression, we still tend to think of it as a mental disorder and treat it with wary suspicion.

However, increasing medical evidence indicates that much (if not all) depression has a biological basis and can be effectively treated with medication. Although medication can't abolish or cure the events that sometimes trigger depression—for example, grief, illness, or loss—it can help a depressed person cope more effectively with such dramatic life events.

All that aside, we still have a tendency to berate ourselves for things we don't have much control over (such as being depressed) and excuse ourselves for things we can do something about (such as pettiness and self-centeredness).

Yet one thing the new scientific evidence shows is that depression isn't a moral failing. In fact, Jesus may have had a taste of depression when he was praying in the Garden of Gethsemane the night before the Crucifixion. His desperate prayer, "If this cup may pass . . . ," has more than a touch of despair in it. If Jesus himself could be depressed, then we need not castigate ourselves when we're similarly affected; rather, we can ask Mary and Jesus to help us find a way out from under what Churchill called "the black dog."

Do I know anyone who's depressed (perhaps myself)?
What am I doing about it?
Have I asked for help through prayer?

1 KNOW THAT GOD IS WITH ME IN BOTH MY
UP-TIMES AND MY DOWN-TIMES.

Mirror

Mirrors figure rather prominently in many folk tales. In *Snow White,* for example, the wicked stepmother/queen relies on her magic mirror to keep her informed of her status as reigning beauty of the kingdom. In *The Snow Queen,* by Hans Christian Andersen, a goblin produces a mirror in which everything beautiful is diminished and everything ugly magnified. In neither case does the mirror, which *should* reflect truth, actually do so.

Often we spend our lives looking in warped mirrors. Rather than seeing ourselves as we really are, we let other people's projections and ideas shape our self-image. If we're lucky, we see ourselves as close to reality, but usually we have our beauty diminished and our ugliness magnified (as in the goblin mirror) or we have our good qualities so overemphasized that we overlook our hardened heart.

Mary shows us that the best way to really see ourselves is to not look at ourselves at all. Mary never points to herself; she allows herself to become transparent so that we can see Jesus through her. Likewise, when we allow ourselves to become transparent to Jesus, we begin to see not ourselves but the life of God within us. And once we can do that, we no longer have need of mirrors, for then we're able to see ourselves with God's own eyes.

Do I see myself as I really am or as other people tell me I am?

I SEE MYSELF THROUGH GOD'S EYES.

Whirled Peas

Sometime during the last decade, bumper stickers reading "Visualize World Peace" began to appear. Since world peace is something nearly every person longs for, this slogan had great appeal for a time. But then one day a cynic pasted a bumper sticker on his (or her!) car that said "Visualize Whirled Peas." One might imagine that driver having a desperate desire for a steaming bowl of split-pea soup!

One thing both bumper stickers have in common is the idea that we can make things happen merely by imagining them. While visualization is an important tool in sharpening various skills—athletes use it to envision themselves winning a race, for instance—visualization alone can't create reality. You can visualize yourself winning a marathon day and night, but unless you put on your running shoes and start training, nothing concrete will happen.

In her appearances, Mary advocates peace, asking her followers to envision a world without war and strife. Yet she also points out that merely *thinking* about peace won't make it happen. She tells us over and over that we must both pray for peace and actively seek peace by living in harmony with those around us.

Am I "at war" with anyone at the moment?
Is there someone with whom I need to forge a peace treaty?

INSOFAR AS POSSIBLE, I LIVE IN PEACE WITH ALL PEOPLE.

Sinlessness

According to Catholic theology, Jesus and Mary are the only two people who've ever lived their entire lives without sinning. There's a difference between the two of them, however. Jesus never sinned because he was God, and as God he was incapable of sin; Mary, on the other hand, was conceived without the tendency toward sin that the rest of us are born with, and because of that special blessing was able to live a sinless life.

The difference may seem to be hairsplitting, but it really isn't. Jesus *couldn't* have sinned. Period. Mary *could* have sinned but didn't. That difference makes all the difference for us, who not only can sin but do sin.

Mary was able to live a life free from the burden of sin because she cooperated fully with the salvation offered by God. While Mary's situation is difficult to understand—indeed, many of the great saints had trouble with the concept, so if it puzzles you, you're in good company—Catholic teaching basically says that Mary had the grace of Christ's saving action applied to her while she was still in the womb.

While theologians can ponder the intricacies of the process, what it all means to us is that Mary stands as an example of faith. Knowing that she was able to cooperate fully with God's will, we can strive to live more fully in the grace that God offers each of us.

Do I try to make it on my own, or do I accept God's help in living my life?

I'M THANKFUL FOR MARY'S EXAMPLE OF A GRACE-FILLED LIFE.

Thanksgiving

Most of the official American holidays commemorate something with a political overtone. The Fourth of July, for instance, recalls our independence from England. Memorial Day is set aside to remember those who've died in the service of our country.

Thanksgiving is the one exception. While its roots lie with the Pilgrims, its purpose is simply for all Americans to give thanks for their blessings. Inherent in the celebration is the assumption that there's someone to whom thanks can be directed. Thus, albeit in a roundabout way, Thanksgiving honors God (and is the only U.S. holiday to do so).

We shouldn't limit our thankfulness to a single day, however. Mary gave thanks every day of her life. We need to cultivate that same attitude of daily thankfulness. We need to set aside a regular time every day to give thanks.

And yes, we need to be thankful even for our difficulties and adversities. Being thankful for trouble doesn't mean that we have to jump up and down with delight when things go wrong in our lives, but it *does* mean that we must recognize God's providence in all that happens to us and give thanks for God's care. In other words, while we don't have to experience the emotion of happiness all the time, we do need to cultivate the mental mind-set of thanksgiving every day.

What three things am I the most thankful for today?
Can I recall a difficulty that turned out
to be a blessing in disguise?

I'M THANKFUL FOR EVERYTHING THAT HAPPENS TO ME TODAY.

Retirement

In A.D. 431, leaders of the Christian Church gathered to debate several burning issues, one of which was whether Mary should be identified as "the mother of Christ as God" or "the mother of the human Christ." The participants couldn't agree on which designation was correct, but they could agree that, according to the Gospel of John, Mary was entrusted to John by Jesus, as he hung from the cross, and that John and Mary went to live in the port city of Ephesus, in present-day Turkey. Today ruins of the home where she's said to have lived can be found at the end of the road leading from the Magnesia Gate to Mt. Bulbul (now known as Mt. Koressos).

How would she have spent those last years of her life? Jesus' work was over, yet Mary continued to live for several—perhaps as many as twenty—more years. What did she do in her "retirement"?

As she had all of her life, she probably brought water from the well and prepared daily meals consisting of vegetables, the occasional small portion of meat, and such grains as barley and wheat. She probably dried flax on the roof, to be spun into linen thread, and bargained with shopkeepers in the open-air market for groceries. In the evening, perhaps she and John sat on the roof and talked about the old days, when Jesus was still with them. They probably never envisioned the future, when John's story of Jesus would be the greatest biography ever written and Mary would be the world's mother. And Mary probably never imagined that once she joined Jesus in heaven, she'd work harder than ever to bring the entire world to salvation!

What do I want to do when I retire? Am I waiting until some future date before I start to really live?

I DON'T WAIT UNTIL TOMORROW TO LIVE TODAY.

Possessions

The Levites (or Temple priests) of the Hebrew Scriptures possessed no land; as priests, their riches were heavenly, not earthly. Jesus himself echoed that sentiment when he agreed with his followers that he was a king but added, "My kingdom is not of this world."

People who dedicate their lives to God often renounce possessions and take vows of poverty, not because land or possessions are bad in themselves but because they can become encumbrances to a free life. We may think that we own our possessions, but in fact our possessions can own us.

If St. Paul had owned vineyards and olive orchards, he wouldn't have left his estate long enough to make his missionary journeys or even pen his great letters. He would have been too busy administering his estate, managing his employees, and shipping his fruit.

If Mother Teresa had invested extensively in Calcutta real estate, she'd be too occupied with rents, leases, and administration to minister to the poor and needy.

And if Mary had been a major Galilean landlord, she wouldn't have been available when Gabriel came to visit her with a message from God; she would have been out collecting her rent and checking the conditions of her buildings.

Most of us need to have a certain amount of possessions, but if maintaining our belongings starts to require so much time that we have none left over for the really important things of life—such as prayer and good works—we need to look to Mary and look again at our own lives.

Do I own my possessions, or do my possessions own me?

I ENJOY WHAT I HAVE, BUT I DON'T LET *HAVING*
BECOME MY REASON FOR LIVING.

Embarrassment

Have you ever been so embarrassed that you wished the ground would open up and swallow you? Most of us have experienced acute embarrassment at least once in our lives. (And for most of us, once is more than enough!)

Sometimes, though, we have to be willing to run the risk of being embarrassed in order to accomplish a major good. Mary, for instance, ran the risk of total embarrassment when she ordered the servants to do whatever Jesus told them to do. What if Jesus hadn't done anything? What if the servants had gone to him and he'd said, "What are you talking about?" What if he'd changed the water into grape juice instead of wine? What if? *What if?*

We can argue that Mary knew what Jesus was going to do, but that may not be true. Her words to the servants show that she wasn't certain what was going to happen. Otherwise, she probably would have said something more along the lines of, "Don't worry about the wine. My son has it under control."

Whenever we put ourselves on the line for others, we run the risk of embarrassment. Yet when we're willing to expose ourselves to humiliation, we give God the opportunity to work miracles. If we weigh the good of a miracle against the possibility of a few moments of embarrassment, the choice doesn't seem so difficult after all.

Have I ever embarrassed myself?
Have I ever been embarrassed by God?

1 KNOW THAT GOD WON'T EMBARRASS ME
WHEN 1 PUT MY TRUST IN GOD.

Sharing

When a group of little kids was asked what *sharing* means, one of them replied, "It means if you got something first, you get to keep it." Another said, "Sharing means if somebody else has something you want, they have to give it to you." While we may chuckle at the way their childish definitions of sharing depend on whether they're the sharer or the sharee, we often act as if we agree with them; we act as if what's mine is mine and what's yours is mine too—because you've got to share.

But as we all know, sharing doesn't mean keeping; it means giving. It means letting go rather than holding on. It means taking what's ours by right and freely, willingly, generously giving it to others.

Mary stands before us as a prime example of true sharing. She not only shared her very life with us so that we could have salvation; she continues to share with us even now. Through her appearances, she shares her insights with us. Through her prayers, she shares her power. Through her love, she shares her son.

If you have trouble sharing (and many of us do, no matter how old we are), ask Mary to help you become more generous, more open, more willing. In doing so, you'll learn that the words attributed to St. Francis of Assisi are indeed true: "It is in giving that we receive."

What do I have the most trouble sharing—
my possessions, my time, or my self?

I SHARE.

Autumn

At this point in the calendar, the year is coming to an end. There's only one more month left before we have to learn to write a new date on our letters and checks. But just as buried in every hello is a final goodbye, so buried in fall is the promise of spring. Even while the land is shutting down for winter, new life is waiting deep within the soil.

Right now we're in the autumn of life on earth. We know that, but that's about all we know. We aren't sure if we're moments away from the first snowfall or have weeks of Indian summer yet to come. All we know, from both Jesus and Mary, is that we're in the fall of life on earth. The end is coming. We don't know exactly when, but we know it's on the way.

Knowing that we're in the final stages of life on earth doesn't mean that we should panic. It does mean that we should start getting ready for the winter that we know will come. We still have time to enjoy what's one of the most beautiful seasons of the year, but we can't become complacent in the fall sunshine. Aware that winter could come at any moment, we should live our lives not in fear but in hopeful anticipation.

Am I ready for the winter of life, whether it's the winter of my own individual life or the winter of the world itself?

I LIVE *IN* THE PRESENT BUT NOT *FOR* THE PRESENT.

Mother and Son

Imagine the scene. It's late one evening. Mary has just banked the fire for the night and is getting ready for bed when she hears a knock at the door. *Who could that be this time of night?* she wonders. She cracks the door and sees, who else, Jesus and a handful of disciples.

"Hi, Mom!" Jesus says breezily. "What's there to eat?"

If you think such a thing never happened, then you haven't had much experience with mothers and sons, even adult sons. The first thing most sons do when they come home is head for the cupboard to see what mom has to eat.

What would Mary have done in such a case? Most likely she would have put some wood on the fire (or told Jesus to do it!), pulled out bread, cheese, and fruit, and given the crew something to eat. She would have known, as do all mothers, that you have to feed the body before you can begin to probe the soul. Then, once everyone was full, she would have begun to ply Jesus with questions: "Where have you been preaching?" "What has been people's reaction?" "Are you attracting many followers?"

Finally, when both body and soul were satisfied, she would have undoubtedly made sure everyone was comfy and then gone to bed, content in the knowledge that her son was once more safely under her roof.

*If I have children, what kind of relationship do I have with
them or would I like to have with them in the future?*

I KNOW THE IMPORTANCE OF FEEDING BOTH BODY
AND SOUL—IN THE PROPER ORDER!

Sunshine

Because the sun rises so late and sets so early at this time of year, many people who live in northern climes have trouble getting enough light to function properly. They may be sleepy all winter, feel testy and crabby, or have a general case of the winter blues. In fact, some people become seriously debilitated by this wintry lack of illumination. Doctors call this condition SAD, or seasonal affective disorder, and often prescribe light therapy to help overcome it.

However, all the artificial light in the world combined would be feeble beside the sun. And our sun's light is weak compared to that of the blazing supernovas. And yet even those are pitiful compared to the illumination flowing from God.

Mary's appearances are almost always accompanied by a glimpse of that radiant light—a light that puts the sun to shame. In fact, in most of her pictures, she's portrayed with a shining halo or an aureole of golden radiance, representing the divine light that emanates from within her. As St. Anthony of Padua wrote, "She is said to be light because she dispels the darkness." When we see Mary, we see also a glimmer of the light that eternally illuminates the heavens.

Perhaps God sends Mary into the world to remind us that when winter comes, spring—Mary's season and the time when sunshine returns—can't be far behind.

Do I let myself be illuminated by the light of truth
that Mary brings to the world?

I REFLECT GOD'S LIGHT TO ALL I MEET.

Rejoicing

When the angel Gabriel appeared to Mary, he announced, as one translation has it, "Rejoice, favored one!" When you think about it, that's a rather odd statement. The angel gave Mary a direct order—but one that would have been rather hard to obey. After all, what does it mean to rejoice? And can a person do it on command?

The word *rejoice* implies more than the mere feeling of happiness. It carries connotations of glory, exultation, triumph, and even revelry. Rejoicing is a wellspring that flows over one's entire being.

Interestingly, unlike happiness, which is an emotion over which we have little or no control, rejoicing is something we can choose to do. We can choose to express glory or triumph, no matter what we're feeling at the moment.

If we need proof that we can always rejoice despite our feelings, we need look no further than to Mary. It's clear that Gabriel expected Mary to rejoice, yet he must have known that she was undoubtedly going to feel anxiety. He didn't expect her to be happy on command, but he did expect her to rejoice.

Likewise, we can rejoice at all times and in all circumstances, not because we feel giddy but because life itself is a celebration. To breathe the air, to see the sky, to merely be alive is more than enough cause for rejoicing, angel command or not.

Do I have an attitude of gratitude toward life?
Do I rejoice even when I don't feel particularly happy?

I REJOICE IN THE FACT THAT I'M ALIVE AND LOVED BY GOD.

Bethlehem

"O little town of Bethlehem, how still we see thee lie." The strains of that beloved Christmas carol conjure up an image of a serene, undisturbed village.

Towns at night—especially when viewed from a distance—always appear still, yet once you take a closer look, you discover that they're teeming with activity.

Bethlehem was no exception. As we know, the village was brimming with folks awaiting the government census. It doesn't take much imagination to picture the scene at tavern and inn: loud laughter, drunken shouts, clanging dishes, barking dogs, travelers demanding a place to stay.

Even down in the stable, with the sheep, goats, cows, and donkeys, it would hardly have been still. There, in the cold and dark, a baby was being born. Anyone who's been present at a baby's birth knows that it's not a particularly still time. Even if, as the early Christian writers suggested, Mary was spared the normal pains and tribulations of childbirth, both she and Joseph had to have been excited. After all, neither of them knew what to expect. What's more, after the baby was born, the night sky was filled with angels, singing "Glory to God in the highest!"

Bethlehem *still?* Hah!

Sometimes our lives are a bit like Bethlehem: still when seen from a distance, but churning and turbulent up close. At those times, it helps to remember the old proverb "Still waters run deep." That night in Bethlehem, when a baby was being born and a world was being re-created, even the commotion was blessed with a heavenly calm.

Am I calm on the inside or merely on the outside?
Do I let the commotion of life cause me to lose
my focus on what's really important?

I'M AT PEACE, NO MATTER WHAT'S HAPPENING AROUND ME.

Angelic Messengers

In recent years, angels have become tremendously popular. Books, plays, movies, and television dramas have featured angels interacting with humanity on a regular basis. Often angels are shown lending assistance—getting people out of trouble or just hovering around saving people from themselves. While angels may do those things, the word *angel* means simply messenger—nothing more, nothing less.

Throughout both the Hebrew and Christian Scriptures, that's exactly what angels do: bring messages. An angel asks Mary if she'll consent to being Jesus' mother, an angel informs Elizabeth's husband that their child will be called John, an angel breaks the news to Joseph that Mary is pregnant, an angel warns Joseph to flee Herod's murderous wrath, an angel comes to Jesus with words of comfort before the Crucifixion, an angel greets the women at the tomb, and an angel tells the disciples to stop staring at the sky and go home after Jesus has ascended into heaven.

In some of her appearances, Mary is seen accompanied by an angel or angels. Actually, an angelic companion is very appropriate for Mary, because she's God's primary messenger to the world. Every day—through her prayers if not her appearances—Mary reminds us of God's love, God's plan for the world, and the necessity for conversion. In fact, Mary is so effective a messenger that perhaps her middle name should perhaps be Angelica!

Have I ever received an angelic message?
Do I ever ask my guardian angel for help and guidance?

¶ PAY ATTENTION FOR SIGNS OF ANGELS.

Focus

Have you ever looked up at the night sky and tried unsuccessfully to focus on a particular star, only to have the star leap into clarity the moment you shifted your vision a little to one side? Science tells us that this phenomenon has something to do with the rods and cones in our eyes, as well as the way our night vision has evolved, but none of that matters when we're trying to see a star. All that matters is that we learn how to look a bit off to the side of the celestial body we want to see and focus on it with our peripheral vision.

Taking our direct sight off an object in order to see it more clearly often works in our spiritual life and our relationship with God as well. If we're having trouble figuring out God's will for our life, maybe we need to focus a bit off to one side—say, on Mary—instead of trying to stare directly in the face of God.

It's ironic, but by looking at Mary and her example, we may be able to see more clearly what God would want us to see. It's as if God suddenly comes into focus, just as a star comes into sight when we stop looking for it. When we stop trying so hard to see, we're actually able to see more clearly.

Do I have difficulty discerning God's will for my life?
Could it be that I'm trying too hard?

I BELIEVE THAT I'LL SEE WHAT GOD WANTS ME TO SEE.

Consecration

After David was anointed king of Israel, but while Saul still sat on the throne, David and his starving army entered the Tabernacle and ate the consecrated bread. This was an infraction of the law of Moses, but it kept Israel's greatest king from dying of hunger. Moreover, God called David "a man after my own heart."

That which is consecrated is set apart for God but available for human use. A bishop, for example, is consecrated, but he remains very much in human interaction. The bread and wine we take at Communion are consecrated, yet we consume them in ordinary fashion. And though Mary was set apart, consecrated for God, she traveled the dusty roads of Judea and Galilee, ate ordinary food, probably slept on the flat roof of her house in Nazareth, and washed the family clothing on a stream bank.

Those who are consecrated to the will of God, such as mystics and contemplatives, don't all live in silent cloisters. Many are in the world, acting as bank tellers and copyeditors and schoolteachers. What sets them apart, makes them consecrated, is their prayer life. These are people who, like Mary, constantly have a prayer either on their lips or in their hearts. This is the essence of real consecration: setting your inner spiritual life apart for God alone, for what's consecrated to God can be used for the good of, but cannot be soiled by, the world.

Do I live a consecrated life? Do I set myself apart for God, or
do I set myself apart for myself, my family, or my work?

¶ CONSECRATE MYSELF TO GOD AND GOD ALONE.

Immanuel

The name *Immanuel*, one of the traditional names for Jesus, comes from a passage in the Hebrew Scripture of Isaiah where God spoke to Ahaz:

Ask for a sign from the Lord, your God; let it be deep as the nether world, or high as the sky!

But Ahaz answered, "I will not ask! I will not tempt the Lord!"

Then he said: Listen, O house of David! Is it not enough for you to weary men, must you also weary my God? Therefore, the Lord himself will give you this sign: the virgin shall be with child, and bear a son, and shall name him Immanuel.

This prophecy, uttered long before Jesus' birth, was restated in the Christian Scriptures as they related that birth: "Behold, the virgin shall be with child and bear a son, and they shall name him Immanuel, which means 'God is with us.'"

Even when we aren't conscious of it, we're never really alone. We live in the communion of saints. God is with us, Mary is with us, and we're linked with all those who've gone before us. In a marvelous, miraculous fashion, we share our lives with all of humanity.

The wonder of God is that God has lived as a man among us, God is indeed with us now, and we're loved by the Lord God Immanuel.

Do I remember to pray for those who've died before me?
Do I ask the saints to remember me in their prayers?

IMMANUEL! GOD IS WITH US!

Gifts

By now the Christmas shopping season is well underway. It would be hard to miss the countdown to Christmas, with its relentless, "Only ___ shopping days left!" We're poked, prodded, coerced, and conned into buying expensive gifts for everyone on our list in order to show our love.

But the best gifts aren't those we buy. They're the gifts that come from the heart, and they always involve a gift of self.

Mary has given a few tangible gifts in her appearances. She filled Juan Diego's cloak with roses, for instance. She presented the Miraculous Medal to St. Catherine Labouré. She's even said to have given the Rosary itself to St. Dominic. While these gifts are important, most of Mary's gifts are intangible—though no less real for their intangibility.

For instance, many of the seers who are believed to have seen Mary have talked about the lasting gifts of peace, serenity, assurance, and hope that she's given them. Even pilgrims who've merely visited sites of Marian apparitions have come away with lasting gifts of peace and wholeness—gifts that they've attributed to Mary. What's common about all of Mary's gifts is that they contain a part of herself. She gives a share of her own peace, serenity, assurance, and hope to anyone who will receive. This gift-giving season, what parts of yourself are you giving to others?

Do I ever try to buy love? Am I tempted to spend more than I should at this time of year in order to prove my devotion?

I MAKE SURE THAT EVERY GIFT I GIVE CONTAINS A PIECE
OF MY HEART, NOT MERELY MY POCKETBOOK.

The Immaculate Conception

The doctrine of the Immaculate Conception is probably the most misunderstood teaching of the Catholic Church. Virtually every non-Catholic (and a good many Catholics as well) thinks that this feast refers to Jesus' conception. The standard misunderstanding is that because Jesus was conceived without Mary's having had sexual intercourse, he was "immaculately" conceived.

It sounds plausible, but it's all wrong. The Immaculate Conception has nothing to do with Jesus. And it has nothing to do with lack of sexual intercourse.

In order to understand the teaching, it's necessary to agree on two important points. First, God exists outside of time and space; tomorrow and yesterday are all the same to God, who lives in an eternal present. Second, God can do anything.

Grounded on those points, the Immaculate Conception states that the saving action of Jesus (which would occur in what we would call the future) was applied to Mary while she was still in her mother's womb. She was conceived in the normal fashion, but she existed from the very beginning in the state of grace that the rest of us achieve through baptism; hence she was immaculately conceived.

If you have difficulty with this doctrine, don't fret. You're in good company. Several saints, including St. Thomas Aquinas, have struggled with the concept as well. Just remember St. Augustine's assertion that a thousand doubts don't a single disbelief make, and you'll be fine.

Have I ever thought that after baptism I have
the same graces given to Mary from her conception?

I BELIEVE GOD CAN DO ANYTHING.

Direction

One of the more popular day-planners offers prelabeled, hole-punched pages for your projects. The idea is to jot down your projects, then make a separate page for each one, listing every detail: all the equipment, materials, and attitudes you'll need to attain success. Once you've set your direction, you're to look neither to the left nor to the right, but march straight toward your destination. If you're a task-oriented person, you might enjoy managing your life in this way. If you aren't, setting such a rigid course might result in more frustration than accomplishment.

Highly creative people often can't set firm end points on projects, because they don't know what direction they're going. For example, Sidney Sheldon, the creator of several TV series (including *I Dream of Jeannie*) and author of several best-selling suspense novels, says that he begins a new book by imagining a character. Next he chooses a setting: perhaps a prison or a palace or an exotic city. Then, when he starts to write, the story unfolds itself to him. Clearly the project-page method wouldn't work for him.

When Mary set out on her journey toward the first Christmas, she carried the words of the angel Gabriel in her heart, but until she actually arrived at the stable in Bethlehem, she had no idea how God would bring fulfillment of the promises. She didn't know at the start that she'd sojourn in Egypt, raise her child in Nazareth, or stand on a hill outside Jerusalem and watch her son die. She allowed God to set the direction for her, and she was totally creative in her acceptance, letting her life-story unfold as she lived it.

> *Am I flexible enough to change my direction if God*
> *shows me a better way?*

I LET GOD HELP ME SET MY GOALS.

Sunrise

A woman who lived above the arctic circle once wrote that she and her children made a celebration of watching the sun rise on the morning of each winter solstice—the first sunrise in many months. Never mind that the sun didn't peep over the horizon until about noon and set a half-hour later; for this family, the curse of total darkness was over. Soon the ice would begin to recede, tiny yellow and white arctic flowers would bloom, and birds would return from the south—and eventually the area would be ablaze with the midnight sun.

Right now your life might feel as dark as the days before the winter solstice, with discouraging circumstances making your life feel like perpetual winter. But the sun is peeping over the horizon in the person of Mary. When you allow her to enter the winter of your soul, the ice will begin to melt, the wind will turn from cold to warm, and you'll be able to shed the overcoat of unhappiness.

Mary is able to bring light into your darkness because she's filled with the light and love that come only to a person who gives herself totally to God. The Bible calls Christ "the Sun of Righteousness," and it's his light that shines through Mary and lights our lives as well.

When I take inventory of the seasons of my soul, am I living in winter or spring? Do I let Mary's light warm my darkness?

I KNOW THAT EVERY WINTER IS FOLLOWED BY A GLORIOUS SPRING.

Desire

Did Mary have any unfulfilled desires? Did she, for instance, wish that she could have had grandchildren? Or did she sometimes grieve because Joseph didn't live long enough to see the Resurrection?

If Mary *did* ever wish that things could have been different, that doesn't mean she wasn't completely accepting of God's will for her life and the lives of those she loved. Wishing and even hoping that things could be different is part of human nature. Jesus himself seems to have wished that he didn't have to die on a cross when he fell prostrate in prayer, asking if the cup might pass from him.

The key to keeping our wishes and desires in perspective is inherent in the last part of Jesus' prayer: "not as I will, but as you will."

It's perfectly okay—in fact, it's more than okay—to ask God to give us the desires of our heart, so long as we remember that God isn't a magic dispenser. We can't put in our prayers and have our desires pop out like cans from a soda machine. We must always be willing to accept God's answer to our prayer, even if the answer is no. We have to be willing to accept the answer, but we don't have to like it; we can wish it could have been different—just as long as we're willing to accept God's will for our lives.

What's the desire of my heart?
Have I asked God to give it to me?

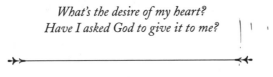

I'M WILLING TO ACCEPT GOD'S WILL.

Our Lady of Guadalupe

One of the most famous—and most beloved—appearances of Mary occurred in 1531 outside present-day Mexico City. There Juan Diego, a Nahuatl Indian, saw a vision of a lovely Indian maiden who told him to climb a hill and pick the roses he would find blooming there. She then took the flowers, tied them in his *tilma* (or cloak), and told him to visit his bishop. When he opened his *tilma* before the bishop, the roses cascaded to the floor; and there on the cloak was a portrait of Mary, dressed as an Aztec queen.

While believers need no proof that Mary presented her portrait, skeptics have to admit that the *tilma* itself presents a bit of a problem. Made of ayate cactus fiber, its normal life-span would have been approximately twenty years, yet after more than 450 years, it looks as new as on the day it was made. Moreover, the image hasn't faded, despite being exposed unprotected to smoke, candles, incense, and other pollutants over the centuries.

Our Lady of Guadalupe shows that faith isn't something we acquire through scientific reasoning. If that were the case, the scientific evidence of the *tilma* would be enough to convince virtually everyone that something miraculous had happened. Rather, faith requires a leap into the unknown, a dive into the realm of the mystical. Before the leap is made, no proof would be adequate. Afterward, no proof is necessary.

Am I a skeptic when it comes to miracles? On the other hand, am I too quick to believe every story that comes my way?

1 HAVE BOTH HEALTHY SKEPTICISM AND HEART-FELT FAITH.

Failure

Positive-thinking gurus often tell us that we should dress for success, plan for success, and strive for success. We should banish the thought of failure from our minds and constantly visualize ourselves as unabashed successes.

While it's true that positive thinking can have a profound effect on our lives, it alone can't guarantee success. And positive thinking doesn't help much when failure does occur.

The fact is that all of us will fail at something. It may be something major, such as a marriage or a job, or it may be something relatively minor, such as meeting a deadline—but everyone fails sometime during life.

Although failure and success are often thought of as mutually exclusive, failure is sometimes merely the precursor to success. Thomas Edison tried time and time again to develop an electric light, and time and time again he failed. Yet we have only to look around our homes to see the evidence of his success.

Mary might have been tempted to think that she'd failed when Jesus died on the cross. All the promises and prophecies aside, when she held her son's dead body in her arms, it had to have felt like failure. However, as we now know, what seemed then to be failure was actually the antecedent to the greatest success story the world has ever known—salvation of humanity and restoration of the covenant agreement with God.

Am I able to see glimpses of God's plan even in my failures?

I LEAVE THE FINAL JUDGMENT OF THE SUCCESS
OR FAILURE OF MY ENDEAVORS TO GOD.

Meditation

Physicians are beginning to prescribe what spiritual masters have advocated for generations: daily meditation. Meditation not only has spiritual benefits, it has medical benefits as well. Individuals who meditate regularly generally have lower blood pressure, less stress, and better overall health than people who don't incorporate the practice into their daily lives.

Meditation got something of a bad name several years ago when it was linked with a particular practice called transcendental meditation. Christians, especially those of a more fundamentalist ilk, denounced the practice as pagan and anti-Christian. But actually nothing could be more Christian than meditation. Over the centuries, most (if not all) of the great saints have practiced meditation in one form or another.

Although we don't have any proof that Mary and Jesus meditated, it's clear from the Gospels that they prayed; and prayer and meditation are closely linked. When we empty our minds and allow nothing but God to enter, we're both meditating and praying. Given what we know about Mary and Jesus, it seems safe to assume that they would have used meditation as an essential part of their prayer lives.

Have I ever meditated on a regular basis?
What kind of experiences did I have?
Do I meditate now? Why or why not?

¶ SET ASIDE TIME EVERY DAY FOR SPIRITUAL RENEWAL.

DECEMBER 15

Love

The love that this good mother bears us is so great that
as soon as she perceives our want, she comes to our assistance.
She comes before she is called.
RICHARD OF ST. LAURENCE

Every parent knows what it's like. You wake in the middle of the night. Not a creature is stirring (not even the proverbial mouse). And yet you instinctively know that something is wrong. You go to your child's room and discover that he or she is sick. Your child didn't have to cry; your love was so great that you knew the need before it was articulated and went to the child before you were called.

Mary's love for us is the love of a parent for a child. She cares so much for each of us that she comes to our assistance as soon as she perceives our want.

If you're in need, try praying Mary's great prayer of petition, the *Memorare:*

Remember, most gracious Virgin Mary, that never was it known that anyone who fled to your protection, implored your help or sought your intercession, was left unaided. Inspired by this confidence, I fly to you, Virgin of virgins, my Mother. To you I come, before you I stand, sinful and sorrowful. Mother of the Word Incarnate, despise not my petitions, but in your mercy, hear and answer me.

When I'm in need, do I turn to Mary as a child
would to its mother?

I BELIEVE MARY, IN HER MERCY, WILL HEAR AND ANSWER ME.

Happiness

Today is the birthday of Ludwig van Beethoven, one of the world's greatest composers. Beethoven's father was an unpredictable man who beat his son into practicing the piano many hours every day, sometimes yanking the boy out of bed in the middle of the night to sit at his instrument.

The elder Beethoven's cruelty can probably be credited to the fact that he had syphilis. We don't know whether the younger Beethoven's early deafness was due to the second-generation syphilitic genes his father bequeathed him or to one of the many blows his father landed on his head.

What we do know is that the composer of nine symphonies and many well-loved piano pieces, including "Für Elise," didn't have a particularly happy life. He never married, not daring to have children; his introverted personality kept him from making many friends; and deafness, the worst thing that could happen to a musician, began to take hold when he was fairly young.

Beethoven could have given up. Perhaps some would say he *should* have given up. Instead, he wrote music that he would never hear, composing his greatest symphony, the ninth, when he was living in total silence. We might have expected that music to be sad or bitter, but its jubilant movements conclude with the vocal quartet "Joyful, joyful, we adore Thee . . . "

Today, rather than looking for happiness to come to you from the outside, find joy within yourself. Perhaps you could begin to seek joy by meditating on the five joys of Mary commemorated in the Rosary: the Annunciation, the Visitation, the Birth of Jesus, the Presentation in the Temple, and the Finding in the Temple.

Which would I rather have: happiness or joy? Do I know the
difference between the two when I experience them?

1 LOOK FOR JOY TODAY AND EVERY DAY.

Scents

Some of our most powerful memories can be evoked by a particular scent or aroma. We may associate someone we love with a brand of perfume or aftershave, for instance, and every time we smell that fragrance, our loved one comes to mind.

At this time of year, we may find ourselves being transported back in memory more frequently than usual, because of the plethora of scents of the season. From the tangy aroma of the Christmas tree to the homey smell of fresh-baked cookies, we're surrounded by memory-recalling fragrances.

One interesting fact regarding scents is that many saints have had particularly sweet-smelling aromas associated with them at the time of death (and sometimes even later). St. Thérèse of Lisieux, for instance, is often associated with roses.

While tradition doesn't assign any special fragrance to Mary, there's no reason you can't make your own connection. One way might be to purchase a distinctively scented candle that you light every time you say the Rosary or meditate upon Mary's life. If you consistently light the candle when you think of Mary, eventually you'll begin to associate Mary with that fragrance. Then, whenever you smell it, you'll remember that Mary is always ready to join you in prayer and to take your prayers to the throne of her son Jesus.

What's my favorite fragrance?
What smells evoke strong memories for me?

I GIVE THANKS FOR MY SENSE OF SMELL.

Absence

Absence makes the heart grow fonder.

Out of sight, out of mind.

Which of these two contradictory statements do you think is more accurate?

For those who've experienced Mary's presence in an apparition, the first seems to be the more compelling. Over and over, seers have said how much they miss Mary's visits after they stop, and how much they long to see her one more time.

Since most of us will never see Mary except through the eyes of faith, we might find the second assertion to be closer to the truth. Because we don't see Mary, we may tend to forget about her.

Although devotion to Mary isn't essential to salvation, it can be one of the best ways to deepen our understanding of the message of Christianity. Moreover, it can result in not just pie-in-the-sky good feelings but a genuine relationship with a loving mother who will comfort and protect us.

In recalling the attempt on his life—he was shot three times at close range on May 13, 1981—Pope John Paul II said,

And again I have become indebted to the Blessed Virgin and to all the Patron Saints. Could I forget the event in St. Peter's Square took place on the day and at the hour when the first appearances of the Mother of Christ to the poor little peasants has been remembered for over sixty years at Fatima in Portugal? For in everything that happened to me on that very day, I felt that extraordinary protection and care, which turned out to be stronger than the deadly bullet.

What part does Mary play in my daily life?

I INVITE MARY INTO MY LIFE.

Advent

It's odd how the meaning of some words gets corrupted in everyday language, while the dictionary definition remains static. Take *commencement,* for example. We've become so accustomed to thinking of commencement ceremonies—in other words, graduation—as the end of one phase of schooling that we've almost obliterated the real meaning of *commencement,* which is "beginning."

The same is true for the liturgical season of Advent, which is celebrated for the four weeks before Christmas. Although the word *advent* means "coming" or "arrival," we've co-opted it to mean waiting. Ask any child. An Advent calendar doesn't have all that much to do with coming; instead, it's a way to count off the days of waiting until Santa arrives.

Yet despite that shift in emphasis, Advent really *is* the time of arrival. At this time of year, we, along with Mary, remember the first Advent, when a teenage girl anticipated the arrival of her firstborn son. But at the same time, we also live in a second Advent, when the world anticipates the Second Coming of that same firstborn son of creation.

This year, as you wait for Christmas, take some time to reflect on the Second Coming. In addition to thinking about the baby who will appear in a manger, consider also the King who will return with his armies, ready to assume the throne that has been his for all eternity.

If Jesus were to return tomorrow, would I be ready?

I AM READY FOR JESUS' RETURN.

Charity

Christmas is coming, the geese are getting fat.
Please to put a penny in the poor man's hat.
If you haven't a penny, a halfpenny will do.
If you haven't a halfpenny, God bless you.

During this season, guilt tends to get the best of us, and we often try to make up for a year of less than optimal charity by cramming our good works and best intentions into a few weeks. If you find yourself in that situation, you're in good company. Nursing homes, retirement centers, soup kitchens, and the like find themselves overflowing with gifts and volunteers right now; but in a few short weeks, their pantries will be like Mother Hubbard's—totally bare.

Mary always encourages us to perform works of charity and kindness, but she (along with the soup kitchen administrators, the nursing home recreation staff, and others) would prefer that we spread our charity out a bit.

If you're feeling as if you should take a poinsettia to the local nursing home or arrange for children to carol at a retirement center, ignore the feeling. There will be plenty of other people to buy poinsettias and sing carols. Instead, flip ahead a month or two on your next year's calendar and write—in pen!—something that you can do during the barren, lonely months when your acts of charity will be not only more appreciated but also more necessary.

Do I do acts of charity out of guilt or out of love?

I MAKE MY ACTS OF CHARITY YEAR ROUND,
NOT JUST DURING THE HOLIDAYS.

Carols

One way we have theology imprinted into our minds is through the hymns we sing. In fact, what we learn in hymns often sticks more than what we learn from any catechism text. For instance, most people could tell you that "a mighty fortress is our God" and it's "grace that set me free."

Moreover, we're told that when we sing, we pray twice—which may be more encouraging for those of us who can carry a tune than for those of us who are tone-deaf.

Nevertheless, this month, as we listen to and sing the special carols of the season, let's not just mouth the words; let's take time to hear and appreciate their words of praise:

"Hark, the herald angels sing, 'Glory to the newborn King.' "

"It came upon a midnight clear, that glorious song of old."

"We three kings of Orient are. Bearing gifts we traverse afar."

"Oh, holy night, the stars are brightly shining. It is the night of the dear Savior's birth."

"Away in a manger, no crib for his bed, the little Lord Jesus lay down his sweet head."

"Oh, come, all ye faithful, joyful and triumphant."

"What child is this, who, laid to rest, on Mary's lap is sleeping?"

> *Which carol is my favorite? Do I play carols that reflect the meaning of Christmas, or do I play music that emphasizes the more secular aspects of the season?*

¶ CELEBRATE THE SEASON IN SONG.

Stables

The nativity is usually pictured as taking place in a stable—a rather clean and antiseptic stable with a couple of sheep, a cow, and a donkey. While the image is deeply ingrained in our collective tradition, Mary probably gave birth in a cave that was under or connected with an inn or a house.

The location of Jesus' birth isn't the only thing about the nativity that we may have wrong. We also generally picture Mary as giving birth with only Joseph and perhaps an angel or two in attendance (even though the Scriptures don't say a word about who was or wasn't present).

If you think about it, Mary's giving birth without a midwife or experienced mother present seems very unlikely. First of all, Bethlehem was Joseph's hometown; that's why he and Mary had to go there in the first place. Since it was his home, he more than likely had some relatives still living there. Even if they didn't have room in their home for the couple to stay, it seems likely that at least one of the women would have noticed Mary's advanced state of pregnancy and kept an eye out to help. Moreover, if the innkeeper's wife knew that Mary was ready to give birth, she undoubtedly would have gone to help— as women have helped each other since the beginning of time. Finally, it's unlikely Joseph would have been much help.

Of course, Mary may have given birth alone or with only angelic help, but if she did have another woman or two to assist her, that help didn't diminish the event one iota. In fact, it's sort of comforting to think that God made sure Mary had help during this potentially difficult and frightening time.

Am I willing to help others when they're giving birth, whether it's to an actual child or to a new life or a new idea?

I'M WILLING TO BE A MIDWIFE TO NEW LIFE.

Preparation

During this time of year, we're told that we need to prepare for the upcoming holidays. In fact, we're told so often that we sometimes spend more time preparing than celebrating.

If you find yourself caught up in the flurry of buying presents, decorating, cooking, cleaning, and all the rest—if you're beginning to feel that Christmas is a lot more work than it's worth—perhaps it's time to stop and ask yourself exactly what you're preparing for.

Many people spend their years acting as if preparing for life to begin is the *purpose* of life. And yet, as a somewhat flip but nonetheless succinct saying puts it, "Life isn't a dress rehearsal." We get only one chance at life; if we waste that chance, we don't get another.

Mary clearly jumped into life with enthusiasm. She was willing to risk everything to believe an angel's promise, she celebrated with abandon, she wept with passion, and she loved with her whole heart. Mary didn't *prepare* for life; she *lived* it. And we need to do the same thing.

If I fail, what's the worst thing that could happen?

I'M WILLING TO ENGAGE LIFE FULLY AND WITHOUT RESERVATION.

Silent Night

Despite the fact that Christianity talks a lot about joy, many Christians are deadly serious. If life is supposed to be a banquet, they act as if they're on a perpetual diet.

Not that faith is a light topic. On the contrary, it's the most important thing in life. But just because something is important doesn't mean it has to be morbidly dull.

Much of what has been written about Mary over the centuries is inspiring, uplifting, and encouraging, but a lot of it is also ploddingly dull. Reading some of the massive tomes written about her, one might think that only scholars and saints could find her interesting.

A favorite story involving Mary centers on the hymn "Silent Night"—perhaps the most beloved of all the Christmas carols. As the story goes, a little boy was singing enthusiastically when he suddenly stopped and asked his mom, "I know all about the mother and child in the song, but who's Round John Virgin?"

If we take Mary too seriously, we might think that she'd be upset or offended by the joke, but if we're willing to concede the fact that Mary might have had a wonderful sense of humor, then we can imagine that she chuckles each time she hears the carol. In either event, the story is a good reminder that faith and spirituality aren't supposed to be deadly serious. In the banquet of life, we're all invited to take a second helping of dessert!

When was the last time I laughed so hard my sides hurt?

I BELIEVE THAT LAUGHTER IS GOOD MEDICINE FOR THE SOUL.

Birth

A while back, someone came up with the saying "It's never too late to have a happy childhood." Although at first hearing, the saying seems silly, it contains an important truth: it's never too late to enjoy life, to live with the excitement and wonder that characterize a happy childhood.

But to have a happy childhood requires a new birth, not literally but spiritually, and that's exactly what Jesus' own birth says to us.

In coming to earth, becoming human, living with his mother Mary, preaching, teaching, and ultimately dying for us, Jesus shows us that we can be reborn—not by reentering the womb but by embarking on a new way of life. The glory and the mystery of Christmas are that we can be born again.

If you could start life all over, what would you do differently? Would you eat more dessert and less spinach? Would you spend more time watching sunsets and less time watching your assets? Would you laugh more and frown less?

Whatever you would do if you could live life again, you can start doing right now. The first day of the rest of your new life is today.

Am I living the kind of life I really want to be living?
What would I change if I could? What's stopping me?

TODAY IS THE FIRST DAY OF MY NEW LIFE.

Swaddling Cloths

She wrapped him in swaddling cloths and laid him in a
manger, because there was no room for them in the inn.

LUKE 2:7

When we read the accounts of Jesus' birth, we may get the idea that swaddling cloths were something special, because Luke goes out of his way to mention them. Actually, though, it's more likely that he mentions them to let readers know how very ordinary everything was at Jesus' birth. *All* babies were put in swaddling cloths. To mention it is a lot like someone today saying, "She put her son in diapers." It's a clever way of showing that Jesus was really and truly a baby—a regular baby who needed to be put in baby clothes.

For a moment, jump ahead in history and imagine St. Luke asking Mary to tell him about the night of Jesus' birth. Perhaps Luke has been thinking that Jesus was extraordinary from the moment of his delivery. Maybe he's wondering whether Jesus was so well developed that he wasn't really a baby at all.

One can almost see Mary chuckling and shaking her head. "No, no. He looked just like an ordinary infant. I had to put him in swaddling cloths just like every other baby."

Luke was either so impressed or so surprised by that fact that he wrote it into his account of Jesus' life. Now, two thousand years later, we can read that account and be reminded that in acknowledging Jesus' divinity we must not forget his humanity. Jesus started life wearing diapers (i.e., swaddling cloths) just like the rest of us.

Which aspect of Jesus' nature—his humanity or his
divinity—am I more inclined to focus on?

¶ GIVE THANKS THAT JESUS WAS REALLY AND TRULY
HUMAN, JUST LIKE ME.

Shepherds

*When the angels went away from them to heaven, the shepherds
said to one another, "Let us go, then, to Bethlehem to see this
thing that has taken place, which the Lord has made known
to us." So they went in haste and found Mary and Joseph,
and the infant lying in the manger.*

LUKE 2:15–16

The shepherds who visited the Holy Family probably tended to be on
the rough, uncouth, smelly side. After all, they spent their days *and*
nights out with the sheep, and it was probably a mighty long time between baths and changes of clothing. But there they came, clomping
into the stable to see the baby—Jesus' first recorded visitors.

What was Mary thinking when they showed up? Did she want to
say, "Don't touch the baby!" when they came to peer in the manger?
Mary probably was tired from the birth, a little dazed by the whole experience, and not in the mood to entertain unexpected guests (much
less a bunch of shepherds and their sheep). However, she undoubtedly
was gracious and kind, allowing the men to look at her son, maybe
even to run their callused fingers across his soft cheeks.

How do you feel when people drop by your home unexpectedly?
Do you open the door and let them in, or do you stand awkwardly in
the doorway, hoping that they'll get the hint and leave? The Hebrew
Scriptures encourage us to afford hospitality to all (even shepherds!),
for in doing so, we may be entertaining angels without knowing it.

Are people comfortable in my home?
Am I comfortable having people in my home?

I MAKE MY HOME A PLACE WHERE ALL ARE WELCOME.

Wonder

The star that appeared over the night sky that first Christmas has never been adequately explained by astronomers. Many possibilities have been suggested, ranging from a comet to an unusual conjunction of certain constellations that might have looked like a single star. In the end, however, we just don't know what the star of Bethlehem was. We're left with the same wonder that Mary, Joseph, and the shepherds experienced as they gazed upward into the clear night sky.

All too often, we try to explain away the wonders of the world. But wonder is what makes life worth living. To reduce the world to scientific explanations is to remove its magic.

Children seem to know this instinctively. Consider this story: A dad with a scientific bent was out one night in the yard with his three-year-old daughter. When she asked a question about the stars, he launched into a lengthy explanation of cosmic gases, the big bang theory, and the redshift phenomenon. The little girl listened intently. When her dad was finished, she looked at him and asked, "Do they twinkle because they're winking at us?"

Life isn't a scientific problem to be carefully researched and solved; it's a mystery to be celebrated. Today give yourself permission to rejoice in its wonder.

Do I approach my life as if it were an equation with a single right answer, or do I see it as a party to be attended?

1 CHOOSE TO CELEBRATE THE UNIVERSE.

Wise Men

> *When Jesus was born in Bethlehem of Judea, in the days of King*
> *Herod, behold, magi from the east arrived in Jerusalem . . . and*
> *on entering the house they saw the child with Mary his mother.*
> *They prostrated themselves and did him homage.*
> *Then they opened their treasures and offered*
> *him gifts of gold, frankincense, and myrrh.*
>
> MATTHEW 2:1, 11–12

Who were the Magi who came to visit the Christ child and his mother? Even though we traditionally think of them as three kings, they were really an unknown number of astronomers from the East— probably present-day Iran—who saw the star and followed it. (As noted earlier, we tend to think that there were three of them only because they brought three gifts.)

But the Magi are more than just quaint figures in the Christmas story. They're symbols to show us that Christ came for all people, not just a select group. Moreover, it's clear that Mary welcomed them into her home. In the same way, Mary welcomes all people. She makes it clear that she isn't just for Catholics or even for Christians; she's an advocate for all who see the wisdom and truth of her son's teachings.

> *Am I willing to do whatever it takes to follow my star?*
> *Do I believe that God will lead me as God led the Magi?*

I TRUST THAT MARY WILL HELP ME FIND MY STAR.

Power

Machiavelli asserted that "power corrupts and absolute power corrupts absolutely." While history would tend to prove him right, power in and of itself isn't evil. In fact, there's nothing inherently wrong with using our rightful authority—the power God gives us.

For example, parents rightly have power over their children. Teachers have power over their students. Humanity has power over the world. It's how we use our power that makes the difference.

Mary clearly understood how to rightly use her power. For instance, she made her twelve-year-old son leave the Temple (where he was obviously having a good time) and return home—right that very minute! She didn't abdicate her power to her child, even though he was God.

Later in life, she knew that she had the authority (she was his mother, after all) to tell Jesus (under the guise of a simple statement: "They have no wine") to do something about a troubling social situation. Even today Mary knows how to use her power. When we ask her for something, she knows she can't grant it on her own. However, she marches boldly to the throne of her son with our requests, fully expecting that he'll do what she asks. And you know what? He does!

*What is lacking in my life right now? Have I asked Mary
to take my request to her son? If not, why not?*

I ACCEPT THE RESPONSIBILITIES OF THE POWER GOD HAS GIVEN ME.

Destiny

There's something you do better than anyone else in the world.

Say it aloud: *There's something I do better than anyone else in the world!*

Do you believe it? You *should*, because it's true. You may not have all the talent, all the gifts, and all the abilities you might want, but you *do* have all the talent, all the gifts, and all the abilities you need to do the one little (or big!) thing you were created to do. God created you to do a job, and God outfitted you with everything necessary to accomplish that task. It's your destiny—a destiny given to you from the beginning.

Mary had a destiny as well. Her destiny may be more obvious and impressive than ours, but because she was human, not divine, she had to discover and carry out her destiny just like the rest of us.

What's your destiny? If you aren't sure, ask Mary to help you figure it out. Then believe with all your heart that she will do so. As Thomas à Kempis wrote, "Mary will most willingly pray for you, and the Son will most certainly grant all his mother asks."

What's my destiny?

I KNOW THAT THERE'S SOMETHING I DO BETTER
THAN ANYONE ELSE IN THE WORLD.